CAMBRIDGE LIBRARY COLLECTION

Books of enduring scholarly value

British and Irish History, Nineteenth Century

This series comprises contemporary or near-contemporary accounts of the political, economic and social history of the British Isles during the nineteenth century. It includes material on international diplomacy and trade, labour relations and the women's movement, developments in education and social welfare, religious emancipation, the justice system, and special events including the Great Exhibition of 1851.

Collection of Reports of Celebrated Trials, Civil and Criminal

A solicitor with offices in Scarborough, William Otter Woodall (1837–1914) was a prominent member of the local community. This work, edited by Woodall and first published in 1873, brings together reports of seven notable and intriguing nineteenth-century civil and criminal trials as case studies for the benefit of the legal profession. (It was intended as the first of a series, but no further volumes were published.) The book includes the case of the so-called 'Quaker' poisoner John Tawell, executed in 1845, who was the first person to be arrested with the aid of the electric telegraph and about whose fate several popular ballads were written; that of Abraham Thornton in 1818 – for the murder of Mary Ashford – who claimed the right to the ancient Norman tradition of trial by battle; and that of Reverend William Bailey, transported for life in 1843 to Van Diemen's Land for forgery. This colourful, engaging work will appeal to anyone with an interest in the law or true crime stories.

Cambridge University Press has long been a pioneer in the reissuing of out-of-print titles from its own backlist, producing digital reprints of books that are still sought after by scholars and students but could not be reprinted economically using traditional technology. The Cambridge Library Collection extends this activity to a wider range of books which are still of importance to researchers and professionals, either for the source material they contain, or as landmarks in the history of their academic discipline.

Drawing from the world-renowned collections in the Cambridge University Library and other partner libraries, and guided by the advice of experts in each subject area, Cambridge University Press is using state-of-the-art scanning machines in its own Printing House to capture the content of each book selected for inclusion. The files are processed to give a consistently clear, crisp image, and the books finished to the high quality standard for which the Press is recognised around the world. The latest print-on-demand technology ensures that the books will remain available indefinitely, and that orders for single or multiple copies can quickly be supplied.

The Cambridge Library Collection brings back to life books of enduring scholarly value (including out-of-copyright works originally issued by other publishers) across a wide range of disciplines in the humanities and social sciences and in science and technology.

Collection of Reports of Celebrated Trials, Civil and Criminal

WILLIAM OTTER WOODALL

CAMBRIDGE UNIVERSITY PRESS

Cambridge, New York, Melbourne, Madrid, Cape Town,
Singapore, São Paolo, Delhi, Mexico City

Published in the United States of America by Cambridge University Press, New York

www.cambridge.org
Information on this title: www.cambridge.org/9781108052986

© in this compilation Cambridge University Press 2012

This edition first published 1873
This digitally printed version 2012

ISBN 978-1-108-05298-6 Paperback

A COLLECTION

OF

REPORTS

OF

CELEBRATED TRIALS,

CIVIL AND CRIMINAL,

EDITED,

WITH INTRODUCTIONS AND NOTES,

BY

WILLIAM OTTER WOODALL,

ATTORNEY-AT-LAW.

VOL. I.

LONDON:
SHAW AND SONS, FETTER LANE,
Law Publishers.

———

1873.

LONDON : PRINTED BY SHAW AND SONS, FETTER LANE.

CONTENTS OF VOL. I.

PREFACE.

My object in preparing this volume of Reports is simply to present for the use of the Profession generally, in a convenient form, a Collection of some of the more important and interesting Trials of modern date. It is well known that there is no publication now in existence which exactly carries out this object. The result is, that if a trial be not published in a separate form at the time, it is afterwards practically inaccessible to any one who for professional or other purposes may be desirous of referring to it. Even when published separately, the Reports are often, after the lapse of a few years, very difficult to meet with, and expensive to purchase. The plan of this work is, therefore, to collect together some of those trials now either scattered abroad in a separate form, and long since out of print, or not reported at all.

In dealing with the Trials thus collected I have endeavoured, whilst eliminating everything that is irrelevant, to preserve almost entire the evidence touching on the main points of the case. Where there have been more than one report I have carefully compared and collated the different accounts together, sifting and condensing the evidence so as to bring the case within a reasonable compass. In this I have experienced the greatest difficulty. To have made the present volume three times its size, inserting only the same Trials, would have been a comparatively easy task : to condense it, and whilst retaining what is essential, reject all immaterial parts, has been a work of much labour. This particularly applies to the Case of the *Wager of Battel,* the Trial of *Smyth* v. *Smyth,* and especially to the Case of *Leotade,* now, I believe, first published in an English form.

Whilst endeavouring thus to make these Reports strictly accurate, I have also endeavoured to make them, to some extent at least, interesting. Therefore, several pieces of evidence, observations of counsel, passages between Judge and Prisoner (as in the case of Leotade), and other matters not strictly material to the point at issue, yet enlivening the Trial, have been retained either in the evidence itself, or inserted in the Introduction. A bare legal Report of a Trial, containing merely sufficient evidence on which to form an opinion, would, without these *loci lætiores,* be found, though perhaps a useful, yet a very uninteresting work.

In venturing to submit this Collection to the perusal of the public I do so with much diffidence. I know that I am treading upon ground, not on which others have feared to tread, but which has been already occupied by abler writers. To follow in the steps of Mr. Serjeant BURKE Mr. TOWNSEND, Q.C., and Mr. BURTON, is not easy. I wish it therefore to be understood that I have no intention of laying claim to the powers which these writers possess of dealing with subjects similar to the ones which I am now attempting to treat. My object is simply to produce a tolerably accurate Report of Trials, which may probably not be either uninteresting or uninstructive to the members of the Profession to which I have the honour to belong, and for whose use more especially it is written.

In concluding these remarks I gladly take the opportunity of thanking those gentlemen who have so kindly placed at my disposal the briefs and papers relating to some of the Cases reported, and who have otherwise afforded me much assistance and encouragement. I particularly wish to acknowledge my obligation in this respect to Mr. SPENCER, Solicitor, of Birmingham, Mr. SADLER, Solicitor, of Sutton Coldfield, and Mr. HOLBECHE, of Sutton Coldfield. These gentlemen, who now represent the firms which were engaged on one side or the other in the Case of *Thornton* and the *Wager of Battel* very obligingly put in my hands all the papers in their possession relating to those Cases. To Mr. WILLIAM BEVAN, Solicitor, Old Jewry, I am also under considerable obligation for the loan of several very interesting reports and papers relating to the Case of *Tawell;* and also for information connected with the Case of much importance and interest, of which, however, I regret I did not feel able to avail myself more fully. Whatever doubt might have been felt at the time as to *Tawell's* guilt was removed by the confession he made after conviction. I therefore did not think it necessary to enter upon any discussion as to the correctness of the medical evidence furnished on behalf of the prosecution. To those to whom the secret of *Tawell's* confession has been confided, the perfect accuracy of some portions at least of this evidence may perhaps be questionable, but no doubt upon this point can at all affect the question of his guilt. For this reason I have not thought it expedient to enter on any inquiry on the subject, or to reveal the details of that confession which *Tawell* requested should not be made public.

August 21*st*, 1873.

NOTE ON THE CASE OF TAWELL.

At page 164 it is stated that *Tawell* at the time of the forgery of the bank notes was a member of the Society of Friends. I have been informed since this work was printed that *Tawell* was " disowned " on the 7th of February, 1809, " for having been married by a priest, and also for very disorderly and immoral conduct." I gladly avail myself of the opportunity of correcting this error, more especially as I believe it to be one largely shared in by the public. The general impression indeed seems to be that as late as the time of the murder in 1845 *Tawell* was a Quaker.

THE TRIAL

OF

ABRAHAM THORNTON

FOR THE MURDER OF MARY ASHFORD,

AT THE WARWICK SUMMER ASSIZES,

BEFORE MR. JUSTICE HOLROYD,

On August 8th, 1817.

Counsel for the Prosecution : Mr. *Clarke*, Mr. Serjeant *Copley*, and Mr. *Perkins*.

For the Prisoner : Mr. *Reader* and Mr. *Reynolds*.

INTRODUCTION.

THERE has probably been no case in the criminal records of this country, during the present century, that has attracted so universally the public attention as the case of Abraham Thornton. Its chief interest is, however, derived not from the trial itself, but from the subsequent proceedings in the King's Bench, after Thornton, notwithstanding·his acquittal, had been arrested a second time on the obsolete writ of *Appeal of Murder*, and it is more especially by way of introduction to those proceedings that the following Report of the trial is here given :—

On the evening of the 26th of May, 1817, the deceased, Mary Ashford, accompanied by a friend of her's, Hannah Cox, went to a dance at a public-house called Tyburn, not far from Erdington, a village a few miles distant from Birmingham. The prisoner Thornton was at the dance ; and about half-past eleven, or from that to twelve, he and the deceased left the house, and went together along the highroad in the direction in which Mary Ashford resided. They were left together on the highroad about midnight. From that time

B

until near three o'clock in the morning nothing was seen of them; but a little before three, a man named Umpage, on his way home, came across the prisoner, whom he knew, and a woman, whom he could not recognise, but who was, beyond all doubt, the deceased, at a stile leading into Bell Lane. Near this stile was a harrowed field, through which it was proved Thornton and Mary Ashford had been in the course of the night, and in which footsteps, undoubtedly those of the deceased and Thornton, were afterwards traced.

Nothing was seen of Thornton after this for some time; but Mary Ashford was traced to her friend's, Hannah Cox's, house in Erdington, *alone*, where she changed her clothes. She left Cox's at about fourteen minutes past four in the morning, and went up Bell Lane; and was last seen alive going in the direction of the harrowed field where the foot-steps were found, at about eighteen minutes past four. She had then some way to go to the spot where her body was afterwards found in a pit of water; and in all probability she could not reach the pit until half-past four at the earliest. Her body was discovered in the pit about half-past six.

The theory of the prosecution was, that Thornton waylaid Mary Ashford on her way home from Cox's, and assaulted her: that she fainted; and that he then threw her body into the pit. In support of this it was sought to prove, from the footmarks in the field, that Thornton had chased, and had ultimately overtaken the deceased, and then violated her, not far from the pit. There was undoubtedly the impress of a human figure on the grass near the pit, and blood was traced from it, without any footmarks, close up to the edge of the pit. It was inferred from this that Thornton had carried Mary Ashford in his arms, and had then thrown her into the water.

Allowing the least possible time for the commission of the crime, the deceased having been last seen alive at about eighteen minutes past four, and then having some distance to go, she could not have met with her death before half-past four, but in all probability not until a quarter to five. At half-past four, however, the prisoner was indisputably proved to have been seen at a distance from the pit, in a straight line, of one mile and a half; but by the nearest road, of two miles and a quarter. He was calm, and did not seem as if he had been running. On being apprehended, he admitted being with the deceased until four in the morning, and that he had been intimate with her, but, as he asserted, with her consent. On this evidence he was, without any hesitation, committed for trial on the Coroner's Inquisition for Murder.

THE trial took place before Mr. Justice HOLROYD on the 8th of August, 1817, at Warwick. The indictment consisted of two counts. The first charged the prisoner with having on the 27th of May, 1817, in the royal town, manor, and lordship of Sutton Coldfield, in the county of Warwick, not having the fear of God before his eyes, but being moved by the instigation of the devil, wilfully murdered Mary Ashford, by throwing her into a pit of water. The second count charged him with having on the morning aforesaid committed a rape upon the body of the said Mary Ashford. To both counts the prisoner pleaded not guilty.

Mr. CLARKE, the senior counsel, then rose and addressed the jury in a short and temperate speech. He said :—" I am of counsel for the prosecution ; and by the indictment, which has just now been read to you by the officer of the court, the prisoner at the bar is charged with one of the highest offences that human nature is capable of committing ;—nothing less than shedding the blood of a fellow-creature. I need not enlarge upon this subject ; the crime itself is incapable of aggravation. It is my painful province, however, to lay before you a statement of the evidence which will be produced in support of that charge · and, as it is not my duty, so neither is it my inclination, to exaggerate anything upon this occasion ; but public justice requires that the whole proof should be brought fully and fairly before you. Gentlemen, the deceased was a young girl of the most fascinating manners, of lovely person, in the bloom and prime of life, and living for some length of time under the protection of her uncle, a small farmer residing at Langley, in this county, and was well-known and well-respected in the village of Erdington. The unfortunate young woman went, on the 26th, from her uncle's at Langley, where she lived, to Birmingham. On her way

she called upon Hannah Cox, at Erdington, and arranged
that she should be back early in the evening, to go to
a dance at Tyburn.   This was an annual feast, and a dance
always followed.   She was not in the habit of attending
dances, but she did attend at this dance.   The prisoner was
there, admired the figure and general appearance of Mary
Ashford, and was heard to say, 'I have been intimate (I
won't use the coarse expression he made use of) with her
sister, and I will be intimate with her, though it should
cost me my life.'   He accompanied her from the dancing-
room, and was seen with her at a stile, about three in the
morning.   At four she called at her friend Cox's, and was
calm, composed, and in good spirits.   On her leaving
Erdington at this time, between four and five in the morning of the 27th, the fatal deed was done which now forms
the subject of inquiry.   Gentlemen, it will be shown to you
that the footsteps of a man and a woman were traced from
the path, through a harrowed field by which she was going
towards Langley.   These footmarks exhibit proofs of running, chasing, and struggling.   They at length led to a spot
where a distinct impression of the human figure was found,
and a large quantity of coagulated blood was also discovered ;
in the same place were seen the marks of a man's knees and
toes.   From that spot the blood was distinctly traced for a
considerable space on the grass ; consequently, had any foot
gone along there, the dew would have been brushed away.
It appeared plainly as if a man had walked along the footway carrying a body, from the extremity of which the blood
dropped upon the grass.   At the edge of the pit her shoes,
her bonnet, and her bundle, were found, but only one footstep could be seen there, and that was a man's.·   It was
deeply impressed, and seemed to be that of a man who
thrust one foot forward to heave the body he had in his arms
into the pit.   When her body was examined there were
marks of laceration upon it, and both her arms had the
visible mark of hands, as if he had pressed them with
violence to the ground.   In her stomach some duck-weeds
were found, which proved that she had breathed after she
had been thrown into the water ; but the small quantity
merely shows that she had not previously been quite dead.

The evidence of a skilful surgeon will show that down to this violation she had been a virgin. It is therefore natural to suppose that the violent agitation and outrageous injury of such an assault stunned her, and deprived her of animation for the moment ; that in this state she was thrown into the water ; and the animation restored for a moment was instantly cut off by drowning. Hitherto, however, the prisoner is not connected with the act ; but you will not only find him with her at three o'clock, but you will also find, by his own admission, that he was with her at four. You will find the marks of a man's shoes in the running and struggling correspond exactly to his. You will find, by his own admission, that he was intimate with her ; and this admission made not before the magistrate, and never till the evident proofs were discovered on his clothes. Her clothes, too, afford most powerful evidence. At her friend Cox's, at four in the morning, she put off her dancing-dress, and put on the dress in which she had gone to Birmingham. The clothes she put on there, and which she had on at the time of her death, are all over bloody and dirtied. The surgeon will tell you that the coagulated blood could not have proceeded except from violence. Therefore, the case appears to have been that he paid attention to her during the night; showing, perhaps, those attentions which she might naturally have been pleased with, and particularly from one her superior in life; but that afterwards he waited for her on her return from Erdington, and first forcibly violated her, and then threw her apparently lifeless body into the pit. It will be attempted to show you that he returned home, and that some other person must have met her and brought her to the dismal end she met with. But, gentlemen, as footsteps were traced through the harrowed field to a stile leading to his father's by the very course he took, and he admits an intimacy with her, that is a circumstance of the utmost importance, and you will bear in mind that he did not admit this till the proofs were adduced against him. [Here Mr. Reader expostulated with Mr. Clarke for making such observations.] Gentlemen, the evidence will be laid before you ; from it you will form your judgment, and I desire you to lay out of view everything I may have said, unless it shall be confirmed by the learned judge who presides at this trial."

Hannah Cox was then sworn and examined by Mr. Serjeant COPLEY. She said :—" I lived in the service of Mr. Machell, of Erdington, in the month of May last. I slept at my mother-in-law's, Mrs. Butler, on the morning of the 27th; her house is nearly opposite to my master's. I was acquainted with Mary Ashford; she lived with her uncle at Langley Heath, about three miles from Erdington. I know her grandfather very well; he lives in the same parish, at the top of Bell Lane, against Mr. Freeman's. I remember Mary Ashford coming to Erdington on the morning of Monday, the 26th of May. She called on me at Mr. Machell's about ten o'clock, on her road to Birmingham market. She had a bundle with her, and said she was going to Birmingham market. In the bundle were a clean frock, a white spencer, and a pair of white stockings. The deceased was dressed in a pink cotton frock or gown, a straw bonnet with straw-coloured ribbons, a scarlet spencer, half-boots, and black stockings. I went with her to Mrs. Butler's to leave the bundle. The deceased then went to Birmingham, having first agreed that she and I should go together that night to Daniel Clarke's, at Tyburn House, to a dance. The deceased returned about six o'clock in the evening, and called on me at Machell's. I went with her to Mrs. Butler's, where she put on the clean dress she had left there in the morning, and a new pair of shoes, which I bought for her at a shoemaker's at Erdington in the course of the day. The clothes she pulled off she made up into a bundle and left at Butler's. We set off for Tyburn between seven and eight o'clock. The dance was at a public-house there, kept by Mr. Daniel Clarke. Tyburn is about two miles from Erdington, and by the side of the turnpike road. I did not pass the whole of the evening in the dancing-room; I might be in the room about a quarter of an hour. Whilst I was there I saw Mary Ashford dancing, but do not recollect that I saw the prisoner there. I left the public-house alone between eleven and twelve o'clock. Mary Ashford was at the room door when I was going; she told me she would not be long before she would follow me. I walked to the bridge, which is but a short distance from Clarke's, and waited for her there some length of time. Whilst I was standing on the bridge Benjamin Carter came to me. I sent him back for Mary Ashford, who came soon after, in company with the prisoner Thornton. All four of us then proceeded towards Erdington. The prisoner and Mary Ashford went on first ; Carter remained talking with me a few minutes, and I then followed them. About ten minutes afterwards Carter overtook me ; he continued with me a short time, and then said he would go back to the dance. Upon leaving Carter I walked on and joined Mary Ashford and the prisoner, and parted with them between Reeves's and the Old Cuckoo, a little before you come to the road on the left which leads to Erdington. I did not go with them to the place where the road separates, but very near it. I walked on first, and took the road to the left of a house called Loars, and I then left them and went home to my mother's to bed."

Were you called up again at any time in the course of the morning?—Yes. Who called you up? Mary Ashford. You got up and let her into your mother's house?—Yes. Do you know what time it was ; did you look at the clock ? —Yes ; it was twenty minutes before five. Do you know whether the clock was right; that is, how was your mother's clock by the other clocks in the neighbourhood?—The clock was too fast. Was the deceased in the same dress then as she had on overnight?—Yes. Did you perceive any agitation or confusion in the person of the deceased?—No. Neither her person nor her dress were disordered?—Not that I saw. The deceased appeared very calm and in good spirits?—Yes. The deceased did not go into another room to change her dress, did she ; she remained in the house all the time, and you stayed with her?—Yes. What did the deceased do with the clothes she took off?—She tied them up in a bundle along with some market things ; she wrapped the boots in a handkerchief, and kept on her shoes. The deceased had some market things, had she?—Yes ; some sugar and other things which she brought from Birmingham market the day before. How long was the deceased in the house altogether?—She might be in the house a quarter of an hour, but I cannot exactly say. The deceased then went

away, and you saw no more of her?—Yes.   What situation
was the deceased in when she changed her clothes; did she
sit down on a chair?—No; she stood up.   Did the deceased
stand up whilst she pulled off her stockings?—Yes.   Did the
deceased do anything more in the house?—She did nothing
more than change her dress.   Did you observe that the deceased's frock was stained?—No; but I did not take much
notice of it.   Did the deceased tell you she had any complaint
upon her?—No, she did not.

In cross-examination by Mr. READER on behalf of the
prisoner, the witness said she was very intimate with the
deceased, and that she (deceased) was about twenty years old.
She knew the father of the deceased; he was a gardener,
and resided at Erdington.   Her grandfather lived near Bell
Lane, about two or three miles off.   The place where the
prisoner and the deceased parted from her the night before
was about two or three miles off witness's own home.
The pit where the body was found was about three or four
hundred yards from the deceased's grandfather's.   When
the deceased called her up in the morning she said she had
slept at her grandfather's.   Did you say anything to the
deceased, when she had called you up, about the prisoner?—
I asked her what had become of him.   What answer did
she make?—She said he was gone home.

On re-examination by Mr. Serjeant COPLEY, witness
said she knew her mother's clock was too fast when the
deceased came to her mother's house.   She could not tell
exactly what time it was, but she thought it wanted about
twenty minutes to five.   She did not observe anything particular about the deceased's dress.

Benjamin Carter was then called, and in reply to Mr.
PERKINS, he said:—" I am a farmer, and live with my father
at Erdington.   On the night of the 26th May I was in the
room at Tyburn House where the dance was.   I saw the
deceased and the prisoner dancing together.   I left the
house between eleven and twelve, and went to the bridge outside the house to Hannah Cox.   I stayed there with her
about a quarter of an hour.   Hannah Cox desired me to go
back and fetch the deceased.   I went, and found the
deceased and prisoner dancing together.   I spoke to Mary

Ashford, and went back to the bridge. In about a quarter of an hour Mary Ashford and Thornton came to us. I went with them a little way towards home, and then turned back towards Tyburn House. I afterwards overtook them all— deceased, prisoner, and Hannah Cox—again between Mr. Reeves's and Mr. Potter's. I then parted with Hannah Cox; she went off another road to go home. I went on with the prisoner and the deceased to the turn in the road, and then went home. I saw no more of them that night."

Having thus laid before the jury evidence to show that the prisoner and the deceased went from the dance together on the night in question, and were left alone near midnight on the highroad leading to the deceased's residence, Mr. CLARKE then brought the case one step nearer home to the prisoner by proving that from that time up to near three in the following morning the prisoner and deceased were together wandering about the fields. The witness *John Hompidge,* or *Umpage,* who proved this, is one of the most important witnesses called during the course of the trial. His evidence was much relied upon, not only by the prosecution, but also by the prisoner.

In reply to Mr. CLARKE, he stated :—" I live at Witton, near Erdington, in the parish of Aston. I remember being in Mr. Reynolds's house at Penns on Tuesday morning, the 27th May last, in the lower part of the house. Whilst I was there sitting in the house I heard somebody talking. It was about two o'clock, or a little after, when I first heard the talking. I continued to hear the talking until a few minutes before I started to go home. I left for home about a quarter before three. When I first got out of doors I did not see anybody, but when I had passed along the footpath over the fields to the 'fore-drove' leading into Bell Lane I saw a man and a woman at a stile at the bottom of the 'fore-drove.' Bell Lane leads to Erdington. When I got up to the stile I knew the man to be the prisoner. I had known him before. I bid him good morning, and he said good morning to me. I did not know who the woman was. I did not see her face; she held her head down so that I could not see it. I left them both sitting against the stile."

On cross-examination by Mr. REYNOLDS, he said:—"I know the pit where the body was afterwards found.   It is about 100 yards from Reynolds's house.   There is another house in the neighbourhood nearly adjoining the close.   I went out of the house a quarter before three.   I came within about 100 yards of the persons at the stile before I saw them."

The next witness, a man named *Thomas Aspree,* proved seeing the deceased going towards Erdington *alone.*   It is material here to observe that the *prosecution* never were able to trace Thornton after this.   The witnesses who next saw him were his own, and called on his behalf.

Aspree said:—" I live at Erdington.   On the 27th of May I was going to Great Barr, passing by Mr. Greensall's house. I crossed Bell Lane, leaving Erdington on my left and Bell Lane on the right, by Greensall's house.   On the right in Bell Lane there is a horse-pit.   I saw Mary Ashford against the horse-pit, going towards Erdington ; she was walking very fast.   It was about half-past three.   She was quite alone.   I looked up Bell Lane in the direction from which she was coming, and I saw no other person."

Cross-examined by Mr. READER.—" She was going towards Mrs. Butler's house.   That will be about a quarter of a mile distant.   I saw no other person."

In answer to Mr. Serjeant COPLEY, this witness said, " Bell Lane is twenty-one yards wide, and straight for a considerable distance."

John Kesterton, a farmers' labourer, the next witness called, saw the deceased after she had left Cox's on her way back home.   His evidence is remarkably clear, and corroborates fully Hannah Cox as to her statement of the time when the deceased left Mrs. Butler's house on her way home. Although it does not appear on the face of the evidence, nor on cross-examination, yet the fact was that this witness was in the habit of going daily to Birmingham for manure, and his watch was set by Birmingham time.   His estimate of the time is therefore more likely to be correct than that of almost any witness called to speak on this point.   He said:—" I live at Erdington, with Thomas Greensall, a farmer.   On the 27th of May I got up about two.   I went first to the stables to fettle the horses; the stable looks towards the road that leads to the village of Erdington. I put my horses to the waggon at about four that morning, and then took them to the pit of water in Bell Lane by the side of the road. When my horses had drunk I turned them round and went straight off for Birmingham through Erdington. I know Mrs. Butler's house; I passed it, and after I passed I turned to look back. I saw Mary Ashford coming out from Mrs. Butler's entry. I knew her perfectly well. I smacked my whip at her. She turned round, smiled, and nodded to me. This would be about a quarter past four. She went up Bell Lane, and seemed in a great hurry. I hardly know the prisoner by sight, but I have seen him. I saw no person like him that morning; nobody but her. The road is broad, and I could see for some distance; but I saw nobody on the road."

Mr. READER then put one or two questions of importance in order to fix the time when the deceased was seen coming out of Mrs. Butler's. The whole defence turns upon this as a starting point. You knew the deceased very well?—Yes. You could not therefore be mistaken in her person?—No. And you saw her about a quarter past four coming out of the entry?—Yes. And you saw nobody else?—No.

The next witness, *Joseph Dawson*, spoke to meeting the deceased at a quarter past four, as near as he could guess, between Bell Lane and Mrs. Butler's. He spoke to her; asked her how she did, and passed on; in respect of time entirely corroborating Kesterton.

Thomas Broadhurst, the last witness that saw the deceased alive, was then called, and said :—" On the morning of the 27th of May, I was on the turnpike road leading from Tyburn. I crossed Bell Lane. Before I crossed, Mary Ashford crossed the turnpike road in front of me. She was going from Erdington towards Penns. She had a bundle in her hand, and was walking fast. I asked a man who was trenching about 200 yards below, what time it was, and he said it was about ten minutes past four. When I got home it was twenty minutes to five, which was a quarter too fast. It would take me seven minutes to get home. It would be half a mile and better from the part of Bell Lane

where I saw Mary Ashford to Erdington." This witness,
after making the allowances he mentions, fixes the time when
he last saw the deceased at eighteen minutes past four,
which is in accordance with and in full corroboration of the
other witnesses.

George Jackson proved finding the deceased's bundle and
bonnet, which led to the discovery of the body.   He said :—
"I live in Hurst Street, Birmingham, and follow the labouring
business.   On the 27th of May I left Birmingham for a
place betwixt Newhall Fields and Sutton.   It was five o'clock
when I was at the top of Moor Street in Birmingham.   I
came past the workhouse at Erdington and turned up a lane
near the workhouse.   I do not know the name of that lane.
I afterwards turned again out of that lane into the fore-drove
leading for Penns.   I went along a footpath and came to a
pit of water.   I observed a bonnet, a pair of shoes, and a
bundle close by the top of the slope that leads down into the
pit.   I looked at them.   I saw one of the shoes all blood.
Then I went towards Penn's Mills to fetch a person to come
and look at them.   I brought a man from the first house ;
he was coming out of his own door-place, and we went to the
pit.   His name is Lavell.   I told him to stand by these
things whilst I fetched some more hands from Penn's Mills,
as nobody should meddle with them.   Going from the pit
along the footpath, I saw some blood about thirty yards from
the pit.   It might be about a couple of yards round, in a
triangle extending zig-zag about two yards.   I went a little
further and saw a lake of blood by the side of the brink.   I
saw some more to the left on some grass ; then I went
forward to the works at Penn's Mills to let them know what
had happened.   I got assistance, and sent to Lavell at the
pit.   I went to Penn's Mills to let them know, and then I
came back again.   I did not stay until the body was found.
I went to my work."

On cross-examination by Mr. REYNOLDS, the witness said :—
"It might be about five miles or five miles and a half from
Birmingham to the pit, as near as I can guess.   There is a
public road the whole way.   I left Birmingham about five,
and it was about half past six when I got to the pit.   It is
about five miles from Moor Street to the pit.   The pit is

close to the footpath, and the footpath is close to the carriage road, separated by a hedge. The pit is close to a stile, and the field in which it is, is a grass field. The field immediately before it, coming as I did from Birmingham, is a ploughed field, through which there is a public footpath. In order to get from this ploughed field into the field where the pit is, it is necessary to get over a stile. The only communication from one field to another is by the stile. The stile is two or three yards from the place where the bundle was. The things I saw were on the edge of the pit. The pit is not very steep, in a middling way; perhaps rather steep than otherwise. Penn's Mills are about half a mile off. Mr. Webster has there a considerable manufactory. I did not see all the men collected at work when I arrived, but I saw several about. Between four and five in the morning is a very common hour for labourers in the fields to be about."

Re-examined by Mr. CLARKE.—How far might it be from the place where the bundle and shoes were to the pit?—It might be about four yards from the top of the slope to the water.

Mr. CLARKE.—What time was it when you got to Mr. Webster's works?—I cannot tell; it was soon after I went to Lavell's. It might be half an hour or three quarters after I first saw the bundle till I got to Mr. Webster's works.

Mr. Justice HOLROYD.—How far were the bundle and shoes from the top of the slope?—About a foot.

William Lavell, the first of the witnesses who spoke to the footmarks, gave some very important evidence. He said:—" I am a workman at Penn's Mills. On the 27th of May, in consequence of what the last witness said to me, I went to the pit. I know the harrowed field through which a footpath from Erdington to Mill Lane goes. It is next the field where the pit is. I went along the footpath to see if I could discover any footsteps. The first I saw were those of a man going from the pit towards Erdington on my right hand, going across the ploughed field towards a dry pit at the corner of the field to the right. I then went higher up the footpath, and at about eight yards distance I discovered a woman's footsteps going from the footpath in the same way to my right. I traced the steps and found they got together in about fifteen yards. I gather from the stride and sinking in of the ground that the footsteps were those of persons running. I traced them up to the right-hand far corner of the field where the dry pit is, running together. When I got to the corner I observed them dodging backwards and forwards; the steps there seemed shorter, as if they had been dodging about. I traced the steps further on to the grass at the corner of the field to the dry pit. They then went from the dry pit to the water pit in the harrowed field; not the one where the body was found. I traced them on the harrowed ground. The footsteps appeared to be of persons walking; sometimes the woman's feet went on the edge of the grass, and sometimes on the edge of the field. I traced the footsteps down to the water pit in the harrowed field, and could trace them no further. I traced the man's foot till it came to the hard road (the footpath), but could not trace the woman's foot because she was on the left of the man on the grass. I could trace them no further towards the second pit, because the road was hard. I afterwards traced the footsteps of a man in a contrary direction back from the pit in the harrowed field. They began at the foot-path and were those of a man running. They were on the harrowed ground. There were no woman's footsteps. I traced these footsteps about three parts up the field; it might be rather better towards the dry pit. The footing then turned down to the left as I was pursuing the track. I traced them down to the gate at the further corner crossing the footpath. They crossed the footpath at the middle of the piece or thereabouts. They appeared to be the footsteps of a man running. They went quite to the corner to the gate. On the other side was a greensward, clover, and I could trace them no further. The gate would lead into some meadows towards Pipe Hall. I know Castle Bromwich. That road would take a person to Castle Bromwich. You could get that way into the Great Chester Road for Castle Bromwich. From Penn's Mill Lane the regular road to Castle Bromwich from the corner of the pit would have been straight across the piece, up the foot-road, and so into Bell

Lane. By the way I traced these footsteps to the corner of the field, a man would sooner get to Castle Bromwich than by going the regular way. From the gate where I lost the footsteps there was no regular way to Castle Bromwich, and to go that way you must go upon trespass. It would make a shorter cut. I afterwards went into the field with a man with a pair of shoes to try the footsteps. Joseph Bird took the shoes. They were the prisoner's. A woman's shoe was also taken, but not at that time. I took that shoe. The shoes were right and left shoes. The footsteps of the man in the field appeared to be made with right and left shoes. I and Bird tried the shoes on the footsteps. We compared them I suppose with about a dozen. The shoes fitted these footsteps exactly. I compared them with the footsteps on both sides of the way. I have no doubt whatever that these footsteps were made with those shoes. I compared them with the footsteps that turned off the road, about eight yards from where the footsteps of the woman turned off. They fitted them. I compared them with those parts where the man and the woman appeared running, and where the dodging was. They agreed in all those parts. Some of the footsteps were covered up with boards at the corner, up by the dry pit. I covered them. One of the shoes was nailed with a nail called a sparrow-bill."

Was there any at the toe of either shoe?—There is not on one side. Which shoe?—The right. Were there any marks of this sparrow-nail on those that you covered?—There was one step trod on a short stick, which threw the foot up, and there were the marks of two nails. I tried the shoe with that footstep. The nails were so small we could not see whether they fitted those marks or not. I afterwards went with a woman's shoe in company with Bird. It was Mary Ashford's shoe. I compared that shoe with the woman's steps I had traced, and with those that turned to the right and with those where the man and woman appeared to be running, and where the doubling was, in every place. The shoe corresponded. We took both shoes. I have no doubt in my mind that the woman's steps all along were made by those shoes. I know the slope of the pit where the body was found. I saw at the edge of the slope one footstep, that of a man ; it appeared to be the left foot sideways, inclining towards the slope. I did not compare the shoe with that. I saw where the bundle was beside the pit. There were also a pair of shoes and a bonnet. The shoes were not tied up in anything. These were the shoes with which I compared the footsteps.

This part of the evidence goes to show that the shoes with which the footsteps were compared were those in which Mary Ashford had been to the dance, and in which she had been walking with Thornton for three hours over, or in the neighbourhood of, this identical field. At Hannah Cox's, it will be remembered, she changed everything *except her shoes.* If she had also changed her shoes, the whole face of this evidence against Thornton might have assumed a very different aspect. It is curious to think what the effect would have been if Mary Ashford had put on the shoes which she had left at Hannah Cox's in the evening on her return from Birmingham, and in which she had *not* been to the ball. In that case, if the footsteps in the field were made by her in the shoes which she had changed at Hannah Cox's in the morning *after* the ball, they would have been conclusive evidence against Thornton. As however they were not, but were made by the shoes which she wore at and after the ball up to half-past three, all which time she was voluntarily in Thornton's company, the value of the footsteps as evidence is much weakened. It is singular and unfortunate that the only articles of dress, the change of which could have thrown any light on the question of the deceased's death, were those which, by some fatality or other, were not changed.

The witness then went on to say :—" Below the gate, about forty yards from the pit, I saw blood. There was blood also about fourteen yards up nearer the pit. I traced the blood for about fourteen yards—a train of blood. It ran straight up towards the pit, across the path, and then about a foot from the path on the clover."

When you saw it on the clover were there any footsteps ? —No. How near the footway were those drops that you saw on the clover ?—About a foot. Was the dew on the clover ? —Yes. Did the blood on the clover appear to be a track of

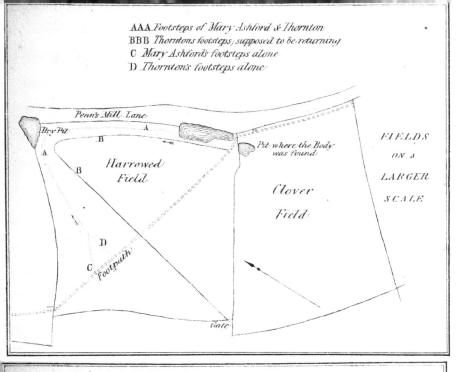

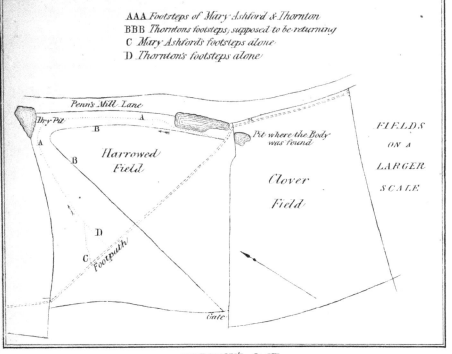

THORNTON'S CASE.

blood or a few drops?—It came in drops at last, but it was a regular run when it first came on the clover—not all the way.

Cross-examined by Mr. READER.—My house is from 200 to 300 yards from the pit. I live next Reynolds, and work at the mill. I had not been at work that morning. The men at the mill collect about half-past six. [This was to show that Mary Ashford *might* have been murdered by one of the workmen on his way to the mill.] None of my family were up at that time. The first I heard of this was by Jackson calling me. I cannot tell whether there had been much rain that morning. There had not been a storm before I traced the steps. I began to trace them about seven o'clock. It might be one on the same day when I traced the man's shoe. It rained while we were going to trace them. I do not know that it had rained before. I covered two of the man's and one of the woman's with a board before the rain began. I put the boards near the dry pit. There were a great many people collected on the ploughed field at one time after another, but not then. I do not think there were more than 1,000 footsteps there. There were a great many footsteps besides the footsteps I traced in the morning, but I will not say there were thousands. There were a great number of footsteps of other persons. I tried the shoes of some of these persons, to see if they corresponded with the marks, and they did not. Did you try the marks of the shoes of any other persons there with what you supposed to be the prisoner's? No (*a*). You say, when you began to trace you first traced the man's shoes in the direction towards Erdington?—No (*a*). You traced them backwards and forwards over different parts of the close towards the dry pit?—Yes. Some appeared to be running and some walking?—No. In the course of this tracing you traced them sometimes running and sometimes walking?—Yes. At times running, and at one time walking?—Yes. You describe them as though you had seen them, but all you mean is that in some places the marks

---

(*a*) These questions in cross-examination seem either to be inaccurately framed or inaccurately reported.

were deeper and the strides greater?—Yes.   Some parts of
the harrowed field were, I suppose, softer than others?
Partly of the same nature all over.   This must have occupied
these persons, walking and running as you describe, a long
space of time, must it not?—Yes.

Mr. Justice HOLROYD.—What was the distance from the
footpath where the tracks were to the dry pit?—About
140 yards.

Mr. READER.—How far from the dry pit to the other?—
Near upon the same length.   I then traced the footsteps
down from the top end to the pit.   The harrowed close is
not the close in which the body was found.   I saw
some blood about forty yards from the pit where the
body was found in the next close of clover.   I saw but one
mark of a footstep on the edge of the pit close to the slope.
I did not measure that.   There had not been a great many
persons near the spot before I found the marks.   *I observed
that one footstep when I got up first.*   I did not observe any
blood in the harrowed field.   I saw a footing go across the
close from the dry pit to the other corner of the close.
That would lead to Castle Bromwich.   A person could, if he
liked, have gone by Tyburn House.   By trespass he might
have gone a nearer way.   He must have got into the Chester
road.   I suppose a person could have got in less time to
Castle Bromwich if he had gone over hedge and ditch.   I
traced the spots of blood that went towards the pit; for
fourteen yards there were no footsteps of any sort, neither
of a man nor woman.   There was a footpath by the
side.   Near the pit was only one footstep, and I could not
tell whether it was a man's or a woman's.

Joseph Bird, the witness who accompanied Lavell in his
examination of the footmarks in the harrowed field, then
gave some corroborative testimony.   It is not necessary to
give the whole of his evidence, which would be merely a
repetition of that of the last witness.   He made one or two
remarks, however, as to the nature of the footsteps which
Lavell had not made, or at least had not given in evidence.
He said:—" The footsteps had the appearance of a heavy man
running.   I gather that from the length of the stride and by
the little scrape of the toe of the woman's shoe, and by the

heels of the man's shoe sinking very deep, as if made by a heavy man." And then some entirely new evidence of considerable importance. " I compared the two footsteps that had been covered with boards. I kneeled down and blew the dirt out of the right footstep, to see if there were any nail marks. There lay a bit of rotten wood across the footstep, which had turned the outside of the shoe a little up, and the impression of that side of the foot was not so deep as the other. I observed two nail marks on that side where it was shallowest. The shoes were nailed, and there was a space of about two inches where the nails were out, and they were nailed again. I marked the first nail on the side of the shoe, and then kneeled down to see if they exactly corresponded, and they did exactly. I could see the second nail mark at the same time, as well as under the shoe, and they fitted in every part exactly. I compared also the tracks of the woman's shoe. Where the running over the ground was, there was a dent or scraping in the ground; and by looking at the shoes the leather of one of them was raised at the toe more than the other, from being wet. The shoes were not alike, and the impressions varied accordingly, agreeing with the form of each shoe." After giving some evidence as to the time when he examined the footmarks, he said :—" By going along the turnpike road, a person must have passed Tyburn House and several other houses before he got to Castle Bromwich; but if he had turned to the right he might have got to that place over the fields, where there is no footpath. There is no regular footpath that way, except a bit of a road that turns off near Samuel Smith's house, which is used by the market people, and goes down to Occupation Bridge, and crosses the canal by the side of Adams' piece. By pursuing that road, a person might have gone to John Holden's either by going down the towing-path of the canal or by the road."

In cross-examination by Mr. Reynolds, the witness admitted that the straight and nearest road was along the turnpike, and that it rained sharpish as he returned from Tyburn House to measure the footsteps. There had been by that time thirty or forty people walking over the ground, but not where the boards were placed. They were ordered off by

Mr. Bedford.   Mr. Bedford came on the ground about nine
or ten o'clock.   At that time there would be about a score
of persons in the ploughed field.

In answer to Mr. Serjeant COPLEY, he said he first saw
the footmarks about seven o'clock, and there had not been
many persons in the harrowed field then.

James Simmonds proved the finding of the body.   He
said :—" I am a labourer.   I was at Penn's Mills on the
morning of the 27th of May last.   I accompanied two or three
persons to the pit; the first thing I observed was a bonnet,
a pair of woman's shoes, and a bundle.   I then dragged the
pit with an eel-rake and a pair of long reins, three or four
times, and succeeded in bringing up the body of Mary Ashford.   There were some leaves and mud about her face.
This was about eight o'clock in the morning."

Mr. *John Webster,* who had taken throughout a very prominent part in the prosecution, was then called.   He said, in
reply to Mr. CLARKE :—" I am proprietor of a considerable
manufactory at Penn's Mills.   I recollect the body of Mary
Ashford being extricated from a pit on the morning of the
27th of May; it was just brought to the edge of the pit
when I arrived.   As near as I can judge, it was about eight
o'clock.   I ordered the body to be immediately taken to
Lavell's house, and the bonnet, bundle, and shoes with it.
I examined the ground on all sides of the pit, and about
forty yards from it, observed a considerable quantity of
blood—as much as I could cover with my extended hand.
On examining the spot more closely, I discovered on the
grass the impression of a human figure; the legs of the
figure were extended, and the arms stretched out to the full
length.   In the centre of the figure was a small quantity of
blood, and at the feet a considerable quantity of coagulated
blood, the same which first caught my attention.   Between
the extension of the legs were the marks of the knees and
the toes of a man's large shoes; I judged them to have been
made by the same person.   I traced blood for nearly ten
yards up the footpath, in the direction of the pit.   A little
further from the pit, and near the stile, on the other side, in
a contrary direction from the harrowed field, there was the
mark of some person who had sat down.   I could not tell

exactly whether it was made by one or more persons. I then retired from the spot to dress, but returned in the course of an hour afterwards. I accompanied Bird into the harrowed field, and there perceived traces of a man and a woman's foot. I sent for the shoes which had been taken to Lavell's house with the body. They were brought; and I examined them with the footmarks on the ground, and they perfectly corresponded. I have not the least doubt in my own mind that the footsteps I there saw were made by the shoes of the deceased. One of the shoes was stained with blood a little on the outside, and the other a little on the inside."

[The shoes of the deceased were then produced by a police-officer, and handed to his Lordship and the jury for examination. They were marked with blood in the manner described by Mr. Webster, who stated them to be the same which were found at the edge of the pit on the 27th of May.]

Mr. Justice HOLROYD.—The black spot observable on the outside of one of the shoes, Mr. Webster, is, I suppose, one of the marks you allude to?

Mr. Webster.—It is, my Lord. The marks of blood were very plain when I first saw them; they are now much darker.

Examination of Mr. *Webster* continued.—" I then went to Lavell's to examine the body of the deceased. I perceived marks on each arm, which appeared to me to have been made by the grasp of a man's hand. I saw the clothes the body had on; they consisted of a red spencer, a pink coloured gown, and a pair of black worsted stockings. The seat was in a very dirty state; and I observed some blood upon other parts of it. These were the same clothes which I had sent from the pit with the body, and intrusted to the care of Lavell's wife. Next day I had them sent to my house, where they were put under lock and key in my possession, until they were given to Dale, the police-officer. I know Butler's house very well. After the first examination of the prisoner at Tyburn, I went to examine her clock. I compared it with my own watch, which I consider to be a very accurate one, and found it to be forty-one minutes too fast. My watch was set by Mr. Crompton's, which I believe keeps time very correctly."

Fanny Lavell, in reply to Mr. Serjeant COPLEY, said :—" I am the wife of William Lavell. I remember the body of Mary Ashford being brought to my house on the morning of the 27th of May. Mr. Webster gave me a bundle of clothes; it was undone by him in my presence. He also delivered to me a pair of shoes and a bonnet. I delivered the whole of them back to him the next day in the same condition in which they were given to me. I undressed the body of the deceased. Her clothes were in a very dirty condition; they were very bloody. The pink gown was particularly so in the seat. The blood had stiffened them so much in some parts that I was obliged to tear some of them off. The front of the shift had a rent of about five or six inches in length."

Mr. Justice HOLROYD.—Did you perceive the marks of blood upon the black stockings?—I cannot say I did, my Lord.

Witness continued.—" I examined the dresses of the deceased. The gown in which she danced had a small drop of blood on the seat; the white stockings, too, had marks of blood upon them; and the back of every other part of the gown was clean, and the muslin spencer appeared to be but little soiled."

[Thomas Dale, the police-officer, here produced a bundle, which he stated to be the same he had received from Mr. Webster. It was sealed up by Mr. Webster before it was given to him. The seal was then broke, and the two dresses of the deceased handed to the jury. The pink gown, as described by Mrs. Lavell, appeared to be much blooded, and the mark of a drop of blood was observable on one of the black stockings.]

Mary Smith said :—" I live at Penn's Mills. On the 27th of May I assisted in examining the body of the deceased. It was then lying at the house of William Lavell, and might be about half-past ten o'clock in the morning. The body at that time was not cold. I did not see the clothes of the deceased taken off. On each arm, just above the elbow, was a black mark, which appeared to have been made by the grasp of fingers."

Mr. *William Bedford,* a magistrate for the county, was then called. He said :—"On the 26th of May I went to Tyburn House and took the deposition of the prisoner. The deposition now produced is the one. It was read over to the prisoner, and signed by him afterwards in my presence." The deposition was then read by the officer of the court. It is a document of some importance, and as some discrepancies exist in the different copies inserted in the published reports, the following has been taken from the brief for the prosecution, and is the same as the copy prepared for the use of the Judge on the trial.

At Tyburn, in the parish of Aston, in the county of War-
wick. The voluntary examination of Abraham Thornton,
of Castle Bromwich, in the said parish of Aston, taken
before William Bedford, Esquire, one of His Majesty's
justices of the peace for the said county :

Who saith that he is a bricklayer; that he came to the
" Three Tuns" at Tyburn about six o'clock last night, where
there was a dance. That he danced a dance or two with the
landlord's daughter, but whether he danced with Mary Ash-
ford or not he cannot recollect. Examinant stayed till about
twelve o'clock. He then went with Mary Ashford, Benjamin
Carter, and a young woman, who he understood to be
Mr. Machin's housekeeper, of Erdington; that they walked
together as far as Potter's. Carter and the housekeeper went
on towards Erdington. Examinant and Mary Ashford went
on as far as Mr. Freeman's; they then turned to the right
and went along a lane till they came to a gate and stile on the
right-hand side the road; they went over the stile and into the
next piece, along the fore-drove; they continued along the foot-
road four or five fields, but cannot tell exactly how many.
Examinant and Mary Ashford then returned the same road.
When they came to the gate and stile they first got over, they
stood there about ten minutes or a quarter of an hour talking.
It might be then about three o'clock, and whilst they stood
there a man came by; examinant did not know who. Had on
a jacket of a brown colour. The man was coming along the
footpath they had returned along. Examinant said good

*morning, and the man said the same. Examinant asked
Mary Ashford if she knew the man ; she did not know
whether she knew him or not, but thought he was one who had
been at Tyburn. That examinant and Mary Ashford stayed
at the stile a quarter of an hour afterwards ; they then went
straight up to Mr. Freeman's again, crossed the road, and
went on towards Erdington till he came to a grass field on
the right-hand side the road, within about* 100 *yards of
Mr. Greensall's, in Erdington. Mary Ashford walked on, and
examinant never saw her after she was nearly opposite
Mr. Greensall's. Whilst he was in the field he saw a man
cross the road for James', but he did not know who he was.
He then went on for Erdington workhouse to see if he could
see Mary Ashford. He stopped upon the green about five
minutes to wait for her. It was then four o'clock, or ten
minutes past four o'clock. Examinant went by Shipley's in
his road home, and afterwards by John Holden's, where he
saw a man and woman with some milk-cans, and a young man
driving some cows out of a field who he thought to be Holden's
son. He then went towards Mr. Twamley's mill, where he
saw Mr. Rotton's keeper taking the rubbish out of the nets at
the flood-gates. He asked the man what o'clock it was ; he
answered near five o'clock or five. He knew the keeper.
Twamley's mill is about a mile and a quarter from his father's
house, with whom he lives. The first person he saw was
Edward Teck, a servant of his father, and a boy. That his
mother was up. He took off a black coat he had on and put
on the one he now wears, which hung up in the kitchen, and
changed his hat, and left them both in the house. He did not
change his shoes or stockings, though his shoes were rather
wet from having walked across the meadows. That examinant
knew Mary Ashford when she lived at the " Swan" at
Erdington, but not particularly intimate with her ; that he
had not seen said Mary Ashford for a considerable time
before he met her at Tyburn. Examinant had been drinking
the whole evening, but not so much as to be intoxicated.*

Mr. *Bedford* then said :—" The deposition was taken about
one o'clock on the 27th May, at Tyburn House, at the house
of Daniel Clarke."

The police-officer *Thomas Dale* was then put forward. On being sworn, he said :—"I am one of the assistant constables of Birmingham. I was applied to on the morning of the 27th of May, to go to Tyburn House. I arrived there about ten.o'clock, and took the prisoner into custody. Daniel Clarke, the landlord, was then in company with him. Mr. Bedford, the magistrate, arrived there about eleven o'clock. The prisoner was then in my custody. The prisoner said, when he was before the magistrate "—

Mr. REYNOLDS.—My lord, I humbly submit to your lordship that my learned friend cannot pursue this course of examination.

Mr. Justice HOLROYD.—Certainly not, if the object is to make an addition, by oral testimony, to the prisoner's written examination taken before the magistrate.

Mr. READER.—My Lord, I know the worthy magistrate before whom this examination was taken too well to believe that a fact of any importance transpired which was not put in the deposition.

The examination of *Thomas Dale* was then resumed.— " After the examination was taken before the magistrate, I took the prisoner up stairs and examined his person. Two persons of the name of Benson and Sadler were present. I examined his linen, and questioned him about the state in which it was in. He then acknowledged to us that he had had connection with the deceased, but that it was with her own consent, and declared he knew nothing of the murder.

The cross-examination is interesting as showing the value of this officer's testimony. The important point really was whether the prisoner had admitted having had intercourse with the deceased *before* he was asked by the magistrate or after.

Mr. READER.—Dale, how long had you been with the prisoner before Mr. Bedford, the magistrate, came to Clarke's ?—An hour or more. Did he confess he had been intimate with the deceased before he was taken to be examined? —I believe he did. Did anyone hear it besides you ?—I can hardly tell ; I think not. Did you tell Mr. Bedford what the prisoner had said before he examined him ?—I believe not.

Mr. Serjeant COPLEY.—Did Thornton tell you this before the magistrate came to Clarke's ?—*I am not quite sure*

whether he said so before or after.   You are sure he did say
so to you, are you?—I am sure he said so when we were
searching him up stairs.   You are quite sure of that?—Yes.
Who heard him make that confession besides yourself?—
Mr. Sadler and Wm. Benson were present.   Who is Benson?
—I do not know.   Did not you know him before?—No; I
never saw him before that morning.   He assisted you, I
suppose?—He was called in by somebody.   I suppose he
went up stairs?—Yes, to search the prisoner.

William Benson was then sworn.   He said, in answer to
Mr. CLARKE :—" I live at Penn's Cottage, near Penn's Mills.
I was at Tyburn on the 27th of May last, and assisted Dale
in examining the person of the prisoner.   What he has stated
is perfectly true.   I was not present when the prisoner's shoes
were taken off.   He was sitting in a chair without shoes on,
and a pair of shoes, which seemed to be his, stood by him.
Mr. Bedford asked me to take up the prisoner's shoes and bring
them to him.   I took up the pair by the prisoner, and the
prisoner did not deny their being his."

Joseph Cooke, sworn.   Examined by Mr. CLARKE :—" I am a
farmer's son, and live at Erdington.   I was at the dance at
Tyburn on the night of the 26th of May.   The prisoner
Thornton was there.   I saw Mary Ashford come into the
room.   Thornton inquired who she was, and I heard
Cotterill say, ' It is Ashford's daughter.'   Prisoner then
said, ' I have been connected with her sister three times, and
I will with her, or I'll die by it.' "

Cross-examined by Mr. REYNOLDS.—" I do not think anybody heard this conversation pass between the prisoner and
Cotterill but myself.   Nobody else was near enough.   I did
not remonstrate with Thornton on making use of this
expression.   Nor did I say anything to Mary Ashford about
what I had heard.   I was not examined at the coroner's
inquest.   I cannot say how that was.   I knew when the
inquest was held.   I was at the house at the time, and
should have gone if I had been called for.   I was not asked.
I did hear that Cotterill denied that he overheard the
prisoner say what I have stated.   He never denied it to me."

Daniel Clarke, the person who kept the Tyburn House,
was then called.   His evidence was shortly as follows :—" I

heard of the body being taken out of the water. In consequence, I went to search for the prisoner. I went on the
road to Castle Bromwich, and met the prisoner near the
chapel on the turnpike-road on a pony. I asked him what
had become of the young woman that went away with him
from my house last night. He made no answer. I said,
' She is murdered, and thrown into a pit.' He said, ' Murdered!' I said ' Yes; murdered.' The prisoner said ' I
was with her till four this morning.' I then said, ' You
must go along with me and clear yourself.' He said, ' I can
soon do that.' We then rode towards my house. I did
not have any conversation with the prisoner about the
murder. *We talked about things we saw, such as farming.*
I said nothing more to the prisoner about the murder.
Though I went a mile at least with the prisoner, neither of
us mentioned another word about the matter. When we got
to my house at Tyburn, the prisoner put up his pony into the
stables, and said he would walk over the ground, the footway
to Sutton. He then went into the house and had something
to eat and drink. Nothing more was said between me and
the prisoner after we got into the house. The prisoner
stopped at my house till the constable came and took him
into custody. He said nothing more about going to Sutton."

Cross-examined by Mr. READER.—" The prisoner and I did
not converse as we went along the road. I did not allude
to the matter at all after what passed between us at first;
nor he either. I do not think the prisoner had heard of the
murder before I told him. On my telling him, he immediately said, ' Murdered! why, I was with her till four
o'clock.' I should not have known that the prisoner had
been with the deceased until four in the morning unless he
had told me."

Mr. Justice HOLROYD.—Did the prisoner appear confused
when you first told him of the murder?—I think he
appeared so a little.

Mr. READER.—You were greatly affected yourself?—Yes.
And the prisoner might have been equally so?—He might:
I cannot say.

George Freer, a surgeon, was then called, who repeated
the medical evidence previously given at the inquest. In

addition, he said :—" The deceased was a strong, well-made girl, about five feet four inches in height."

Mr. *Fowler*, on behalf of the prosecution, and *Henry Jacobs*, on behalf of the defence, both land surveyors, having produced and sworn to the accuracy of the plans laid before the jury, the case for the prosecution closed.

Mr. Justice HOLROYD then addressed the prisoner. He said :—" Now is the time for your making your defence. Your counsel have done all they can do for you. They cannot address the jury on your behalf. All they could possibly do they have done, by cross-examining the several witnesses brought forward in support of the prosecution. The Court and jury will now hearken with patience and attention to anything you have to say."

Prisoner.—My Lord, I shall leave it all to my counsel.

The following witnesses were then called :—

W. Jennings.—" I am a milkman and live at Birmingham. I buy milk of Mr. Holden, of Erdington ; myself and wife were at his house on the morning of the 27th of May. I remember seeing the prisoner coming down the lane which leads from Erdington to Mr. Holden's. He was going towards the house. It was, as near as I can judge, then about half-past four. I had no watch with me. We milked a cow a-piece in the yard after we saw him, which might occupy us ten minutes. My wife then asked Jane Heaton what o'clock it was. The prisoner was walking very leisurely. My wife saw him as well as I."

Cross-examined by Mr. CLARKE.—" I was standing in the lane within about thirty yards of Mr. Holden's house on the great road when I first saw Thornton. I had been standing there about ten minutes. When I first saw the prisoner, he was within twenty yards of us, coming down the lane between Mr. Holden's house and the canal lane. I cannot tell whether he came down the towing-path of the canal or down the lane from Erdington. I did not see him until he was within twenty yards of me. I had been standing there about five minutes before I saw him."

By Mr. READER.—" I could see down the towing-path from where I stood 300 or 400 yards. If the prisoner had come that way I think I must have seen him."

Martha Jennings.—" I saw the prisoner on the 27th of May walking gently along the lane leading to Mr. Holden's house. I then went to milk the cows, and inquired of Jane Heaton the time of day a little while afterwards. Between the time of milking the cows and seeing the prisoner might be a quarter of an hour. I was standing near Holden's house when he passed me."

Cross-examined by Mr. Serjeant COPLEY.—I was standing in the road when I first saw the prisoner. We were looking at a cow that was running at a great rate down the lane. When she had passed us, we turned to look after her, and then we saw the prisoner. Then, as your backs were towards the prisoner, he might have come along the towing-path without your seeing him?—Yes.

By Mr. REYNOLDS.—" We came that morning to Holden's by the towing-path from Birmingham not many minutes before I saw the prisoner on the road. I could see some distance along the towing-path and I saw no one. The prisoner was walking leisurely, and did not seem in a hurry, or the least confused."

Jane Heaton.—" I live servant with Mr. Holden. I was getting up at half-past four on the morning of the 27th of May. My bedroom window looks into the lane which leads from Erdington to Castle ·Bromwich. I saw a man, whom I supposed to be the prisoner, walking towards Castle Bromwich. He was walking quite slow. About a quarter of an hour after, Jenning's wife came and asked me what time of the day it was. I looked at the clock, and observed that it wanted seventeen minutes of five. The clock was not altered for several days after that."

John Holden.—" I was at home on the 28th of May last, when Mr. Twamley came to examine my clock. I believe it to be a very good one. I do not know whether it kept Birmingham time. The clock had not been altered since the day before."

John Holden, jun.—" I am son to the last witness. I live with my father. I remember Jennings and his wife being at our house on the morning of the 27th of May. My mother was ill in bed at the time. I had been to the field to fetch the cows for Jennings. I met the prisoner about 200 yards

from my father's house.   I knew him very well by sight.
He was then proceeding very slowly towards Castle Bromwich.   I cannot say what time it was, but it was early
in the morning."

Mr. *William Twamley.*—"I live at Newhall Mills, near
Sutton Coldfield, and within three miles of Castle Bromwich.
I caused the prisoner to be apprehended.   I compared my
watch and Holden's clock on the 28th of May; they were
exactly alike as to time.   From Mr. Holden's I immediately
went to Birmingham, and my watch agreed exactly with
St. Martin's Church-clock there."

John Haydon.—" I am gamekeeper to Mr. Rotton, of Castle
Bromwich.   I left my own house about ten minutes before
five of the morning of the 27th of May.   As I passed by
Mr. Z. Twamley's, I heard Mr. Rotton's stable-clock strike
five.   About five minutes after I saw the prisoner.   He was
then coming towards Mr. Twamley's mill, as if from Erdington to Castle Bromwich.   I knew him very well.   I asked
him where he had been.   He said, 'To take a wench home.'
After stopping with me a quarter of an hour he went on in a
direction to his own house."

Mr. Justice HOLROYD. — What is the distance from
Mr. Holden's to the spot where he met the prisoner?—It
is, my Lord, as near as I can guess, about half a mile.

John Woodcock.—"I am a miller.   I work at Mr.
Zachariah Twamley's mill.   I know the prisoner.   I saw a
man whom I thought to be him talking to Mr. Rotton's
gamekeeper near the flood-gates; it was then ten minutes
past five."

Cross-examined by Mr. Serjeant COPLEY.—" I know the
prisoner very well.   I was not certain that it was him, but I
thought it was at the time.   I heard the clock strike five just
before the prisoner came up to Haydon.   I had been into a
field belonging to Mr. Smallwood, and back again to the mill
after the clock struck.   I have walked the distance over since
then at my usual pace, and find I can do it in ten minutes."

W. Crompton.—"I saw Mr. Webster on the morning of
the 27th of May in the field in which were the footsteps.
We rode to Castle Bromwich together.   Mr. Webster compared his watch with mine; we perfectly agreed.   Our watches

were according to Birmingham time. We found our watches were fifteen minutes slower than Mr. Rotton's stable-clock. The Birmingham clocks and those at Castle Bromwich differed fifteen minutes."

James White.—" I remember seeing the prisoner near to Mr. Wheelwright's, in Castle Bromwich, about twenty-five minutes past five on the morning of the 27th of May; he was then on his road to his father's house, which was about half a mile distant."

William Coleman.—" I live at Erdington. I am the grand-father of the unfortunate young woman who was found in the pit. She did not sleep at my house on the night of the dance."

This closed the case for the defence. The question of the alibi, though the outline of it was doubtless known to the prosecution before the trial, had assumed an importance that was not fully anticipated in the first instance.

Mr. Justice HOLROYD then proceeded to sum up the evidence (a). He commenced by impressing upon the jury the duty of dismissing from their minds everything they had heard relative to the case before they came into court, and not to suffer prejudice to interfere with their duty. In order to convict the prisoner, he observed, the evidence must be such as not to carry in their minds a reasonable doubt of his guilt. The counsel for the prosecution did not insist that they had produced any direct and conclusive evidence that the prisoner had committed the murder. They had inferred his guilt prin-cipally by combining all the circumstances attending the case, and it remained with them well to consider in what degree those circumstances furnished satisfactory proofs against the prisoner. Crimes of the highest description, it was certain, might be proved by circumstantial evidence only, and sometimes that kind of evidence was the strongest of all others. But then it must be taken and compared in all its parts and considered in all its bearings. Witnesses

---

(a) The summing up of the learned judge is given here in full from the shorthand notes taken at the time, and published in *Cooper's* report of the trial.

might vary in their testimony in stating the appearances of the same things; but facts could not be altered; they always spoke for themselves, and would not give way to opinions.   But these circumstances, he must observe, must be clear, full, and perfect.   Nothing should be wanting to complete the connection, or the whole would necessarily fall to the ground.   They must therefore examine with the greatest care all the circumstances on which the proofs of guilt depended, and whether they amounted only to mere presumptions and probabilities instead of positive and real facts.

If, on considering maturely all the circumstances of the case, they should be of opinion that no reasonable doubt existed, and that Thornton was the person who committed the crime, in justice to the public the conviction of the prisoner must follow.   But if that should not be the case, if they should have good reason to doubt of his guilt, though they could not consider him blameless, that would be a ground of acquittal.

Probably the jury might think, considering the time as spoken to by the last witnesses, that a good deal of the mystery of this transaction had been unravelled.

That this young woman was at the dance on the night of the 26th, and that this transaction happened on the morning of the 27th: that the prisoner was with her at the dance and during great part of the night, was perfectly clear.   It was clear, too, that he had had connection with her, not merely from circumstances, but from his own acknowledgment.   One point material for their consideration was whether that connection took place with or against her consent.   If the connection took place against her consent, and a rape had been committed, that would be ground for the guilty party to wish to get rid of her testimony.   If there were no rape, and the intercourse took place with the consent of the deceased, whether that consent was obtained by great importunity or not, that would make it less likely that he should commit murder.   The conduct of the prisoner, too, when he was taken up, was very material to be attended to in considering the probability or improbability of his having been guilty.

But in one point of view—with a view to infer the probability of his guilt—it would be very material to consider at what time the connection took place, whether before the deceased went and changed her dress at Mrs. Butler's, or afterwards. Because, if they thought the connection took place previous to that time, then the deceased coming to Hannah Cox's, and making no complaint at all against the prisoner, would show that if it had taken place before, it had taken place by her consent, or that the inference would be too uncertain to form any argument against the prisoner. He mentioned these things because they would be material in considering whether, at the periods of time at which the prisoner was proved to have been at considerable distances, the connection could have taken place after that time, that is, if the witnesses for the prisoner had spoken the truth.

It was a very commendable thing on the part of Mr. Webster and Mr. Twamley that they had taken such pains to ascertain the time, which was sometimes the main ingredient in ascertaining facts.

In reciting Hannah Cox's testimony, his lordship observed it was not material to repeat all the circumstances about the deceased changing her dress, and going to Birmingham. After alluding to what had occurred previous to her calling at Mrs. Butler's, his lordship said he then came to a part more material, namely, the time at which she called there. Now, according to Hannah Cox's evidence, when the deceased called at her mother's it was about twenty minutes before five by her mother's clock. Her mother's clock was forty-one minutes faster than Mr. Webster's watch, and his watch was agreeable to Birmingham time. It was very material to see at what time the deceased came to Mrs. Butler's house, and what time she left; and, therefore, what space of time there was for the transactions to take place between that time and the time when the prisoner was seen three miles and a half from that place. It was twenty minutes before five by her mother's clock; that would be one minute before four by the Birmingham time when she was called up.

The gown and stockings which the deceased took off there

D

were both bloody.   Her dress did not seem disordered, and
she appeared calm and in good spirits.

It would be ten minutes or a quarter past four when the
deceased went away again.   It was between two and three
miles from thence to her uncle's, where she lived.   The
deceased said she had slept at her grandfather's, to make an
excuse to her friend for having been out all night.   Her
grandfather's house was about a quarter or half a mile from
the place where Hannah Cox parted with her on the preceding night; and when they parted she said she was going
to her grandfather's.

Benjamin Carter's evidence, his lordship said, only went
to the transactions of the night before at the ball, and until
they parted.

On Umpage's evidence the learned judge remarked that
if the persons whom this witness heard talking in the night
while he sat in Reynolds's house were the prisoner and the
deceased, it must have been previous to the time when she
called at Hannah Cox's.   He first heard the voices about
two o'clock, and continued to hear them until a few minutes
before he left.   He set out from Reynolds's house about a
quarter before three.   Soon afterwards he saw them against
a stile in the fore-drove.   The pit was distant about 100 yards
from Reynolds's house, and they must have come down
there, agreeably to the account which the prisoner gave in
his examination before the magistrate.   The deceased, when
this witness came up to them, appeared to wish not to be
known, by her hanging down her head; but that was not
unlikely whether anything had taken place between them
or not.

The period of time of their being together being about
three o'clock, it must have been previous to the deceased
having returned to Hannah Cox's, at which period they
certainly had been in one or more of the closes where the
footmarks were afterwards discovered.

Asprey saw the deceased about half-past three o'clock
going towards Erdington, and walking very fast, at which
time the prisoner was not with her; this must have been
when she was going to Hannah Cox's, and at that time
nobody was seen up the lane.

When Joseph Dawson saw the deceased it must have been after she had changed her dress, and was returning from Hannah Cox's; and, making an allowance for Mrs. Butler's clock, it would then be about ten minutes after four; so that she was then seen going on without the prisoner, and there was no evidence of any person seeing her with the prisoner after she had changed her dress.

In remarking upon the testimony of George Jackson, his lordship said there were no footsteps on the slope down to the pit, except one of a man, which was not compared; nor was this footstep seen until after Jackson had been there, and whose footstep it was did not appear. Nor did it appear how the bundle, the bonnet, and the shoes came there; that was a mystery which was not explained by any part of the evidence.

Supposing the connection had taken place at a prior time, before the deceased had returned to Hannah Cox's, then a question arose whether there had been a fresh attack upon her. How she came there, or for what purpose, or how she came into the pond, did not appear; but this footstep was upon the very top of the slope leading down to the pit, which was rather steep than otherwise, and there were no other marks of footsteps.

The bonnet, the bundle, and the shoes, were found on the grass about a foot from the top of the slope; and it would seem very extraordinary if the deceased, in despair, had thrown herself into the water, how she came to take off her bonnet and her shoes. How, therefore, the circumstance took place—whether she had fallen in, whether she threw herself in, or how she came there, there was no evidence to give information; the evidence was not positive on that point, and the conclusion, therefore, must be collected from comparing together all the circumstances of the case.

William Lavell's evidence, his lordship said, was material as to what was going on in the course of the night between the prisoner and the deceased. He described the footsteps of a man going out of the path leading towards Bell Lane, and also the footsteps of a woman leading the same way. These footsteps did not go off the path from the same place; but about fifteen yards from the path they joined, or came together, and from their appearance, this witness thought they had been running. He traced these footmarks together up to the corner of the field. It was not improbable but that the deceased, if she was coming that way, on seeing the man, had turned to run, and that they had both run together. There was a good deal of dodging about; this dodging was in a harrowed field, and therefore the footsteps could be easily traced. The witness traced the footmarks up to the grass by the dry pit; the same footmarks he traced down towards the water pit in the same field. It was material that he could not see the footsteps of the woman on the grass, while on the edge of the pit the footsteps on the grass were plain to be seen. He then traced the footsteps of a man running in a contrary way, which turned to the left, and went down to a gate at the opposite corner of the field, making a shorter cut. The inference to be drawn from these circumstances was that the person, whoever he was, that had done the act ran away, and that those were his tracks.

From the circumstance of there being no footsteps to be seen near the pit where the body was found, and from some of the blood being there, the inference was that the blood had fallen from a body carried; but it was questionable, on the other hand, whether the person whose blood had flowed there might not have walked, because she could not be tracked in other places on the grass where there were no marks of blood.

When Mary Smith examined the body, which was about half-past ten in the morning, she states that it was not then cold, from which circumstance it was probable that the act was committed so much the later in the morning.

In commenting upon the deposition of the prisoner taken before the magistrate, his lordship observed, it was a circumstance deserving consideration, that the prisoner acknowledged having had connection with the deceased before he was compelled to make that disclosure, to account, on the examination of his person, for the appearance of his clothes.

When Daniel Clarke first saw the prisoner, and told him that Mary Ashford was murdered, he immediately answered, " Murdered! I was with her till four o'clock:" so that the jury would perceive in neither of these instances was there any concealment.

After concluding the evidence for the prosecution, his lordship remarked it did seem that these persons, the prisoner and the deceased, were upon the stile about three o'clock; so that they had been together during the night about the spot where these transactions took place. He was inclined to suppose that the connection had not taken place before the deceased went to Hannah Cox's. If it happened before, then the prisoner was never seen with her by any person after she left that house. The jury were to consider whether it could or could not have happened after; and if after, then whether the prisoner was the person who committed the act.

In commenting upon the evidence of William Jennings, his lordship said it seemed, by his examination, that the prisoner might have come down by the canal towing-path through the meadows, and it certainly was possible that he might have done so. But then he must have gone the distance of three miles and a half from a quarter past four o'clock, and all this pursuit and the transactions which followed must have taken place within the period of time within which he was afterwards seen. It would have taken up no inconsiderable space of time, including the running and pursuit, and he thought it could not be done in a quarter of an hour. If the prisoner had been running there would have been an appearance of warmth in his person; but he was seen walking slowly, and without any appearance of heat or confusion (a).

After going through the evidence for the prisoner, his lordship said this was one of those mysterious transactions in which justice could not be done but by comparing most carefully all the facts and circumstances of the case, all the

---

(a) It is material here to observe that Thornton was a short and remarkably thick-set man, with " legs as thick as hovel-posts," according to his own attorney's description of him in his instructions to counsel. Taking, therefore, into consideration the hedges and ditches intervening, and assuming the time spoken to by the witnesses to be correct, the probability of his being able to accomplish the distance in the time allowed is much lessened.

circumstances for, as well as those against, the accused ; and before they could convict the prisoner they must be fully satisfied that he was guilty of the murder.   If any fair and reasonable doubt arose in their minds as to his guilt, the prisoner was entitled to the benefit of the doubt.   But if they were convinced that the evidence was satisfactory, and that the crime was fully proved against the prisoner, they were, in justice, bound to pronounce him guilty.   Yet, in coming to this conclusion, it was their duty well to consider whether it was possible for the pursuit to have taken place, and all the circumstances connected with it, and for the prisoner to have reached Holden's house, a distance of nearly three miles and a half, in so short a time—a period of not more than twenty minutes.

In concluding, his lordship observed to the jury that the whole of the evidence lay before them, and by that evidence only they were to be guided in their decision.   It were better that the murderer, with all the weight of his crime upon his head, should escape punishment than that another person should suffer death without being guilty.

The jury, after consulting about six minutes, returned, by their foreman, without retiring, a verdict of " Not Guilty."

Immediately after the verdict, Thornton was put on his trial before the same jury for the rape ; but the counsel for the prosecution having informed the Court that no evidence would be offered, Mr. Justice HOLROYD directed the jury to acquit him.   Thereupon a verdict of " Not Guilty" was returned, and Thornton was discharged.

THE APPEAL OF MURDER.

WILLIAM ASHFORD *v.* ABRAHAM THORNTON.

KING'S BENCH, NOVEMBER 6TH, 1817.

Counsel for the Appellant: Mr. *Clarke*, Mr. *Gurney*, Mr. *Richardson*, and Mr. *Chitty*.

For the Appellee: Mr. *Reynolds*, Mr. *Reader*, and Mr. *Tindal*.

INTRODUCTION.

THE verdict of a jury in all criminal cases is now considered final, and though where the prisoner is found guilty the sentence may be, and in some instances is, modified or remitted by the Crown, in the event of an acquittal the prisoner is never again put on his trial for the same offence. This, in practice, prevailed as much in Thornton's time as it does now, but the law was different. It was open then to the heir-at-law of a murdered person, or of a person considered to be murdered, to *appeal* the person suspected of the murder. This appeal signified nothing more than a summons or challenge to the person suspected. It was, in fact, a criminal prosecution put in force by one private subject against another; and it had this material distinction from a public prosecution, that it sought to have the offender punished, not because the crime was a public offence, but because it was a private injury. In the earlier days it was no doubt chiefly used as a means of extorting compensation, but as civilization advanced, and offences were no longer redeemable by money, this private process was, in rare instances, put in force in order to ensure the infliction of some punishment at least on the person suspected, though no pecuniary compensation might be allowed. In Thornton's time, though the right of appeal was undoubtedly in existence, in practice it was quite obsolete, the last instance, in a case of felony, being as far back as the reign of George the Second (*a*).   Of its legality, however, there could be no doubt; and, in fact, the decision of the King's Bench in this particular instance showed that both *Appeals of Murder and Wager of Battel* were at that time undoubtedly the law of the land.

The acquittal of Thornton on the two indictments tried at Warwick gave rise to a great deal of dissatisfaction, not only in that county, but throughout England.   An opinion was formed, and rapidly gained ground, that a great failure of justice had taken place; that the verdict had been given against evidence; and that the witnesses for the prisoner had, in the matter of the alibi, wilfully and deliberately committed perjury.   It is not, perhaps, to be wondered at that public opinion should have been against Thornton.   The evidence was strong and, to persons not able or willing to criticise evidence, convincing.   The crime, too, assuming murder to have been committed, was a most brutal one.   In addition it was stated and believed that Mary Ashford's case was by no means the first in which Thornton had been concerned; that he had been on other occasions placed in a similar predicament; but that the offence had always been condoned by money, and large sums paid by his father in order to avoid the disgrace of a conviction.   Of the truth of these assertions there was no proof; but the public did not require and certainly would not pay any attention to proofs that did not coincide or harmonize with their own preconceived convictions.   The result was, that a great and unreasonable prejudice was raised up against Thornton. When he appeared in his own neighbourhood again, and especially when he was seen in Birmingham, crowds followed and insulted him.   On all sides a desire was expressed to get the case re-opened.   Funds were raised by subscription, and ultimately it was determined at all hazards to get Thornton, by means of the obsolete *Writ of Appeal of Murder*, put a

---

(*a*) *Bambridge and Corbett's Case*, 1730, State Trials, 17, 398.

second time on his trial, in the hopes that a jury would be found who would not, like the previous jury, have any hesitation in convicting him.

The only way by which this could be accomplished was by getting the heir-at-law of the deceased Mary Ashford to institute the proceedings. Though both her father and her grandfather were living, neither of them could claim as heir, for, according to the law as it then stood, no inheritance could lineally ascend. But Mary Ashford had left brothers her surviving, the eldest of whom, William Ashford, would be her heir-at-law. He was a young man barely of age, by occupation a labourer. He was seen, and consented to the proceedings proposed. The trial had taken place in August. By October all the preliminaries were arranged, and on the 9th of the same month a writ, signed by the Secretary of State for the Home Department, was directed to the sheriff of Warwickshire, the Hon. Henry Verney, commanding him to cause Abraham Thornton to be re-apprehended.

In the course of the next day Thornton, who, ever since the trial had been at his father's house at Castle Bromwich, was arrested, by virtue of a writ issued by the high sheriff, and lodged again in the custody of the gaoler at Warwick. Upon being informed of the nature of the charge against him, he quietly submitted without making the least remonstrance.

On Thursday, the 6th day of November, 1817, the first day of Michaelmas Term, this extraordinary case came before the King's Bench, Lord Ellenborough (Lord Chief Justice of England), Mr. Justice Bayley, Mr. Justice Abbott (afterwards Lord Tenterden), and Mr. Justice Holroyd, being the Justices present. After some formal matters had been disposed of, Mr. CLARKE, the senior counsel for the appellant, was called upon by the Court.

Mr. CLARKE said he appeared on behalf of William Ashford, on an *Appeal of Murder* against Abraham Thornton; and after some preliminaries, in the course of which both Ashford and Thornton were brought into court and placed opposite each other, and the different writs and returns read, he moved that Thornton be placed at the bar in the

custody of the marshal of the Marshalsea, and the count
of appeal put in by William Ashford be read. This was
accordingly done, and the count, of which the following is a
short abstract, was read.

It commenced by stating that Abraham Thornton was
attached to answer the appeal of William Ashford, who was
the eldest brother and heir-at-law of Mary Ashford, and
then proceeded to charge Thornton in terms very similar to
the indictment with the murder of Mary Ashford on the
27th of May last. It concluded with averring that if
" Thornton denied the felony and murder, then that he,
Ashford, was ready to prove the same, and had found
pledges to prosecute."

Mr. READER.—My lords, the defendant has had no notice
of this proceeding, and certainly, with regard to myself, as
the papers were only sent to me late last night, I have had
no sufficient opportunity to look into the subject. From the
rareness of cases of the kind, it will not, perhaps, be
expected that I should be at all points prepared; and it is a
matter requiring great consideration.

Lord ELLENBOROUGH.—What time do you wish for?

Mr. READER.—I trust that by appearing now for the
prisoner it will not be considered that I waive any objections
I might be entitled to take in his favour. In the case of
Bigby, widow, v. *Matt. and Pat. Kennedy* (a), the Court of
its own act adjourned the proceedings to a future day,
directing that the parties accused should, in the meantime,
remain in the custody of the marshal. The counsel on both
sides declined moving for an adjournment. I hope the same
course will be adopted to-day, and that the subject will be
postponed until some time in the next week. May I be
permitted to ask if in cases of this sort, by the practice of
the Court, any time be allowed to the defendant to plead?

Lord ELLENBOROUGH.—In the case you have referred to a
week's time was given for the defendant to plead.

Mr. Barlow, the secondary in the Crown-office, informed
his lordship that the delay was allowed generally, not

(a) 5 Burr. 2643, and 2 Blackst. 714.

for the purpose merely of giving the defendant time to plead.

Mr. Justice ABBOTT.—The week's time to plead was given in another case, not in that.

Lord ELLENBOROUGH.—Giving that time will not prejudice you when you come up under the rule on the *dies data* ; you will be heard without any consideration that you have prayed the delay. What time will be convenient ?

Mr. READER.—Monday se'nnight. In the meantime it will be necessary for me to pray, on behalf of the prisoner, oyer and copies of the original writ, the return, and the declaration.

Lord ELLENBOROUGH.—You shall have access to them at any time for your convenience for the purpose of collecting the contents ; but I do not know that the Court is prepared to say that copies ought to be delivered to you.

Mr. READER.—In one of the cases now in the hands of your lordships it was permitted.

Mr. CLARKE.—The case alluded to by Mr. READER was long before the authority in Douglas, where it is said that the Court will not grant oyer of the original writ.

Lord ELLENBOROUGH.—The last case is that of Bonner; but the proceedings there were *ore tenus*, and the Court did not grant oyer. You may have it read, so that you can take down what is necessary for your purpose.

Mr. READER requested that the officer would read the document slowly, that it might be taken down in shorthand.

Lord ELLENBOROUGH.—This is a proceeding in which, perhaps, a copy may be very material ; but it is important that we should adhere to the established course, or the privilege might be claimed in all criminal cases.

The original writ of appeal was then read aloud by the officer of the Court, as well as the return and the count of the plaintiff appellant. After this had been concluded, Mr. READER applied to know if on the future day the prisoner must attend.

Lord ELLENBOROUGH.—Let him be committed to the custody of the marshal of the Marshalsea, and be brought up again on Monday se'nnight, and the same day the plaintiff appellant must appear.

With this adjournment the proceedings on the first day terminated, and Thornton was removed in the custody of the marshal of the Marshalsea.

On Monday, the 17th, the case again came on for hearing. The Court was crowded to excess, and long before the doors opened a great number of persons were assembled on the outside, in the hope of admittance. It was only with great difficulty, and after strong resistance, that the avenues to the Court were cleared. The same counsel appeared as on the former occasion. Thornton was brought into court in custody of the tipstaff and the keeper of the Marshalsea Prison, and placed in the centre of the front row of barristers, behind the King's counsel, Mr. READER being upon his left hand, and Mr. REYNOLDS behind him.

Mr. Le Blanc, the master of the plea side, then rose and read the count delivered in by Ashford on the first day of term, an abstract of which has been already given; and, addressing Thornton, said :—" Abraham Thornton, how say you; are you guilty of the felony and murder whereof you are appealed, or not guilty ? "

Mr. READER immediately put a paper into Thornton's hand, on which were written the following words :—" *Not Guilty; and I am ready to defend the same by my body.*" Thornton read out these words to the court, but rather inaudibly. He then took from his counsel, Mr. READER, a pair of new buckskin gloves or gauntlets, of antique form, and embroidered in a peculiar manner, one of which he put on his left hand, and the other he flung down upon the floor of the court into the " well " between the front row, where the King's counsel were sitting, and the bench. In falling it struck Ashford, who was in front of the King's counsel, facing Thornton, on the head, and then fell at his feet. Ashford stooped to pick it up, and at one moment there was a possibility of the challenge being really accepted ; but a very audible whisper of " Let it lie " induced Ashford to relinquish his intention. Mr. READER then moved that the gauntlet be kept in the custody of the officer of the court, which was accordingly done (a).

Mr. CLARKE then rose, and said that he appeared on the part of the appellor.

Lord ELLENBOROUGH.—The appellor must be called.

Mr. CLARKE.—He is in court.

William Ashford then stood up, but Lord ELLENBOROUGH said that he must be formally called into court, which was done by Mr. Le Blanc: and Mr. CLARKE, the counsel for Ashford, then addressed the bench as follows :—

Mr. CLARKE.—My lords, I did not expect at this time of day to have heard this sort of demand made in answer to the charge that has been brought against the prisoner, viz., that the issue should depend, not upon a trial before a jury, but upon a trial by battel. At least, we may say that it is an obsolete practice, and it may be considered a very extraordinary and astonishing circumstance that a person charged with the crime of murder should be permitted to repel that charge by committing another murder; such a proceeding is both ancient and barbarous; but I shall exhibit the appellor before your lordships, and you will see that he is not a person—

Lord ELLENBOROUGH (interposing).—I wish only to correct an expression you have used. You say, " by committing another murder." If it be the law, what the law authorizes is not murder.

Mr. CLARKE.—I beg your lordship's pardon. I should have said, " by killing the brother of the person murdered." I apprehend that on inquiry your lordships will find that the allowance of this plea is in a great measure discretionary, viz., whether they will permit battel in this case to take place. I do not say that it is a matter entirely discretionary, but that it depends in some degree upon the reason of the

---

(a) The gauntlet, the fellow of the one thrown down, and the same that Thornton put on his left hand, is now in the possession of Mr. R. Sadler, of Sutton Coldfield, whose grandfather acted for Thornton in this appeal. Neither in the Queen's Bench, Crown Office, nor Record Office, can any trace now be found of the gauntlet ordered to be filed, or of the papers in the case. Probably they were all destroyed or lost when Paper Buildings were burnt down.

case. If the court, on the exhibition of the appellor, finds that he is of weak body, and on that account incapable, that, I believe, is sufficient.

Mr. Justice BAYLEY.—Have you any authority for so stating?

Mr. CLARKE.—The authorities I have are only examples of what may be an answer to the claim of trial by battel.

Mr. READER.—The court will not suppose that I mean unfitly or unpleasantly to interrupt Mr. CLARKE, but I apprehend that he is now adopting a new course of proceeding, not warranted by any authorities. If there be any objections to the wager of battel demanded by the appellee, they must be made by counter-pleading, and not by statement of counsel.

Lord ELLENBOROUGH.—Do you wish, Mr. CLARKE, to counter-plead?

Mr. CLARKE.—Certainly; and we further request that time may be allowed to enable us to prepare our counter-plea.

Lord ELLENBOROUGH.—In a proceeding so antiquated and obsolete, to grant time is certainly a matter of strict justice to you. I do not apprehend that any resistance would be made to it on the part of the appellee.

Mr. READER.—Certainly not.

Lord ELLENBOROUGH (to Mr. CLARKE).—What time would be convenient to enable you to prepare your counter-plea?

Mr. CLARKE.—I fancy we should be ready by Thursday next.

Lord ELLENBOROUGH (after consulting with the other judges).—Perhaps Friday might be more convenient to the court.

Mr. CLARKE.—Any day after Thursday that may be appointed will answer our purpose.

Lord ELLENBOROUGH again consulted the rest of the bench, and said that Saturday would, on several accounts, be preferable.

Mr. READER then addressing their lordships, said:—"I have to pray the indulgence of the court for one word, the object of which is to put the defendant in the situation in which he is entitled to be placed, both before your lordships and the public. It has been our only and for myself I may say anxious duty to consider and advise the appellee what course he ought to adopt; and I have no difficulty in declaring that we determined to recommend him to take this step, on account of the extraordinary and, I may add, unprecedented prejudice disseminated against him throughout the country in regard to this unfortunate transaction."

Mr. READER having made this undoubtedly true explanation of the reasons for adopting the course determined upon, Lord ELLENBOROUGH ordered that the prisoner should be remanded, and be brought up again on Saturday, when the other side would be ready with the counter-plea.

Mr. GURNEY observed that in consequence of the confusion prevailing at the time in court, the precise terms of the prisoner's plea had not been heard. He therefore requested that the master, to whom the paper had been handed, should read the contents distinctly.

Mr. READER said that the appellee pleaded *ore tenus*, but in order to avoid mistake the precise form had been written down.

Mr. Le Blanc then read these words, *"Not Guilty; and he is ready to defend the same by his body."*

Lord ELLENBOROUGH.—Mr. CLARKE, as this is a matter of strict form, the court wish to know whether you pray time to counter-plead, or whether you pray time generally.

Mr. CLARKE.—To counter-plead, my lord.

With this the proceedings for the day terminated, and Thornton was removed in custody, to be brought up again on the day fixed for the adjournment.

Accordingly on the next Saturday, the 22nd November, the court again met, and all parties appearing, the appellant, by his counsel, put in his counter-plea, which he verified on oath, and it was then read. It is a very lengthy document. In substance it was to the following effect:—That Thornton ought not to have wager of battel, because there were violent presumptions that he was guilty of the murder. That on the morning of the 27th May, at about seven, Mary Ashford was found drowned in a pit of water, with marks of violence upon her, and her clothes torn. That about forty yards from the pit there were the impress on the clover-grass of a human body and the marks of blood, and blood and marks also on the clover-grass leading from the impression in the direction of the pit; but no marks of footsteps over the said clover-grass, which was wet with dew. That on the previous evening Mary Ashford and Thornton had been at the dance at Clarke's house, and that Thornton had made use of a coarse expression concerning her, and that they left together about twelve and went towards Erdington. That about three they were seen together at a stile near Bell Lane. That about four Mary Ashford went to Mary Butler's house for her clothes which she had left the previous day, and remained there about a quarter of an hour, and appeared in good health and perfect composure of mind. That she then left (about a quarter past four), and a quarter of an hour after was seen going in the direction of Langley, where she lived. That to get to her residence she had to pass along a footpath leading from Bell Lane across a newly-harrowed field, next adjoining the close in which was and is the pit where the body was found. That there were footsteps on the said field, which, being carefully examined by divers credible witnesses, corresponded with the shoes worn by Mary Ashford and Thornton respectively; and that it appeared from such footsteps that Mary Ashford had been endeavouring to escape from Thornton. That Thornton had overtaken her, and that they had walked together in a direction leading to the said pit, and towards the spot where the impression of a woman's figure was found. That the footsteps ceased at about forty yards from the pit on account of the hardness of the ground. That Thornton's footsteps were traced also back from the said pit, and that near the edge of the pit was the mark of a man's left foot. That Thornton had on, on that morning, shoes that were fitted for his right and left feet respectively, and that his person was examined, and his clothes found bloody. Such was the substance of the count put in by the appellant, setting forth, in fact, the more salient points on which the prosecution had mainly relied to convict Thornton on the trial, and it prayed that Thornton should not be admitted to wage battel.

On the application of Thornton's counsel time to reply was granted, and the case adjourned until the second day of Hilary Term, the 24th January, 1818, when, Thornton being again brought into court from the King's Bench Prison, the proceedings were resumed.

Mr. CLARKE.—My lord, I attend here as counsel for the appellor, William Ashford, who was ordered by the court last term to attend to-day to hear the replication of Abraham Thornton, the appellee, to his counter-plea.

Mr. READER.—I also appear, my lord, as counsel for the defendant.

Mr. CLARKE.—I believe the proper description of your client is—the appellee.

Mr. READER.—I am told I should have said, I appear on behalf of the appellee. Be it so. I attend on the part of the appellee, who is ready with his replication, and prepared to verify the same on oath.

Thornton then stood up and swore to the truth of the contents of his replication, which was handed to Mr. Le Blanc to read. In length it greatly exceeded the counter-plea of the appellant. In substance it was shortly as follows :—

That there were strong and violent presumptions of his innocence, for that on the morning in question Mary Ashford, alone and unaccompanied, left the house of Mary Butler at a quarter past four. That she was seen shortly after in Bell Lane, and again, crossing the highroad going towards the footpath, Thornton not being in her company. That the road was broad, and that he (Thornton), if with Mary Ashford at the time, might have been seen at a considerable distance. That at half-past four, and not later than twenty-five minutes to five he (Thornton) was seen walking slowly along a lane leading from Erdington to Castle Bromwich, close to John Holden's house, being his (Thornton's) direct way home ; and that after going a mile further on the same road he was seen by John Haydon, at ten minutes to five, with whom he stopped and conversed for a quarter of an hour, and then went home. That the distance from Mary Butler's house to the pit by Bell Lane, and across the harrowed field, was one mile two furlongs and thirty yards ; and the distance from the workhouse at Erdington, the nearest part of the village of Erdington, to Holden's farmhouse along the road leading to Castle Bromwich was one mile three furlongs and sixty-two yards; and the distance from the pit round by Erdington to Holden's house was two miles and four furlongs at the least. That the nearest way from the pit to

E

Holden's, and the shortest in time was from the pit across some closes into the Chester Road, near the garden wall of John Hipkins, then across the road and across certain other inclosures into a lane leading by Mr. Laugher's house, and so along another lane to Holden's, and the distance by this route was one mile seven furlongs and 170 yards (fifty yards short of two miles), and the distance in a straight line was one mile four furlongs and sixty yards. That there was no footpath along the latter route, and from intersections and inclosures it would require far more time than the road secondly pointed out. That the time of Mary Butler's clock and the clock at Holden's farmhouse were both on the same day noted, and the time above given was the true time as kept at Birmingham on that day. That on his apprehension he voluntarily made a statement, reduced afterwards to writing, in which he gave an account of the several places at which he had been on the night of the 26th of May, and morning of the 27th, and that no fact stated by him had been contradicted, but that on the contrary his statement had been wholly confirmed.

It then set out at full length the indictment for the murder of Mary Ashford, and also the indictment for rape, and the acquittal on both; and in conclusion, submitted that the facts set forth by him in his replication were stronger, and afforded stronger and more violent presumptions of innocence than those set forth by the appellant, and prayed that he might be admitted to wage battel.

The appellant demurred to this replication, and the case was again adjourned until the 29th of January, when Mr. CLARKE put in his demurrer. Thereupon Mr. READER joined issue, first verbally and afterwards in writing, and the 6th day of February was fixed for the hearing of the demurrer, it being understood that on that day the real arguments in the case would commence. Thornton, who was stated to have listened most attentively to the proceedings, and whose conduct and demeanour generally are described to have been on the whole decidedly prepossessing, was then removed again in custody.

On the 6th day of February, 1818, the Court of King's Bench was again thronged, both inside and out, by numbers of persons anxious to catch a glimpse of Thornton, and to hear, if possible, some of the arguments.

On the Bench were the Lord Chief Justice of England, Lord Ellenborough, Mr. Justice Abbott, Mr. Justice Bayley, and Mr. Justice Holroyd. In the interval since the last adjournment the counsel on both sides had been reinforced. On the side of the appellant, Mr. Chitty, a most able and learned lawyer, appeared for the first time ; and on the side of Thornton Mr. Tindal, afterwards Chief Justice of the Common Pleas. According to custom the case was argued on both sides by the junior counsel.

At the sitting of the court, when Thornton had been placed at the bar, Mr. CHITTY rose and addressed the court on behalf of his client. His arguments took several hours in delivery, and many days of anxious and laborious investigation had no doubt been previously employed in their preparation.

He commenced by observing that the right of appeal had its origin in common law, but that from time to time many exceptions having been allowed to it, the right was eventually confirmed by the Statute of Gloucester (6 Ed. 3, c. 8), provided the appeal was brought within a year and a day after the deed done. That subsequently a practice had arisen not to put persons on their trial until the time limited for the appeal had expired, which, being found a great practical injustice, was remedied by another Act (3 Hen. 7, c. 1), providing that no previous acquittal on an indictment should be a bar to the appeal. This statute, Mr. CHITTY submitted, expressly recognized the right the heir had at common law to bring an appeal for the death of his ancestor, and particularly that the acquittal of the defendant was no bar to the suit. And he urged that the only point to consider was whether the appellee (Thornton) having in answer to that appeal pleaded his right to wage battel, that right had been at any time taken away.

In support of the proposition that the right had been in fact taken away, Glanville, writing in the time of Henry the Second, was cited as an authority. In his book (lib. 14, c. 1)

E 2

Mr. CHITTY showed it was laid down that in the case of an appeal, if it appeared that there was probable ground of suspicion, the party was not to be allowed to try the question by battel, but by ordeal, and that the accuser might decline battel, either on account of age or mayhem. Bracton also, he said, had laid it down that if the defendant, being accused of a crime, denied it, he might have the option whether he would place himself on his country or defend himself with his person; and that it was the duty of the judges *ex-officio* to inquire into the matter and cause of the appeal, and if found correct, then to award trial of battel; but with this important proviso, that if there were any violent presumptions of guilt against the defendant which could not be proved away—as if any one were found over a dead body with a bloody knife—wager of battel could not be awarded him. And this, Bracton said, was the usual custom in cases where no proof was required. But where there was a violent presumption of guilt against the appellant, there was no occasion to prove it either by the body or by the country.

Lord ELLENBOROUGH.—Then according to this, a man who may be found standing over the body with a bloody knife must of necessity be held to be guilty.

Mr. Justice ABBOTT.—And a person coming accidentally by, and finding the man wounded, draws the dagger from his body with a view to saving his life; if that person is found with the bloody dagger in his hand, he is of consequence guilty of the murder.

Mr. CHITTY.—That hasty construction of guilt was abandoned afterwards; I merely state the case with a view of showing that where the fact was considered self-evident, the party was pronounced guilty, and that the same principle now leads to persons being sent to a jury.

Mr. Justice BAYLEY.—He certainly has a right to explain the fact of his being found with a knife in his hand, and there is no other way of doing it but by a trial before a jury.

Mr. CHITTY.—Subsequent writers so explained these terms.

Lord ELLENBOROUGH.—What I infer from Bracton is, that

he considered there was no occasion for trial, either by battel
or the country, in cases where the fact exists of a bloody
knife being found in the hand of the accused.

Mr. CHITTY.—It is that for which I contend; but I wish
my argument to apply only to cases of trial by battel.

Mr. Justice BAYLEY.—Suppose the appellee denies that he
had the bloody knife in his hand, how is he then to be
tried?

Mr. CHITTY.—By his country.

Mr. Justice BAYLEY.—Then Bracton is at variance with
himself; for he says that if that fact is alleged, the appellee
is not entitled to trial either *per corpus* or *per patria.*

Mr. CHITTY.—Bracton further says : — " Likewise if a
person shall have lain in any house at night, alone with any
other, and he shall have been murdered, or if there have been
two or more there, and they shall not have raised a hue and
cry nor received a wound from the robbers, or others who
committed the murder, in endeavouring to defend themselves,
nor yet have pointed out from among themselves or others
the person who slew the man, they shall not have it in their
power to deny the death. In these cases the appellee shall
not have his choice whether he will put himself upon the
country, or defend himself by his body."

Lord ELLENBOROUGH.—There is no exception there to the
case of a man being asleep at the time a murder might have
been committed in the house in which he was. A man may
have been asleep all the time, and yet summary justice is to
follow without trial of any sort.

Mr. CHITTY.—Such seems to have been the law, my lord.

Lord ELLENBOROUGH.—I do not contradict it; but one
retires with a degree of horror from the consideration of
such laws.

Mr. Justice BAYLEY.—It appears that in those times a
man could not escape capital punishment, unless the justice
thought fit that the truth ought to be inquired into by a
jury of the country.

Mr. CHITTY.—What I mean to urge from the authority
I have quoted is that where a man's character is blackened
by evident appearances of guilt, he is not entitled to his
wager of battel.

Lord ELLENBOROUGH.—Even a trial by jury was within the merciful consideration of the justice. What was to be done if a man was refused his trial by battel or by his country?

Mr. CHITTY.—The ordeal was not then practised; he was therefore hung. Where there was a degree of doubt, the justice allowed the trial *per patria.*

My next authority is Horne's Mirror, p. 158, written in the time of Edward II., A. D. 1307. It is there laid down as follows :—"And there are divers causes to oust the defendant in the appeal of battel, for it is said that if an infant within age bringeth an appeal, or if a woman bringeth an appeal of the death of her husband, the defendant shall lose the advantage of battel; for he cannot combat or do battel with a woman. And if a party be indicted of the felony or murder, he shall not wage battel."

Lord ELLENBOROUGH.—Then the appellee is not entitled to wage battel if a bill of indictment has been preferred against him?

Mr. CHITTY.—If the bill has been found by the grand jury, that was considered a presumption of guilt. The next extract I shall cite is from Staundforde's Pleas of the Crown, published in 1567, entitled "Trial by Battel, and Counter-Plea to Battel." The extract is as follows :—"Trial by battel is another trial which the defendant in appeal of felony may elect; that is to fight with the appellant by way of trial, whether he is guilty of the felony or not; and if the event of such battel be so favourable to the defendant that he vanquish the appellant, he shall go quit with respect to the appellant, and bar him of his appeal for ever. And this is an ancient mode of trial in our law, and one much used in times past, as appears by divers precedents in the time of Kings Edward III. and Henry IV.; a mode which is not disused, but may be brought into practice again at this day if the defendant please, *and there be nothing to support the counter-plea of the other party.*

"The reason why a man shall be admitted in a case of appeal to try his cause by battel seems to be this, that no evident or probable matter appears against him to prove him guilty, but only a bare accusation. For in that the appellant demands judgment of death against the appellee, it is more reasonable that he should hazard his life with him for trial of the cause if the defendant require it, than put him on the country, which for want of evidence may be ignorant of the matter; and that he should leave God, to whom all things are open, to give the verdict in this cause, by awarding victory or defeat to one or the other party according to his pleasure. And hence our books are that if there be anything which can serve the plaintiff for presumption or testimony that his cause is true, he shall oust the defendant of his trial by battel; as, for instance, where one is taken with a bloody knife over the dead body, in which case he is not allowed to deny the death, nor is any other proof requisite by long-established decision."

Mr. CHITTY then proceeded to read an extract from the same author, for the purpose of showing that a man charged with a felony and breaking prison after he was arrested, was ousted of his wager of battel. He might however plead his pardon, and be restored to that right. Vehement presumption of guilt, the infirmity or imbecility of the appellant, were also grounds for ousting an appellee of his battel; and he then read to the court some extracts from Hearn's Antiquarian Discourses, an author of considerable celebrity, who collected all the arguments on the subject, urging on the court that trial by battel was only permitted where there was an absence of evidence to establish the appellant's charge. Several other authors were also cited, to show that where there were notorious presumptions of guilt against the appellee, as if he were discovered in the act, or had been indicted, the right of wager of battel was taken away. The curious and interesting case of *Slaughterford* was quoted amongst others, and was in its circumstances very similar to Thornton's. *Slaughterford* had been tried for the murder of a young woman, and acquitted. The brother of the deceased then appealed him of the murder, and he was tried a second time before Lord Chief Justice HOLT, convicted, and executed. This was strongly urged in the court as showing that an indictment and acquittal would oust the appellee of his battel. In an antiquarian point of view these cases and arguments are no doubt both interesting and instructive, but it is not necessary to give them here in full. The main point,

or one of the main points in the case was, whether assuming
a presumption of guilt was sufficient to oust the appellee's
right of battel, that presumption of guilt was fully set up by
the counter-plea.   To this point Mr. CHITTY then addressed
himself.

It is shown, he said, in the counter-plea that on the 27th
of May, Mary Ashford was found dead in a pit of water;
that she had been recently alive and had come to her death by
drowning; that her arms had been forcibly grasped, and that
there were stains of blood about her body, and that she
had been murdered by throwing her into the pit.

Mr. Justice BAYLEY.—You have said nothing from which
it is to be inferred that she had been thrown in.   What is there
to show that she did not throw herself in, or tumble in?

Mr. CHITTY.—We show marks of blood, and marks upon
the dew, from which it was manifest that some one had been
carried in the arms of another person.   She could not have
walked herself, or the trickling of blood would have been
closer than was evinced by the footsteps.

Mr. Justice BAYLEY.—You do not allege that the clover
was not marked before ; you do not state whether the blood
was there before the dew came or after.

Mr. CHITTY.—We state that it was not brushed away,
except by the blood.

Mr. Justice BAYLEY.—You cannot by that mode of statement exclude the party from his legal claim.   You have not
positively stated that the dew had been displaced by the
blood.

Mr. CHITTY.—My lord, in forming a counter-plea the
same strictness is not required as in an indictment.   We
only state the probability of the facts, and it may be true
that we state them with less particularity than in the indictment itself.   Here is a distinction between the counter-plea
and an indictment.

Mr. CHITTY then went on to read the counter-plea as
follows :—" That the appellee had declared on the preceding
night, in gross and obscene language, that he would have
criminal knowledge of the said Mary Ashford.   That he was
seen with her about three o'clock on the same morning near
the spot where the murder was committed."

Mr. Justice BAYLEY.—You omit to state the fact that she left a particular house at twelve at night, and that at three o'clock she was seen near a stile in Bell Lane, near a harrowed field.

Mr. CHITTY.—The counter-plea states "that his footsteps were traced near to the pit where she was drowned, and that it was manifest that he had then recently pursued her, and that she had attempted to escape, but that he had overtaken her."

Mr. Justice BAYLEY.—You have not alleged that he ran from the pit, but he ran across that field in a direction from the pit.

Mr. CHITTY.—The counter-plea then states "that there were marks of footsteps running away from the pit, and that these marks resembled those of the defendant, and that near the edge of the pit there was the mark of a man's left foot."

Mr. Justice BAYLEY.—It is not described as a recent impression. It states that it was the impression of a man's left foot, but you do not show that it corresponded with the foot of Thornton.

Mr. CHITTY.—We state that he wore shoes on the night in question manufactured for his right and left feet respectively.

Mr. Justice BAYLEY.—You do not say that the left shoe of the appellee was compared with the impression at the side of the pit, nor do you state that it was impossible for a comparison to have been made from the state in which the impression then was. It was easy to have stated that a recent impression on the dew might have been displaced, and that it was impossible to tell by comparison whether Thornton's shoe fitted it or not.

Mr. CHITTY.—We might have stated this, but we did not feel ourselves justified in going beyond the evidence that was before us. The counter-plea then goes on to state " that on the morning of the said 27th of May, when the said Abraham Thornton was apprehended, he was stripped, and that the inside of his clothes was marked and stained with blood." The appellant then avers that he is prepared to prove these allegations by several credible witnesses, and he has verified his

plea by affidavit, which if not true, of course exposes him
to a prosecution for perjury. This statement, I submit, affords
strong presumption of guilt. The coarse declaration also of
the defendant, and his subsequent admission of a carnal
knowledge of the deceased, accompanied with other circumstances of the case, afford strong evidence of guilt. I rest
with confidence for the decision of the court in my favour,
upon the declaration of the appellee himself of his intention
to have illicit intercourse with the deceased; his subsequent
admission that this intercourse had taken place; the state of
his linen, and the variety of other suspicious circumstances,
which all tended to confirm the supposition of his guilt, and
to point out the necessity, as well as the probable ground of
another investigation before a jury of his country. It now
remains for me to establish, that the replication of the
defendant is insufficient. No case can be found in the books
in which an appellee has been permitted to reply, or has even
attempted to reply, fresh facts by way of counter-presumption of innocence. The only answer he can give to the
counter-plea is a traverse of the facts upon which the presumption of guilt is founded. The appellant's counter-plea
establishes a *primâ facie* case sufficient to go to a jury, and
therefore sufficient to preclude a trial by battel; it at least
establishes sufficient to excite suspicion.

Lord ELLENBOROUGH.—Do you contend that a case of suspicion is sufficient to oust the appellee of his right to wage
battel?

Mr. CHITTY.—Yes, my lord.

Lord ELLENBOROUGH.—You have fallen then from the high
ground which you first took, on which you establish your right
to resist the claim of the appellee upon a case of strong proof
of guilt. Now it is suspicion merely.

Mr. CHITTY.—All I contended for or meant to urge was
that strong pregnant suspicion, and presumption of guilt,
were sufficient to establish a case for rejecting the claim of
battel. I have already shown that this is a mode of terminating the prosecution not to be resorted to unless there be an
absence of evidence. If the defendant be prepared to prove
an alibi, he may trust his case with a jury, and ought not to
resort to a mode of trial which must by every one be repro-
bated. But supposing that it was competent to the defendant

to reply other facts, in order to establish a counter-presumption of innocence, still I submit that the facts as pleaded do not amount to a sufficient alibi or negative of guilt. It is observable that the defendant states that Mary Ashford left Mary Butler's house about half an hour after four o'clock in the morning, and that within a quarter of an hour after that time she was seen near the pit. It is then averred that not later than twenty-five minutes before five the defendant was seen near John Holden's house, which is afterwards shown in the replication to be, in the nearest direction, not less than one mile, four furlongs, and sixty yards from the pit. There is no averment of the precise time when Mary Ashford was last seen; but the time is carefully stated under a videlicet, and a few minutes would have afforded ample time for the commission of the violation and murder, and the arrival of the defendant at John Holden's house, so that admitting all the allegations in the replication to be true, it by no means follows that an alibi is established. There is no averment in general or particular terms that the defendant was not at the pit, or could not have been there at the time of the death, or that there was not time enough between the instant Mary Ashford was last seen and when the defendant was seen at John Holden's for the defendant to have escaped from the pit to that place. It is not averred that the defendant used no horse or other expeditious mode of conveyance.

Mr. Justice BAYLEY.—How can a man prove a fact at which there could be but two persons present, one of whom is dead, and the other could not be a witness for himself.

Mr. CHITTY.—He has not avowed that he was not near the pit.

Mr. Justice BAYLEY.—He raises the fact, and upon that creates a question whether the illicit intercourse with the deceased did or did not take place before she went to Mary Butler's?

Mr. CHITTY.—From the situation in which the violence was committed, which was apparent from the imprint of her body upon the ground, it was impossible that he could have accomplished his purpose before she went to Mary Butler's. He has not averred, however, that such was the fact.

Mr. Justice ABBOTT.—Nor have you averred that the violence took place after she quitted Mary Butler's.

Mr. Justice BAYLEY.—You only allege that *some* person had carnal knowledge of her, without averring positively that the appellee was that person.

Mr. CHITTY.—We have only stated that which has been sworn. It appears to me that the defendant has not succeeded in establishing in any respect an alibi, nor has he answered in a satisfactory way what became of him between half-past three o'clock and ten minutes to five, when he was seen at Holden's.

Mr. Justice BAYLEY.—You do not state it quite accurately. The facts are these,—Mary Ashford left Mary Butler's about a quarter past four, and near a quarter of an hour afterwards she was seen on foot in Bell Lane.

Mr. CHITTY.—We are considering whether there is sufficient presumption of guilt to warrant the rejection of his wager of battel. It is clear by his own showing that fifteen minutes remained to him during which he might have committed both the violation and the murder.

Mr. Justice BAYLEY.—He says, even supposing him to have been with Mary Ashford at the time she was seen going towards Bell Lane, that he had to get her to the place where the criminal intercourse happened—then to carry her to the pit, and throw her in, and be by John Holden's, which was a distance by the nearest way of at least a mile and a quarter, and by the readiest road nearly a mile and seven furlongs; and all this must have happened, too, at a time of day when there were a good number of people about.

Mr. CHITTY.—There were marks of running footsteps from the pit.

Mr. Justice BAYLEY.—The difficulty is whether those steps were imprinted before four o'clock or after, the appellee and the deceased having been seen walking publicly together towards the pit. Whether before four or after was the question.

Mr. CHITTY.—There is no allegation on the part of the defendant making out his alibi. He has not averred that he had not been at the pit, nor could have been there. There is no averment what became of the appellee between half-past five and seven; he might have gone back and accomplished his object in that interval. I do not put this proposition as one in which I have any confidence; but merely to show that even if the appellee was entitled to plead an alibi, he has pleaded it insufficiently. All I have to consider is whether there is enough of presumptive evidence to induce the court to avoid this mode of trial; and I submit that on these grounds the replication to the counter-plea was insufficient, and that the defendant ought not to be admitted to wage battel with the appellant, but must submit to the constitutional trial of the charge by a jury of his country.

On Mr. Chitty's sitting down, Mr. Tindal rose for the purpose of addressing the court in support of the replication; but the court, after remaining for some minutes in consultation, intimated, on account of the lateness of the hour, that it would be better the defendant's counsel should be heard tomorrow, to which day the court was adjourned accordingly.

On the next day, the 8th of February, Mr. Tindal commenced his arguments on behalf of the appellee, Thornton, who was again brought up in custody. They are well worthy of perusal, and it is to be regretted that space will not allow of more than a few extracts being given.

"On the part of the defendant in this appeal, it is my duty to contend that on the face of this record, and upon what appears in the case, you are bound to give the judgment that battel must be waged between these parties, unless I can, in the course of the argument, convince you, as I feel I shall be able to do, that the proper judgment will be the final judgment that the appellor shall take nothing by his writ, but that the appellee shall go without day. It is not my intention to devote so long a period to the argument as was yesterday devoted to it by my learned friend Mr. Chitty; for I apprehend, as to many of the authorities cited by him, and also as to many parts of his argument, it will not be necessary for me to make any reply; for I apprehend you will not declare the law of this country as it is laid down in foreign writers, or in the writings of speculative men, but that you will rather decide according to the older authorities of this country; and therefore if I can show you by the Year-book, and authorities, the proper way is the wager of battel, then I apprehend I shall receive the judgment of your lordships in favour of that mode, whatever impression that judgment may make on the opinion of other men."

" The course I shall adopt will be this :—First, I shall show you that the trial by battel is the undoubted right of the defendant in an appeal, and not the right of the appellant. I shall then show you that the case contained in the counter-plea does not bring the case within the exceptions to the wager of battel which the law allows ; and I shall contend that the counter-plea is too vague and uncertain to call upon us for an answer, and therefore I might stop here by saying that if the counter-plea is bad, the appellant has no case in court. But, thirdly, if the counter-plea is admissible, then I shall contend that the replication contains a complete answer to it ; and I shall, lastly, conclude by calling your attention to the reason of the thing, and shall state authorities to show you the proper judgment is that the defendant shall go' without day."

" As to the first point, that the right to wage battel is a right given to the defendant, and not to the appellant, in an appeal, I shall call your attention no further to the introduction of this mode of trial into this country than by stating that it was brought into this country by the Normans. For if you look at the Collection of the Saxon Laws, by Barnard, or as they are referred to by Selden, you will find that although in the 4th volume Selden's remarks occupy a considerable portion of the work, there is no mention whatever of the trial by battel. The Saxon laws themselves are equally silent upon the subject. The Saxon laws being silent with respect to the trial by battel, you will then turn to the laws of William the Conqueror, where you will find that the trial by battel is of Norman origin. It appearing that before the Norman conquest this mode of trial was not known, and that at the conquest it was introduced by the Normans, I conclude it is a practice originating in the introduction of the Norman law."

" Then my next point is that it is a right given to the defendant only. In the grand Coustumier of Normandy there is a title ' *De suite de Murder.*' It is there stated that suit of murder ought to be made in this manner : R. complains

of T. that he hath murdered his father feloniously, in the
peace of God and the duke, which he is ready to make
appear at some hour of the day, '*un hœur de jour;*' for
your lordships know that if the battel lasted till the evening
star appeared, there was an end of it; and therefore the
appellant was to prove the guilt of the defendant in some
hour of the day. The passage goes on to say, 'If T. denies
this, and offers his pledge, then he ought first to take the
pledge of the defendant;' and then there is this note,
'It appears the defendant ought to throw first his gage, and
then the appellor;' so that it is clearly the right of the
defendant. The next authority is that of Bracton, who of
all the early writers is the most full; he has embodied into
his work all the writers down to Staundforde. He clearly
proves that the wager of battel is the defendant's right. In
chap. 18, fol. 137, he is talking of persons being brought
into court, and expressly states that the defendant '*habebit
electionem utrum super patria se ponebit, vel se defendendit
per corpus suum, &c.,*' so that you see the right of this battel
is the right of the defendant, and not the right of the plaintiff. Fleta, in his 2nd book, c. 41, follows nearly in the same
words, so that it is only necessary to call your attention to
them. Fleta brings his authorities down to Edward I. He
must have written sometime about or immediately after the
Statute of Westminster the 2nd, for he refers to it. The last
author I shall state is Lord Coke, who, in the Second Inst. 247,
says in a case of life or appeal of felony, the defendant may
choose either to put himself upon the country, or to try
it body to body, that is, by combat between him and the
appellant. So that you perceive there is a regular chain of
authorities from the earliest writers of the law down to the
latest text book, proving that the right of trial by battel is
the defendant's right. Then if it is his right, it is the duty
of the appellant to cite him to show that he brings the case
within some of the exceptions; and my second point is
that the counter-plea does not bring the case within the
exceptions."

Mr. TINDAL then, after citing several cases to show that
the only grounds on which an appellee could be ousted of
his wager of battel were his being taken in the *mainour*,—that

is with stolen articles upon him—or breaking prison, or if the
appellant were maimed, or an infant, or above sixty years of
age, proceeded next to discuss the sufficiency of the counter-
plea of the appellant.   He objected that it was so framed
that no issue could be taken on it.   It commenced by stating
" that from various circumstances there were violent and
strong presumptions of the prisoner's guilt."   Now presumptions were nothing, Mr. TINDAL said, but inferences which
were to be drawn from proofs preceding them.   What sort
of issue could be submitted to the consideration of a jury
merely upon the ground of presumptions with which the
facts themselves were mixed up?   There was nothing stated
in the counter-plea as a fact, except such things as appeared
merely to others to be so.   It stated, for example, " that it
manifestly appeared to divers persons that certain marks
upon the arms of Mary Ashford were recent, and occasioned
by the pressure of a person's hand."

Lord ELLENBOROUGH.—The names are not even mentioned.
It is only said " that it appeared, and was manifest to many
persons."   How could an issue be taken on such allegations?

Mr. TINDAL then proceeded to read that part in which it
was stated " that the deceased came to her death by drowning, and that forcibly."   He contended that no facts were
stated.   The different allegations were merely mentioned as
things which appeared manifest to credible witnesses.   It
was stated that the print of a footstep was seen which
" appeared" to be that of the defendant, and he objected to
it, as stating only what appeared.

Lord ELLENBOROUGH.—That is sufficient.   The footstep
could be only matter of appearance.

Mr. TINDAL contended that even admitting all the defective part of the allegations in the counter-plea to be struck
out, still there did not remain sufficient *primâ facie* evidence
against the defendant.

"Then as to the third point, namely, that if the counter-plea
was a good one, the replication was also a sufficient answer to it.
The objection taken was that it pleaded upon uncertainty.
The first objection taken to the alibi was the statement that
the defendant left the house of Mary Butler at four o'clock
in the morning.   The next was that a former acquittal was

no ground upon which to presume the innocence of the defendant. The third and principal objection was, that under the circumstances of the case it was not right to set up a counter-presumption at all. This was arguing that the plaintiff had a right to counter-plead a statement from which guilt might be inferred, while the defendant was to be deprived of the same opportunity of alleging any reasons upon which to establish his innocence. It was said in the replication that they left the house of Mary Butler at a quarter past four; in the counter-plea four was the hour mentioned. They could not know the hour at which the parties left the house. Taking it to be a quarter past four, what was the fair import but this, that the time was uncertain as to a few minutes? Supposing it to be fifteen minutes, more or less, the only inference could be that a small space remained undetermined on one side and the other. The next objection was, that they had no right to plead the former acquittal. The ground upon which the objection went was the statute of Henry VII.; nothing, however, was intended by that statute, but merely to save parties their right of suing an appeal. The statute was meant to redress a grievance which existed at the time by reserving the right of the appellant. Lord Bacon, speaking of the statute, said it was ordained for this purpose, that suit by indictment be taken within a year and a day, not prejudicing the parties suing. Acquittal, in the present case, was not the only ground taken. There was abundance of other proof to show the impossibility of the defendant's having committed the crime charged against him."

" It appeared from the replication that about a quarter past four Mary Ashford left the house of Mary Butler. She had then a mile and a half to go to the pit; and he thought he should not be allowing too much time for a woman to go such a distance in saying twenty minutes. Then she reached the pit at twenty-five minutes before five. He would now ask, according to the replication, where was Thornton at that time? The answer would be, taking the latest moment, that at twenty-five minutes before five he came up with another person a mile and a half from the pit. When Mary Ashford arrived at the pit, the circumstances of

F

rape and murder, according to the counter-plea, were yet
to happen; events which, according to the experience of
courts of justice, must have occupied at the smallest compu-
tation a quarter of an hour. This brought them to ten
minutes before five, at which precise moment they had
Thornton meeting another person, namely John Haydon, a
mile further from Holden's farm, and two miles and a half
from the pit. From thence he was traced still departing
from the pit until he reached Castle Bromwich; so that, in
point of fact, it was utterly impossible for Thornton to have
committed the facts imputed to him, if the statement in the
replication were correct. There were some other points urged
by his learned friend (Mr. CHITTY) which were hardly worth
notice: one of these was as to what had become of the
appellee after five o'clock. Of this no doubt ever existed,
and therefore it was not necessary to meet it."

Mr. Justice BAYLEY.—Mary Ashford was not seen near
the pit after half-past four, and you trace Thornton till
twenty minutes after five.

Mr. TINDAL then concluded his argument as follows:—
"Now as to the last part of my argument the object is to show
that under all the circumstances of the case, the judges have
not alone the power of setting aside the counter-plea, and
allowing the appellee his wager of battel, but also the power
of ordering that the appellor should take nothing by his writ,
and that the appellee should go free without day. In a case
brought before Lord Chief Justice MONTAGUE it was decided
that in appeal of a woman for the murder of her father,
although the defendant offered no objection, the court overruled the appeal on the ground that the wife could only
appeal the death of her husband. From this I infer that
judgment of the court, where a plea failed, was not always
the one way. In fact, it seems to be inconsistent with the
exercise of reason and common sense, where it appears evident to the judge that the appellee cannot by possibility be
guilty of the crime of which he is appealed, that he should
give judgment for battel. Suppose a woman appeals the
death of her husband; that the appellee demands his wager
of battel; that the appellor counter-pleads, and that in
reply the appellee produces the husband supposed to have

been murdered, alive, in court, would the judges, I ask, in such a case have no alternative but be obliged to award battel, and thereby risk the shedding of innocent men's blood? This is not a fancied case, for such a one actually did take place, and is to be found in the Year-book of the 8th Hen. IV., and then the woman was sent to prison until she paid a fine to the king, and her husband was allowed to go free. There is another case in point in Bracton, where the very defence urged in the present replication was made— I mean that of alibi. The judge there dismissed the appeal and discharged the appellee, upon the ground that it was impossible for him to have committed the crime imputed to him from the remoteness of his situation at the time when it was alleged the offence had taken place. Finally, upon the general question of the barbarous practice of wager of battel, and of its unfitness to be pursued at the present enlightened era, I am quite convinced, if your lordships see there is sufficient ground shown for giving the appellee his battel in this case, that you will not compromise your duty, but administer the law as it existed. I trust, however, that I have shown enough to your lordships to induce you, on giving judgment, to come to the conclusion that the appeal ought to be discharged, and the appellee allowed to go free without day."

At the conclusion of the able arguments of Mr. TINDAL, Mr. CHITTY intimated that it would be impossible for him to get through his reply in the course of the day, and the court thereupon again adjourned the further hearing until the 16th of April. An application was made on behalf of Thornton for bail, but as it appeared no sureties were in attendance the court made no order, and Thornton was removed in custody.

On the 16th April the further hearing of the case was resumed.

The prisoner was brought into court shortly before nine o'clock by the private passage, and was placed at the bar. His confidence seemed unabated; he looked extremely well, and his appearance generally was that of a man whose mind was perfectly at ease. Soon after he had taken his seat, an amusing incident occurred. Two women found admission to the court through the door destined for the use of the bar, and placed themselves by Thornton. They were about to enter into conversation with him, unconscious of his being a prisoner, when the usher asked Thornton if they were friends of his. Thornton looked at them, and answered " *No, they are no friends of mine.*" One of the women immediately rose and said, " *Please sir, I am William Ashford's aunt.*" They were accommodated with a situation in another part of the court. The anxiety of the public to be present at the proceeding was manifested as heretofore by the presence of a crowd far greater than could gain admission to the court.

As soon as the court was formed, Lord ELLENBOROUGH called upon Mr. CHITTY, who proceeded with his argument in reply. He admitted that wager of battel was the choice of the defendant, and gave up that point in favour of Thornton, but contended that violent presumption of guilt was sufficient to take it away. His arguments in support of this proposition were very similar to those set up on behalf of the appellant in the first instance, and there is no necessity to repeat them. On the question of the sufficiency of the counter-plea and how far it had been met by the replication, Mr. CHITTY entered into some very learned and technical arguments, and then addressed himself to the alibi, and how far that defence was consistent with wager of battel. On this point his remarks are well worthy of consideration.

" I contend that the fact of the supposed alibi can only be brought forward as a defence on the trial; the counter-plea establishes a *primâ facie* case sufficient to go to a jury, and therefore sufficient to preclude trial by battel. The very allegation in the replication that the defendant is prepared to prove his alibi by competent witnesses establishes that this is not a case in which a trial by battel ought to be admitted, for I have already endeavoured to show that that is a mode of terminating the prosecution not to be resorted to unless there is an absence of evidence. If the defendant be prepared to prove his alibi, he may trust his case to a jury, and ought not to be allowed to resort to a mode of trial which is a profane appeal to the Almighty, upon the supposition that He will interfere. The replication is also substantially defective, for it does not sufficiently aver an alibi. There is no averment of the precise time; there is no averment that the defendant was not present at the time of the death, or that he could not have been there; and it is a remarkable fact that although the village of Erdington, where Thornton alleged he left Mary Ashford, as well as the country between that place and John Holden's, is populous, and the working people must have been about at that time in the morning, there is no averment that he was seen by any person in that village, or between it and the neighbourhood of John Holden's, though immediately he arrived there, he alleges that he was seen by several persons. There is no averment in the replication upon which issue could be taken, and if found by a jury would decide upon a strict alibi, for all the allegations are, '*that about such a time he was at such a place, &c.*' The replication ought to have averred in express terms that Thornton was not at the pit, or present at the time of the murder, and then have stated the facts and evidence in order to corroborate such allegation. We might then have taken issue upon the express averment of the alibi; but it was impossible to take issue upon loose allegations, uncertain in point of time, and which, if found by a jury to exist, would still have left it uncertain whether or not the defendant was present. What is a defence founded on an alibi? It is an allegation: I am not guilty, because I was not at the place at the time the offence was committed, but was at another place, and therefore could not be guilty. Any plea, therefore, of an alibi should contain these allegations."

Mr. CHITTY then proceeded to remark upon the position taken by Mr. TINDAL, that supposing the counter-plea defective or the replication sufficient, the appellant should go without day, and be wholly exempt from any mode of trial, even from trial by battel for which he had prayed, and then to discuss the facts of the case as shown on the record. On this point his arguments were not received with much favour by the court, and he was frequently interrupted by the learned judges, who took exception to several points. The opinion of the bench on the question of the guilt or innocence of Thornton was very evident from the remarks that fell from them.   They observed that there was nothing to show that the defendant was with Mary Ashford after three o'clock, nor was there anything stated from whence it might not be inferred that his connection could not have taken place before that period : that it was not stated that marks of a human figure on the ground—the drops of blood—the footsteps near the pit, could not have been produced antecedent to Mary Ashford's calling at Mary Butler's, or before the dew had fallen; and that there were modes, too, by which Mary Ashford might have come to her death consistent with the innocence of the defendant ; she might have destroyed herself, or might have fallen in from weakness.   Upon the whole, the opinion of the bench seemed unanimous that there was sufficient doubt upon the case, if not altogether to free the defendant from suspicion, yet at least to prevent the court from coming to that conclusion as to his guilt which should go the length of depriving him of his wager of battel.   Mr. CHITTY contended generally that there was no foundation whatever for the supposition that Mary Ashford had deprived herself of life, and that all the circumstances collectively went clearly to establish the guilt of the prisoner; but on this point the court was clearly against him, and he therefore retired from a contest which the observations of the learned judges clearly showed to have been hopeless.

The court then, having remained in consultation for about a quarter of an hour, delivered their opinions *seriatim*.

Lord ELLENBOROUGH.—A multitude of cases and authorities have been cited on both sides, into which the court have most anxiously looked, in order to ascertain what is the mode of trial by law in cases of appeal; and they are of opinion that unless the present case falls within some of the exceptions therein mentioned, with that degree of certainty in point of fact which excludes all possibility of doubt, it is impossible to refuse this defendant his wager of battel.   It is not necessary for the court now to enter into a minute examination of the circumstances of this case, but it is sufficient to say that such degree of certainty as is analogous to the case put in Bracton does not exist in the present case. The rule there laid down applicable to such case of exception, " *That an appellee may defend himself by his body on being appealed, unless some violent presumption make against him, which does not admit of proof to the contrary,*" cannot take place on the present occasion, and therefore the usual constitutional trial (liable to all the objections which apply to cases of appeal and to the trial of battel) must, according to the course of law as it now stands, take place, unless (the plaintiff having declined this mode of trial by his counter-plea) the defendant is entitled to go altogether without day. That is a point, however, upon which we do not pronounce any judgment, leaving that matter to be argued hereafter. The court, upon that argument, will consider that point, but at present the court feel themselves ready, upon consideration, to pronounce that this is a case in which, under the law as it now stands, the trial by battel ought to take place.

Mr. Justice BAYLEY and Mr. Justice ABBOTT having concurred,

Mr. Justice HOLROYD, who was also of the same opinion with the rest of the court, then added a few words touching the really important questions of the guilt or innocence of Thornton. He said :—" Upon the counter-plea this appears, ' *That the prisoner and Mary Ashford had been together during the course of the night, and that several of the circumstances which are stated to have taken place, from which a suspicion arose against the prisoner, might have occurred before they separated.*' It appears by the counter-plea that in the course of that night they separated, because the counter-plea states the fact of her going to Mary Butler's ; but it goes on to state also that she returned alone. It appears therefore that though they were together they had separated, and there is no allegation that they ever met again. There is no circumstance stated in the counter-plea inconsistent with the fact of the deceased having come to her death by accident—either by her being at the brink of the pit, and having slipped in accidentally, or from dizziness occasioned by loss of blood, having fallen in. Now that is quite consistent with everything stated in the counter-plea and the replication. I will not go out of these to anything that might have appeared upon the trial ; but it is consistent

with the counter-plea and the replication that all the circumstances stated from which the suspicion arose against the
prisoner might have taken place before she went to Mary
Butler's and before they were separated.   That there was a
separation was proved in evidence, and all the several
circumstances alleged against the prisoner might have taken
place before the separation.   Why, then, if that were so, there
was no motive or inducement to commit the murder.   Besides
this there is another circumstance to be taken into consideration, namely, the proof by various witnesses of an alibi,
from which presumption may be drawn inconsistent with the
supposed fact that he was the person who committed the
murder, if any murder was committed."

Lord ELLENBOROUGH added.—The general law of the land
is, that there shall be a trial by battel, in case of appeal,
unless the party brings himself within some of the exceptions.
However noxious I am myself to the trial by battel, it is the
mode of trial which we in our judicial character are bound
to award.   We are delivering the law as it is, and not as we
wish it to be; and we must pronounce our judgment that
the battel shall take place, unless the party reserves for our
consideration, whether, under the circumstances of the case,
the defendant is entitled to go without day, which is a point
for further consideration.   At present we pronounce,—" *That
there be a trial by battel, unless the appellant show reason
why the defendant should not depart without day.*"

Mr. GURNEY then craved time to consider of the propriety
of applying for the judgment of the court upon this point;
and the court adjourned until the 20th April, on which
day the defendant was brought up to hear the final judgment
on this appeal.

A report prevailed, and obtained credit to a certain extent,
that the appellant had determined to accept the defendant's
challenge, and that the court would be reduced to the
necessity of awarding the combat; and curiosity was at the
highest pitch to learn the manner of battel, and the time
and spot where it would take place.   All speculation, however,
on the subject was put an end to immediately on the sitting
of the court, when the Chief Justice called on the appellant's
leading counsel,

Mr. GURNEY, who said.—Your lordships were pleased to

give us till to-day to consider whether we would pray your lordships' judgment on this appeal, or whether the defendant should be allowed to go free and without day. Having duly considered your lordships' judgment, that the defendant is entitled to his plea of wager of battel, on the part of the appellant I have nothing further to pray.

Mr. READER.—Then, my lord, I submit the appellant must be called; and that he must either accept the wager of battel, or consent that the defendant be permitted to go free without day.

Lord ELLENBOROUGH.—Very well, let him be called.

Mr. Barlow, clerk of the Crown-office, was proceeding to call William Ashford to appear in court, or his writ of appeal would be lost, when

Mr. GURNEY said the appellant did appear in court, though he did not pray anything, but left his case with their lordships, who had to consider whether any and what effect would attach to him for not praying judgment in consequence of any future proceeding on the part of the defendant. The appellant had no objection to offer against the defendant's being permitted to go free.

Mr. READER said, on the part of his client, that there was no intention entertained by him of praying anything against the appellant.

Mr. Justice BAYLEY.—You, Mr. Gurney, will, I suppose, pray that judgment be stayed.

Mr. GURNEY.—Yes, my lord.

Mr. READER.—I certainly shall not pray anything else.

Mr. RICHARDSON.—My lord, it cannot be considered that we abandon the appeal; the appellant is in court though he does not pray anything.

Mr. READER.—Mr. Gurney, do you consent, on the part of the appellant, that the defendant be discharged, and allowed to go free without day.

Mr. GURNEY.—I do, on the part of the appellant, give such consent.

Mr. READER.—Then I have only to pray the court that he be so discharged.

Mr. Justice BAYLEY.—I conceive the course now to be pursued is this:—The appellant prays nothing. The defendant, therefore, as far as the appellant is concerned, goes free;

but he must now be arraigned at the suit of the Crown; so that you will plead the trial and acquittal which has already taken place, but of which, upon the present proceedings the Crown must be supposed ignorant, although it is a fact well known to the parties.

Lord ELLENBOROUGH. — This is a proceeding between individuals of which the court knows nothing. He must be arraigned at the suit of the Crown, to which he may plead the record of his former acquittal. The attorney general must be present, and will perhaps give his assent to this plea.

Mr. READER said he would send for the attorney general, and would also produce the record of acquittal if necessary.

In the course of a few minutes the attorney general came into court.

The prisoner was then arraigned for the murder of Mary Ashford, and pleaded "Not Guilty."

Mr. READER, in reply, put in a copy of the record of the trial and acquittal at Warwick on the 8th of August last.

The attorney general having admitted the fact of the defendant having been already tried and acquitted on this charge, the judgment of the court, "that the defendant be discharged from this appeal, and that he be allowed to go forth without day," was then delivered by Lord ELLENBOROUGH, and the defendant was discharged.

In the following session an Act of parliament was passed (59 Geo. 3, c. 46) entirely abolishing both *appeals of murder* and *wager of battel*. Thornton left this country shortly after his discharge and went to New York, where he is reported to be still living.

THE TRIAL

OF

JOSIAH PHILLIPS

FOR A LIBEL ON H. R. H. THE DUKE OF CUMBERLAND,

BEFORE LORD CHIEF JUSTICE DENMAN,

IN THE KING'S BENCH,

On June 25th, 1833.

Counsel for the Duke of Cumberland: Sir Charles *Wetherell*, Mr. *Pollock*, Mr. *Follett*, and Mr. *Jelf*.

For Mr. Phillips: Mr. *D. Wakefield*.

INTRODUCTION.

THE trial of Josiah Phillips for a libel on the Duke of Cumberland is inserted in this collection on account of the peculiar interest that at the time attached, and in some measure still attaches, to the circumstances connected with the death of Sellis in 1810. It is scarcely possible to represent at the present day the excitement that was caused on the morning of the 31st May, 1810, by the announcement that the life of His Royal Highness the Duke of Cumberland had been attempted in the course of the previous night; that the duke had been most seriously and dangerously wounded; and that the assassin, finding himself foiled in his intention of murdering the duke, had ultimately frustrated the ends of justice by destroying himself. At first the report was believed to be entirely without foundation; but on further inquiry being made at St. James's Palace, where the duke occupied apartments, it was found that the rumour was indeed true. In the course of the next day an inquest was impanneled on the body of Sellis, and the facts connected with the unfortunate transaction were then clearly brought to light.

From the evidence that was given at the inquest it appeared that the duke, on the night of the 30th of May, returned to his apartments in St. James's Palace about twelve o'clock. After dismissing the page-in-waiting, Neale, the duke retired to bed. After having been some time asleep he was awakened about three in the morning by repeated blows on the head. At first the duke imagined that the blows were caused by a bat flying against him, but their being again repeated with violence, showed that he was in reality in the hands of an assassin. His Royal Highness immediately rose and made for the door, defending himself all the time as well as he was able with his arms and hands. Notwithstanding, however, his endeavours to ward off the blows, he received several wounds of a severe description on the head. Neale, the page, was called to the duke's assistance, and the assassin, who all throughout the attack had kept the most guarded silence, escaped from the room through a door leading into the yellow drawing-room, which had been locked on the previous night, but was afterwards found open.

The duke's surgeons, Sir Everard Home, and Sir Henry Halford, were then sent for, and the wounds examined and dressed. Sir Everard afterwards published a statement of what he observed on that occasion, which, owing to the subsequent proceedings in this case, and to Sir Everard's dying before he could give evidence, is of some importance. He stated that he found " the duke lying on his bed still bleeding, and his shirt deluged with blood, and the coloured drapery above the pillow sprinkled with blood from a wounded artery. This could not," Sir Everard said, " have happened unless the duke's head had been lying on the pillow at the time. The wadded nightcap he wore, and the scalp and skull also, were obliquely divided, so that the pulsations of the arteries of the brain could be clearly seen." In all it appeared that the number of wounds the duke had received was seventeen, some of them very severe, and most of them of such a character as showed at once to the most superficial observer that they could not be self-inflicted. It was evident therefore that they had been inflicted by some assassin, and that the assassin must have been some one well acquainted with the duke's apartments, and also with the palace generally. The outer gates were at once guarded to prevent any escape, and a minute examination of the duke's bedroom, and the rooms adjoining, immediately instituted.

On the floor of the bedroom, near the door by which the assassin had escaped, was found a sabre recently sharpened, which turned out on examination to be the duke's own regimental sabre. In a closet in a small room adjoining the bedroom was found the scabbard, a pair of slippers, a dark lantern, and a bottle of water. The key of this closet was in the inside, and it was evident that the assassin had concealed himself in the closet the previous night, and had then locked himself in.

Suspicion in the first instance almost immediately attached itself to Sellis, one of the valets in the duke's service. The alarm had scarcely been given before the duke's porter and several other servants went in a body to Sellis's door. The door was found locked; and though they knocked repeatedly and called Sellis by name, no answer was returned. There were two ways of access to Sellis's room, one by the gallery leading from the great staircase, and the other through the dressing-room attached to a bedroom adjoining the armoury. The servants had proceeded to Sellis's room in the first instance by the ordinary way, which was along the gallery, but finding they could not get in, it was decided to try the other entrance through the dressing-room. Some slight *detour* was necessary for this, which would not how-ever occupy more than five minutes. On arriving at the door leading into Sellis's room, and before knocking or opening it, a strange gurgling sound was heard, and on an entrance being effected Sellis was found lying on the bed, outside the clothes, with his throat cut from ear to ear, and the blood still frothing from his throat. His arms and hands were stretched straight down by his side, and a bloody razor was found lying on the floor. There was no appearance of any struggle. The drawer where Sellis kept his razors was open, with the key in it; the razor-case itself was on the table, and one razor, similar to the razor found on the floor, was wanting.

About six or seven feet from the head of the bed was a chair, across the back of which Sellis's coat was found spotted with blood. It was not possible that these spots could have been caused by the spurting of Sellis's own blood, because in the intervening space between the bed and the chair there were no marks of blood. If the blood had been sprinkled by a wounded artery from Sellis's bed to the chair, some drops at least must have fallen on the carpet. What, however, was most conclusive as to this was that the bloody side of the coat was *inside*, and the side outward next the bed had no blood on it. It was therefore clearly impossible that the blood on the coat could have been Sellis's own blood. The inference was that it proceeded from the duke when endeavouring to ward off the blows. The duke's blood had in fact spurted eight feet in height round the wall of his own room, sprinkling a portrait of Pichgru with large drops of blood, and it was most likely, and indeed almost certain, that drops of blood must in the attack have fallen on the assassin as well.

On the previous evening Sellis, contrary to his usual custom when not on duty, did not sleep in his family apartments in another part of the palace, alleging as a reason for not doing so, that he was going with the duke next morning to Windsor, which was false. He pretended instead to be going to sleep in the room in which his body was afterwards found, for at a quarter before ten o'clock the housekeeper, who was in a room opposite, was asked by Sellis to bring him some water. She had previously filled the jug with water, but found on bringing the second supply that it was empty, though there was no appearance of any having been used. Sellis had in all probability poured it into the bottle which, it will be remembered, was afterwards found in the duke's closet, and which he had taken with him for the purpose of refreshing himself in the event of feeling faint whilst shut up for so long a time in a narrow closet. When the housekeeper brought the water, Sellis drew back the curtains of the bed, turned down the clothes, and wished her good night, his intention being to leave her under the impression he was going to bed. Instead of that, however, he was found by another servant at 11 o'clock in the duke's bedroom, but his presence there attracted no attention, as it was assumed he was on duty. He had in his hand a bundle of linen, in which in all probability the dark lantern afterwards found in the closet was concealed.

In the course of the investigations next day, it was ascertained that the servants, during the later part of the evening, were alarmed by a footstep overhead whilst sitting below in the rooms under the duke's apartments, as of some one walking in slippers. In the closet a pair of slippers were found, and inside them was Sellis's name. The footsteps would, therefore, be caused by Sellis on his way furtively from his own room to the duke's. A small oil lamp usually kept burning below was missed, and it appeared that the lock of the closet where Sellis concealed himself and of the doors leading to the duke's bedroom had been recently oiled. No one in the palace knew of these locks having been oiled, and the most reasonable explanation of the circumstance is that Sellis himself oiled them.

It is scarcely necessary to allude, so conclusive are all the above facts against Sellis, to any further evidence of his guilt, but there is one other circumstance worth noting. The assassin, whoever he was, fled from the duke's room by a room known as the west yellow room, then along the ballroom, then through the east yellow room, and then through the armoury. The finger plates of all the doors which it would be necessary for him to open on his way were marked with blood. Now this course was the most direct road from the duke's apartments to Sellis's own room, and on the right hand of the door-post leading from the armoury into Sellis's room itself there were marks as of a bloody sleeve having rubbed against it. This mark no one but Sellis could possibly have caused; and it is obvious it could not have been his own blood but must have been that of the duke which had spurted on his sleeve during the attack.

One point only, a point under ordinary circumstances no doubt of great moment, but in this instance quite capable of explanation, was noted, tending to weaken the chain of evidence against Sellis. The razor with which Sellis's throat had undoubtedly been cut was found on the floor on the *left* side of the bed. It had evidently been used with the left hand. Now Sellis was not what is generally known as a left-handed

man, though found to be so at the inquest, but, what is far
more uncommon, he was ambidextrous, and could use both
right and left hand equally well.   A very unfounded and
unjust suspicion was undoubtedly caused at the time by this
circumstance, but the testimony of Sir Everard Home, quite
irrespective of the other damnatory evidence against Sellis,
is quite sufficient to prove that Sellis's death was caused by
his own hand.   And such was the view taken of it by the
inquest, when, after a long and careful investigation, the jury
retured a verdict of *felo de se*.   In the course of the day
the body of Sellis was buried in the manner then customary
in cases of suicide, and as is generally supposed, in Scotland
Yard.

Such is briefly an outline of the facts as proved by the
depositions of the witnesses connected with the death of
Sellis.   It is impossible to deny that comments were from
time to time made on the transaction that were not favourable to the principal persons concerned.   On one occasion
the attorney general of the day thought it his duty to
file an *ex-officio* information against a paper called *The Independent Whig*.   But the accusations then made, and the
inferences drawn, were as nothing compared to what was
published in the work out of which the proceedings in this
case arose.

In the month of March, 1832, a book called *The Authentic
Records of the Court of England for the last Seventy Years*,
was published by the defendant, Josiah Phillips.   It was a
small octavo volume of about 400 pages, now become
exceedingly scarce, and it contained undoubtedly the most
scandalous assertions against His Royal Highness the Duke
of Cumberland.   To suffer such a work to be circulated was
of course impossible, and in the following month a motion
was made by Sir CHARLES WETHERELL on behalf of the
duke for a criminal information against the publisher.

Sir CHARLES, on applying for the rule, read from the
affidavits filed the portion of the work relied upon as containing the libel.   It certainly cries aloud, and spares not.
In the following extract some portions have been omitted : —

" The memorable year 1810 was ushered in under dis-
tressing and unsatisfactory circumstances.   The royal family

PLAN OF THE DUKE OF CUMBERLAND'S APARTMENTS.

CLEVELAND ROW

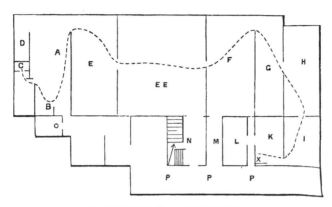

KITCHEN COURT

EXPLANATION OF THE ABOVE PLAN.

A. The Duke's Bed-room. B. The Alcove in which the Bed was placed. C. Closet in which Sellis was supposed to have hidden himself the previous evening, and where his Slippers, Lantern, &c., were afterwards found. D. Dressing-room. E. West Yellow Room, leading to E. E., the Ball-room beyond. F. East Yellow Room. G. Armoury. H. Bed-room. I. Dressing-room. K. Sellis's Bed-room, having two entrances, one from the Dressing-room, the other from the narrow Corridor separating Sellis's Room from (L.) another bed-room, occupied on the evening in question by the house steward. The straight line in the corner of Sellis's room is where the bed was placed on which Sellis was afterwards found with his head toward the Corridor, and the razor on his *left* side where the cross + is placed. The dotted line from C. to B., and from thence to K., is the route supposed to have been followed by Sellis previous to and after his attack on the Duke. M. A Passage leading into (F.) the East Yellow Room. N. Lobby communicating with (E. E.) the Ball-room and the main Staircase. O. The Bed-room occupied by Neale, one of the Duke's pages. P. P. P. Gallery leading to other apartments in the Palace. It has not been thought necessary to show the windows in the different rooms set out in the Plan, as nothing turns upon them. In the Ball-room were six windows, reaching nearly to the ceiling. The shutter of one of these windows was found open on the morning after the attack, and it was assumed Sellis had opened it on the previous evening, in order to give him light on his way back to his own room.

(*To face page* 80.)

were divided among themselves, and every branch seemed to have a separate interest. Under these circumstances, it was not a matter of surprise that truth was now and then elicited. The King was at this time labouring under a severe attack of mental aberration : the situation of the country, his children, and his own peculiar sorrows, made impressions on his mind of the most grievous description.

" Alternate gleams and clouds succeeded each other. In May a new and indescribable sensation was excited by the announcement of an attempt to murder His Royal Highness the Duke of Cumberland. It was said to have been the result of malice on the part of the duke's valet, named Sellis; but, as faithful historians, we give the particulars of these authenticated facts.

" Early in the morning of June 1st an inquiry was made at the Palace (St. James's) for the apprehension of certain individuals then presumed to have escaped in consequence of an attempt to commit a most dreadful and then unaccountable murder.

" At an early hour after midnight the Duke of Cumberland retired for the night to his bed-chamber, after his attendant Neale had served the usual drink for the night, and had retired.

" About half-past two o'clock Neale was awakened out of his sleep by the shrill cries of some person in much agony. He hastily arose and proceeded to his master's bedroom, on entering which he saw the duke, in an apparent quiet attitude, standing in the middle of the room. ' Neale,' said the duke, ' send for Sir Henry Halford; I am severely wounded.' His Royal Highness then laid down upon the bed, and would not permit any of his wounds to be examined until the arrival of Sir Henry Halford. The temper of the duke was too well known to admit of any questions or inquiries, and as soon as Sir Henry arrived every person left the room. When Sir Henry had finished the examination of the royal patient, and prescribed suitable restoratives for his immediate use, he retired, and the servant Neale was ushered into the duke's presence.

*　　　*　　　*　　　*　　　*

" We presume that the following statement of the Cum-

G

berland stratagem may give energy to the mind and activity
to the determinate resolution of our fellow-countrymen.

*   *   *   *   *

" On the morning of June the 1st an astounding communication was made by the daily papers that His Royal
Highness had been surprised in the night, and that his life
had been attempted by one of his valets, namely, Sellis.
Many reports were circulated, and the general opinion was
that the duke was the murderer. Of course, the high Tory
party took no small pains to propagate the opposite sentiment; but the former was most generally believed from the
analogy of attending circumstances. We shall give both
sides of the question, and leave the unbiassed reader to judge
for himself. The first account states that early after midnight of May 31st, an alarm was given by the duke to his
servants, by his screaming aloud, 'Murder!' That a valet
named Neale was the first person who heard the duke's cry,
and ran to his assistance : he found His Royal Highness
bleeding from wounds recently inflicted, and saying some
person had attempted to murder him! Surgical assistance
was immediately rendered, the wounds dressed, and the royal
patient pronounced out of danger. The several apartments
were searched, and in a room appropriated to the use of
Sellis, a most awful spectacle presented itself. The body of
this unfortunate man was lying on the bed, his throat cut,
and life quite extinct. The report went on further to state
that it was believed Sellis had intended to murder his master,
and then to rob; but finding himself detected by the duke
being aroused before he had finished his deadly purpose, he
hastily retired to his own room, where he committed the
rash act of suicide, to prevent detection, and consequent
punishment.

" Afterwards the daily accounts spoke of the dreadfully
wounded state of the duke, and every expression was used to
convey an idea of the murderous intention of the deceased
valet, and the improbability of the duke being any blamable
party in the transaction. The selection of the jury, and the
chosen evidence, produced considerable disgust in many persons who were acquainted with the more private life and
habits of the duke.

"A very considerable time after this tragical event, Sir Everard Home published the following declaration relative to it :—

" 'Much pains having been taken to involve in mystery the murder of Sellis, the late servant of His Royal Highness the Duke of Cumberland, I feel it a private duty to record the circumstances respecting it that came within my own observation, which I could not do while the propagators of such reports were before a public tribunal.

" 'I visited the Duke of Cumberland upon his being wounded, and found my way from the great hall to his apartment by the traces of blood which were left on the passages and staircase, and found him on the bed still bleeding, his shirt deluged with blood, and the coloured drapery above the pillow sprinkled with blood from a wounded artery, and which puts on an appearance that cannot be mistaken by those who have seen it. This could not have happened had not the head been lying on the pillow when it was wounded; the night ribbon, which was wadded, the cap, scalp, and scull were obliquely divided, so that the pulsations of the arteries of the brain were distinguished. While dressing this and the other wounds, report was brought that Sellis was wounded, if not murdered; His Royal Highness desired me to go to him, as I had declared His Royal Highness out of immediate danger. A second report came that Sellis was dead. I went to his apartment, found the body lying on its side on the bed without coat or neckcloth, the throat cut so effectually that he could not have survived above a minute or two; the length and direction of the wound were such as left no doubt of its being given by his own hand. Any struggle would have made it irregular : he had not even changed his position; his hands lay as they do in a person who has fainted; they had no marks of violence upon them; his coat hung upon a chair, out of the reach of blood from the bed; the sleeve, from the shoulder to the wrist, was sprinkled with blood quite dry, evidently from a wounded artery, and from such a kind of sprinkling the arm of the assassin of the Duke of Cumberland could not escape. In returning to the duke I found the doors of all the state apartments had marks of bloody fingers on them. The Duke of

Cumberland, after being wounded, could not have gone anywhere but to the outer doors and back again, since the traces
of blood were confined to the passages from the one to the
other.

" ' (Signed)   EVERARD HOME.'

" We now present the other side of the picture, not drawn
at random, nor coloured too highly.

" Royalty has a profusion of attendants, it is at all times
able to command obedience to any express wish if in the
power of a vassal to obtain.

" An individual then in the household of the duke, who
most probably is now alive (information of which fact
might be ascertained by application to the King of Belgium),
was inclined to give his deposition upon the subject in the
following terms, alleging as his reason the very severe pangs
of conscience he had endured through the secrecy he had
manifested upon this most serious affair.

DEPOSITION.

" ' I was in the duke's household in May, 1810; and on the
evening of the 31st I attended his Royal Highness to the
opera; this was the evening previously to Sellis's death.
That night it was my turn to undress his Royal Highness.
On our arriving at St. James's I found that Sellis had
retired for the night, as he had to prepare his master's
apparel, &c., and to accompany him on a journey early in
the morning.

" ' I slept that night in my usual room, but Neale, another
valet to the duke, slept in an apartment very slightly divided
from that occupied by His Royal Highness. A few days
previous to this date, I was commanded by my master to lay
a sword upon one of the sofas in his bed-chamber, and I did
so; after undressing His Royal Highness I retired to bed. I
had not long been asleep when I was disturbed by Neale,
who told me to get up immediately, as my master, the duke,
was nearly murdered. I lost no time, and very soon entered
His Royal Highness's bedroom. His Royal Highness was
then standing in the middle of the chamber, apparently quite

cool and composed; his shirt was bloody, and he commanded me to fetch Sir Henry Halford, saying, 'I am severely wounded.' The sword, which a few days before I had laid upon the sofa, was then lying on the floor, and was very bloody. I went with all possible haste for Sir Henry, and soon returned with him. I stood by when the wounds were examined, none of which were of a serious nature or appearance; that in his hand was the most considerable.

" ' During this period, which was nearly two hours, neither Neale nor Sellis had been in the duke's room, which appeared to me a very unaccountable circumstance. At length, when all the bustle of dressing the wounds (which were very con-siderable) was over, and the room arranged, the duke said, ' Call Sellis.' I went to Sellis's door, and upon opening it the most horrific scene presented itself. Sellis was lying perfectly straight in the bed, the head raised up against the head-board, and nearly severed from the body; his hands were lying quite straight on each side of him; and upon examination I saw him weltering in blood, it having covered the under part of the body. He had on his shirt, waistcoat, and stockings; the inside of his hands was perfectly clean, but on the outside were smears of blood. His watch was hanging up over his head wound up; his coat was carefully folded inside out, and laid over the back of a chair. A razor covered with blood was lying at a distance from his body, but too far off to have been used by himself, or to have been thrown there by him in such a mutilated condition, as it was very apparent death must have been immediate after such an act.

" ' The wash-basin was in the stand, but was half full of bloody water; upon examining Sellis's cravat it was found to be cut; the padding which he usually wore was covered with silk, and quilted; but what was most remarkable, both the padding and the cravat were cut as if some person had made an attempt to cut the throat with the cravat on, then finding the woollen or cotton to impede the razor, took it off in order the more readily to effect the purpose.

" ' During the time the duke's wounds were being dressed, the deponent believes Neale was absent in obedience to arrangement, and was employed in laying Sellis's body in the form in which it was discovered, as it was an utter impossibility that a self-murderer could have so disposed of himself.'

" Deponent further observes that Lord Ellenborough undertook to manage this affair by arranging the proceedings for the inquest, and also that every witness was previously examined by him. Also that the first jury being unanimously dissatisfied with the evidence adduced, as they were not permitted to see the body in an undressed state, positively refused to return a verdict; in consequence of which they were dismissed, and a second jury summoned and impannelled, to whom severally a special messenger had been sent requesting their attendance, and each one of whom was directly or indirectly connected with the court or the government. That on both inquests the deponent had been omitted, and had not been called for to give his evidence, though it must have been known from his personal attendance and situation upon the occasion that he must necessarily have been a most material witness. The second jury soon returned a verdict against Sellis, and his body was immediately put into a shell and conveyed away a certain distance for interment. The duke was privately removed from St. James's Palace to Carlton House, where His Royal Highness manifested an impatience of manner and a perturbed state of mind evidently arising from a conscience ill at ease. But in a short time he appeared to recover his usual spirits, and being hurt but in a very trifling degree, he went out daily in a sedan chair to Lord Ellenborough's and Sir William Phipp's, although the daily journals were lamenting his very bad state of health, and also enlarging with a considerable expression of sorrow upon the magnitude of his wounds and the fears entertained for his recovery.

" The further deposition of this attendant is of an important character, and claims particular consideration. He says :—

" ' I was applied to by some noblemen shortly after this dreadful business, and very strongly did they solicit me to make a full disclosure of all the improper transactions to which I might have been made a party upon this solemn subject. I declined many times, but at length conceded, under a binding engagement that I should not be left destitute of comforts, or abridged of my liberty, and under special engagements to preserve me from such results, I have given my deposition.' "

Sir Charles then read an affidavit of His Royal Highness, denying the truth of the libel, and evidence of the identity of the defendant with the publisher having been given, the court granted a rule *nisi*, which in the following month was made absolute. A criminal information was then filed, to which the defendant pleaded not guilty, whereupon issue was joined, and the case came on for trial in the King's Bench, before Lord Chief Justice Denman and a special jury, on the 25th of June, 1833.

Sir CHARLES WETHERELL, in opening the case to the jury, after a few preliminary observations, said:—

" Before I proceed to state to you in detail the peculiar facts and circumstances of the case, I shall take the liberty of shortly explaining to you the nature of the proceeding which leads to this trial.

" You are perhaps aware that an information filed by the attorney general *ex-officio* is not supported by the affidavit of any person who complains of a libel; but it is a proceeding which emanates from and is founded alone upon the authority of the attorney general, who has a right, by virtue of his office, in cases where he may deem it necessary, to exercise his authority, and in his own name to file a criminal information in the Court of King's Bench.

" Gentlemen, the information which is now under your consideration is not of that description, but it is what is called a private information at the suit of the Duke of Cumberland, who personally, and as a private individual, applies to the Court of King's Bench.

" Perhaps it will not be deemed superfluous for me to remind you—for upon the present occasion it is in many views material for you to bear in mind—that in order to obtain an information of this kind, the person who applies to the court for the rule to grant it must himself make an affidavit or procure the affidavit of other persons to be made, denying the truth of the libellous matter which he makes the subject of complaint. The consequence of this invariable rule of the court you will have already anticipated, namely, that His Royal Highness the Duke of Cumberland, as a ground for applying to the Court of King's Bench to grant this information, made himself an affidavit, and others were also made, denying in the strongest and most solemn manner the truth of the atrocious charges against him contained in the libel in question.

" You are aware also that in cases of libel there is another mode in which a person whose character is attacked may proceed, that is, by an indictment. But I need scarcely remind you, that the individual who prosecutes by an indictment is not bound to swear that the libellous matter is untrue. There is still another mode of redress, by a civil action. But for various and I think the most obvious reasons, it was impossible in a case of such a peculiar description as this for the illustrious duke to proceed in that manner (a).

" Gentlemen, the time when the imputed transactions occurred, in the year 1810, a valet or servant of His Royal Highness, of the name of Sellis, was found stretched on his bed lifeless, with his throat cut, in his room at some distance from the royal duke's apartments in St. James's Palace, and the royal duke was found in his own bedroom most severely wounded. So extraordinary a transaction could not fail to excite all that curiosity and attention, and to lead to all that investigation which must naturally belong to it. And you will find that, according to the ordinary course of law, the coroner within whose jurisdiction the case fell summoned a jury, and the finding of that jury was that Sellis had murdered himself. This took place in 1810.

" Gentlemen, this transaction at the time became a subject of a great deal of criticism, and of close investigation, independently of the legal proceedings before the coroner. The apartments in the palace were thrown open and examined by a great many persons, and everything which the nature of

---

(a) Sir Charles might have cited an instance of a royal duke bringing an action for libel against a private subject if he had chosen— that of His Royal Highness the Duke of York, who brought an action against Titus Oates, and recovered 100,000l. damages.

such a case required was submitted to the eye of public curiosity and scrutiny.

" Gentlemen, you will probably concur with me in the remark that few persons of high station in this country, if they happen to belong to any particular party, fail to be made the subject of some sort of attack more or less. I might perhaps go the length of saying that there is no public man so fortunate as to be entirely exempt from some kind of personal attack; and the mode of carrying it on is usually to do the most mischief by getting into circulation rumours and insinuations, and by so contriving vague calumnies, that they cannot be met by positive and distinct refutation. By contrivances of this kind suspicions of the most foul nature may be thrown round the character of any man, and in such a manner that he may be left entirely defenceless, and even without any opportunity of vindication. It has so happened in the case of the illustrious individual in question. Ever since 1810, upon several occasions, rumours have indirectly been given out, and mysteriously kept up, that Sellis was murdered, and that His Royal Highness was the guilty man. There has been much dexterity in all this. Some obscure individual has been set to work, whenever it served the purpose of the secret enemies of the duke, and the calumny has been so managed that it has been equally impossible to grapple with the expressions and insinuations through which it has been circulated as with the secret authors of them."

After referring to the publication of the work in question, Sir Charles proceeded to comment upon it with considerable force and effect. " The first page," he said, " exhibits an engraving of the royal arms with a motto ; not indeed the royal motto, but that moral maxim which we must all allow to be sacred, ' *Magna est veritas.*' From this we are to conclude that in 1810 the truth of the transactions in which His Highness is implicated was not investigated; and that between 1810 and 1832, the candid anonymous author has been able to detect it. His diligence, accuracy, and investigation have enabled him, in the year 1832, to lay before the public a statement of facts which had been wilfully suppressed, or mysteriously concealed, or improperly perverted, in the year 1810. He performs a meritorious service in the cause of truth. His invincible attachment to it impels him to drag into daylight, and to hold up to public scorn, an individual, who, by his own stratagems, assisted by the frauds and the wickedness of the tools and instruments employed by him, contrived to elude punishment as an atrocious delinquent.

" Gentlemen, I concur in the sacredness of the duty which this lover of truth assumes. I applaud the conscientious motive. I am ready to eulogize it in the strongest language, because my sentiments upon that subject would be as elevated as those of the anonymous author. I should go along with him in saying,—Let not ten or twenty or thirty years screen a great delinquent, because he holds so high a rank in society, but let justice be ultimately established. I say with this author, be he who he may, the truth will prevail. And I would assist in detecting it, though it has so long been surreptitiously kept from the public. But the question you have to try is, whether this author, who boasts so much of divulging the truth, is really applying himself to the performance of this honourable duty, or whether this publication is produced from a very opposite motive, than which nothing can be more base, namely, that of going back to a period of more than twenty years since, for the purpose of making statements which he cannot fail to know are fabrications and falsehoods, in the hope that the distance of time may prevent his own gross misrepresentations from being detected.

" Gentlemen, the publication in question, as you will soon perceive, whoever is the author of it, is composed with no small degree of art and attention in its arrangement, and in the general form of it. It is obviously the production of some person who has bestowed no small pains upon it; and, gentlemen, I shall further say that the art with which the libel itself is contrived is demonstrative of its bitter malignity. The mode in which it is done is to pretend to state the case, in which the royal duke is implicated, two ways. First, to state the case as it did actually appear before the jury, and then to state that there was an individual, who, if he had been called upon as he ought to have been, would have made a distinct and positive deposition, and that if he had appeared to make that deposition, and it had been submitted to the jury, it would have established a clear case which would have falsified the verdict, and have shown that the royal duke was the murderer of Sellis, instead of Sellis being a self-murderer."

Sir Charles then read at length the portion of the work complained of as containing the libel, an extract from which has been already given. With reference to the depositions inserted in the book for the evident purpose of giving an air of truth and plausibility to the narrative, and which the defendant had stated in his affidavit, when showing cause against the rule, was furnished to him as proceeding from a person named Jew, then in the employment of the King of Belgium, Sir Charles observed :—" Now, gentlemen, through the medium of that deposition, which the writer tells us this individual, formerly in the service of the Duke of Cumberland, would have made—from this supposed statement—you may learn the criminal charge which is sought to be made against the Duke of Cumberland. The statement I am about to read is headed by the word ' Deposition.' This individual here alluded to is a person of the name of Jew. There certainly was a person of that name in the service of the duke at that time. It is also correct that he was afterwards a servant in the family of the King of Belgium. Now let us see what his intended deposition is. (Here Sir Charles read the deposition as given at page 84). Now I will undertake to demonstrate to you that there is literally not one word of truth in any part of this alleged deposition. Gentlemen, the faithful historian may not know whether this person is alive; I rather conjecture he supposes him to be dead. But he is mistaken; I know him to be alive, not in Belgium, but now walking in Westminster Hall, outside of the court; and what is more, I shall presently call him into court, and he will tell you that in this long narrative, in this long supposed deposition, there is not one word of truth from one end of it to the other."

Lord Chief Justice, interposing.—I do not think we can hear him if he is called as a witness; the truth is not put in issue here.

Sir CHARLES WETHERELL.—My Lord, I apprehend that is a point which for the present I need not discuss.

Mr. WAKEFIELD.—There is no danger of his appearing, I will undertake to say. I understand Sir Charles Wetherell to allude to the witness whose deposition he has been reading. I will undertake to state that he will not appear.

Sir CHARLES WETHERELL.—I will undertake to say, then, that he shall appear.

Lord Chief Justice.—I will undertake to say that he can hardly be a witness; I do not quite agree in your view of the nature of the case. Supposing the jury shall be of opinion he published this libel, the question of the truth has been before the court already.

Sir CHARLES WETHERELL.—I will not trouble your lordship with an argument as to the points to which he may be examined. There are several cases on this point.

Lord Chief Justice.—I know what you allude to, as to the introductory statement: the second count omits that introductory statement. I am of opinion the party has no right to put this in issue on such an averment.

Mr. POLLOCK.—Your lordship is aware there are some facts which are very material, not only to be stated in the information, but to be proved in evidence before a jury, because a publication of this description will have one character under one set of circumstances and a totally different character under another; and it is desirable that the fact, if of the larger kind, should be found by the jury, that fact being put into question.

Lord Chief Justice.—At present I only give my general impression.

Mr. POLLOCK.—I wish only to state why some of these facts were put into question.

Sir CHARLES WETHERELL. — I do not know who has instructed my learned friend to say that the witness will not appear. He has been subpœnaed; I shall call him, and he will be tendered by me to the court for examination. If it shall be his lordship's ultimate judgment, when the point is discussed, that he cannot be examined, his non-examination will depend on the legal rule only. If his testimony must be rejected, it will be by the direction of my Lord Chief Justice, who will, by-and-by, correctly lay down the rule of law for our guidance. At present I will only say that I am ready to go along with the faithful historian in attending to the statement of his own pretended witness— the alleged maker of the deposition I have read. I will make him my witness; I will examine him to every tittle of the matter contained in this spurious narrative, and will submit it to the jury as far as the law will allow. My learned friend, therefore, will permit me to say, that whoever told him that Jew will not appear, has told him that which is not accurate. Jew will appear—Jew shall appear; and it is the Chief Justice alone whose authority shall prevent his examination before you. To his lordship's authority we shall bow. If he tells us that the rules of law will not permit me to examine him on my side, I will then make a present of him to the faithful historian, whose learned counsel may make any use of him he can on his side.

Proof of the publication of the libel having been given, General Sir *Benjamin Stephenson* was sworn. He said:—" I remember on the morning of the 31st of May hearing of the attack that had been made on the Duke of Cumberland. I in consequence went to St. James's Palace, where I saw the duke. He was in bed, and severely wounded on the head, and I think on both hands also. I did not see the wounds, as the head was bound up. There was a great deal of blood about the duke's bedroom in many parts, and the bed itself was nearly covered. There were marks of blood on the door, on one door certainly, and indeed, to the best of my recollection on both doors. I afterwards went to the room where the body of Sellis was. It was a considerable distance from the duke's room, and I think, to the best of my recollection, there were four rooms to go through. I saw the body of Sellis lying on the bed with its throat cut, and some blood about the room. I particularly remarked that he had no slippers or shoes on his feet. I remember in a room adjoining the duke's room where there was a long narrow closet seeing a pair of slippers. They were afterwards found to be Sellis's slippers. I was not examined at the inquest."

Sir *W. Waller*, the next witness, proved seeing the duke shortly after hearing of the attack. He said:—" I found His Royal Highness in bed, covered with blood, the room full of people I did not know. I was desired to get the room cleared, which I did. The duke told me the state he was in, and requested me not to leave him, which I never did night or day either. I took my station by him until he was quite recovered. At my earnest request the duke was removed to Carlton House the same evening. The wound had been dressed before I arrived. With great difficulty we got His Royal Highness into a chair and removed him to Carlton House. I walked by his side all the way. I was in attendance upon him as a friend at Carlton House until the 4th of August, when the duke went to Windsor. I had ample opportunities of seeing the wounds; they were never dressed without my being present. They were so severe that as to the wound on the head, I saw the pulsations of the brain, and the late King was so affected that he fainted away."

By the Lord Chief Justice.—In your judgment could these wounds have been given without an attempt to assassinate?—It is utterly impossible, for they were severe beyond all description, and the suffering of the duke afterwards was such as I have never seen equalled. It was to that extent that I dare not walk across the room. If I accidentally touched the bed clothes he screamed with agony, and he could not even bear the scratching of my pen when I was writing in the room.

Samuel Thomas Adams, the coroner for the verge of the palace, was then sworn. He said :—" I summoned as coroner a jury to form an inquest on the death of Sellis. I did not summon the jury from the verge of the palace; in the verge of the palace, but not of the palace itself. I am aware that the statute of Henry VIII. requires yeomen of the household to be summoned on the jury in the case of a death in a royal palace, but I did not summon them from that class of persons in this instance, but from persons in connection with the palace. Mr. Francis Place, of Charing Cross, was foreman. No prior inquest had been summoned, only the one of which Mr. Place was foreman. There was no jury that refused to give a verdict before this jury. The inquest was held at the palace, and I presided as coroner. Several witnesses were examined. It was an open court, and every reporter who applied was admitted. I should think there would be as many as fifty or sixty persons present, and several reporters who took notes. The jury examined the duke's room and Sellis's also. I went with them. Sellis's body was still lying on the bed. The jury examined it most minutely. All persons who could give any information were also examined. The inquest lasted about two hours. The case was so plain that the jury did not require me to sum up the evidence at all. A verdict was returned of *felo de se.*"

Mr. *Francis Place,* the foreman of the jury, was then called and sworn. His evidence corroborated in every respect that of the coroner as to the inquest. He spoke to having examined the duke's bed, and that some of the hangings had been cut apparently with the point of a very long sabre, and added some particulars as to the examination of the body.— " I examined Sellis's body. The room in which it was laid was a very small room, with a door at one end which went down three stairs, and a door at the other end; it was so small that not more than four persons could examine the body at the same time. I stayed in during the whole of the examination; I examined the wound, lifted up the body, and examined the back of it. After all the inquest had seen it once, I went round again, and turned it right and left, and there was no other wound except the large one in the neck. I was there the whole of the time. I noticed Sellis's cravat, which I turned round, and saw there was a slit cut in it which penetrated the whole of the folds, and the inside fold was tinged with blood. I saw the sword and the razor. The razor was found on the left-hand side of the body; and we found the man was a left-handed man. Fifteen of the jury concurred in the verdict; one said he could not concur in the verdict, for although he had no doubt the man had cut his own throat, he considered no man ever did it when he was sane; another said he could not make up his mind whether the man was sane or insane, and he therefore gave no opinion as to that point. But the jury concurred in the fact of self-destruction, though two doubted the fact of sanity."

Joseph Jew, sworn :—" I was in the service of His Royal Highness the Duke of Cumberland at the time the attack was made upon him in St. James's Palace. I have seen this book, which purports to contain a deposition from an individual in

the household of the duke.   The facts contained in the
deposition were never given by me to anybody.   What this
deposition contains as regards me is false.   It is not true that
I was directed by the Duke of Cumberland to lay a sword
upon one of the sofas in his bed-chamber.   I did not see the
duke shortly after he was wounded.   I went for the doctor,
Sir Henry Halford, and did not see the duke again till he
was at Carlton Palace; all that is stated here of my seeing
him at St. James's, and remarking the wounds were not
deep, is untrue.   I do not know how deep the wounds were;
I never saw the duke till after they were dressed in Carlton
House.   I did not see him at Saint James's Palace at all.
It was not my duty to be in the room with the duke.   I was
footman, not valet.   I went into the room where Sellis's
body was lying some time after.   The duke did not tell me
to call Sellis.   I never gave any deposition to any one, nor
ever was asked to give a deposition."

His Royal Highness the Duke of Cumberland, sworn.—
Did your Royal Highness sleep in your apartments at Saint
James's Palace on the night of the 31st of May, 1810?—
Yes, I did.   In the course of the night was your Royal
Highness awoke by any blow struck upon your forehead, or
any other part of your person?—I was awoke by a blow upon
my head (pointing to the right side of the head).   I should
state, when I was awoke at first, I was in a sort of half
sleep; that I really at first did not conceive it was anything
else than like a blow, as if something had just tumbled upon
my head—that was my first impression; but then the blows
were repeated, and that made me wake.   Now, was one of
these blows a blow which made any incision on the back
of your head?—O yes; a violent one.   Will your Royal Highness be so good as to point it out to the jury?   [His Royal
Highness exhibited the back of his head to the jury.]   Did
it produce any effusion of blood?—An immense effusion.
Were you capable of seeing by what instrument the blow
was inflicted?   No; I had not the least idea; I could not
see that, except that the first idea that I had was that I was
atacked by somebody, and this calls to my idea the time that
it must have happened.   The bed was placed in a position
that there was a looking-glass exactly opposite, and through

a faint light from the window-shutter I saw a sparkling as from a sword, in the glass. That made me first think that I was attacked by a robber, and that made me make a dash at him. I grappled with him and got this slit in my thumb, and afterwards several other cuts; in all I think I had seventeen wounds. The moment I perceived myself attacked, I jumped out of bed, and seized the sword, which gave me these cuts. At that instant it was impossible for me to know whether I had one or more persons in the room. I consequently, knowing the position of the room, made for the door; the room was so constructed that in order to get to my servant's room I was obliged to open two doors, one to me, and the other from me; and in that I got that second violent blow that I received here at the back. I then first of all called my servants, and at that moment a man of the name of Neale came. I sent for Sir Henry Halford and Sir Everard Home. I have applied to Sir Henry Halford to attend upon this occasion. On account of a misfortune that has happened in his family, it is impossible for him to attend. I was in a state of agony, I suppose, from six weeks to two months from the wounds; in short, it was not, I believe, till the beginning of August that I was able to leave my house. I have read over the publication which forms the subject of this prosecution.

The Lord Chief Justice.—I do not think you can go into that. His Royal Highness has made an affidavit upon that subject.

Sir CHARLES WETHERELL.—Then if your lordship rules that I have no right to put to the duke the negative of this act imputed to him, I do not put the question if your lordship so rules.

The Lord Chief Justice.—I think that that is not at all in issue on the present occasion.

Sir CHARLES WETHERELL.—Then I will take the liberty of putting that question to His Royal Highness, and your lordship will have the goodness to tell me that I have no right to put it.

The Lord Chief Justice.—I feel it my duty to say that that is not at all the present matter of inquiry, and it cannot be gone into.

Did your Royal Highness make an affidavit upon which the rule was made absolute for this information ?—I did.

Sir CHARLES WETHERELL.—We need not trouble your Royal Highness further.

This closed the case for the prosecution, and Mr. Wakefield then rose to address the jury on behalf of the defendant. His speech is well worthy of perusal. It was of course impossible for him to contend that there was no libel on the Duke of Cumberland, and on that point he necessarily had to abandon his client. His address, therefore, was directed more with a view to mitigation of punishment than to obtain an acquittal, which was obviously impossible. Mr. Wakefield said :—" I own that I stand before you in rather a difficult position to-day, and the difficulty of that position arises from several causes. In the first place, no small cause is the very obscure or rather the no station at all which I occupy in this court, from the very little time during which I have belonged to the bar. Another cause arises from seeing my learned friends, whom I have seen here to-day, arranged against me. In this or in any other court, none could have been selected more remarkable for their intelligence, their knowledge, their experience, and their acuteness in their profession. I mention these circumstances, because, although I have not gained a name in my profession, I hope to gain a name ; and it might be supposed that I was unaware of the difficulties which surround me if I did not take the liberty of adverting to a matter which is purely personal to myself.

" Gentlemen, you have heard the very able and eloquent speech made by my learned friend on this occasion; and you have heard from him a doctrine laid down as to public morals, and as to the investigation of truth, in which I beg leave to say that I most cordially concur. I concur in every word that was uttered by my learned friend on that subject, and I think that doctrine more excellent could not be uttered ; but I would wish you to consider whether that position which he took up, namely, the position of a prince, which, he said, was one that a philosopher would deplore, was not to be aggravated by attacks like those in the publication which is now before you. I would ask you to consider whether that position does not cut two ways ; because if publications like

these do give pain, and do aggravate that situation which my
learned friend has called an unfortunate one, I take it that
the person who takes pains to call public attention to such
matters, to fix the public mind upon that which it would
otherwise have entirely forgotten, is himself greatly to blame
for his own indiscretion. Not the same quantity of blame,
of course, can be meted out to him as to the author of these
publications; but when he is complaining of them he ought
to reflect whether he has exercised that sound discretion which
all men would exercise, in abstaining from referring to a
subject which might otherwise, and which must otherwise,
have been buried in complete oblivion. Another thing is to
be considered. Gentlemen, I take it that in your character
of jurors you have a duty to perform over and above that
of merely considering whether this publication entitles the
prosecutor to a verdict or not; you have to consider all the
circumstances attending the publication. You are judges of
the law and the fact, according to the words of the Act of
parliament relating to the law of libel; and in weighing all
the facts and all the circumstances which surround this case,
I apprehend that I am not going beyond the strict truth
when I say that it is a part of your duty to consider whether prosecutions like these do conduce to the maintenance
of that public morality which was alluded to by my learned
friend. I cordially agree, as I told you, with all he said upon
that subject; but I do consider that a discretion which is
anything but sound has been exercised in bringing this
matter into court. And I think so, not only as relates to
the individual prosecutor, but also as relates to the public in
general. I think as relates to the individual prosecutor, that
it will fail in attaining the object for which it was instituted;
that these proceedings will fail in attaining that object; and
I also think that very great evil is likely to result from their
discussion in all classes of society.

"Now something was said by my learned friend as to the
mode in which this prosecution had been conducted. He
told you, if I understand his argument correctly—and I think
I did understand it correctly, because he made use of the
same argument when the rule was made absolute in this
business, and it was this—that the Duke of Cumberland

might have proceeded by many other means to endeavour to
obtain a remedy for any injury which he had sustained;
but that he thought proper to take the mode which he has
adopted, that of proceeding by way of criminal information,
because it afforded him an opportunity of putting upon record
his absolute denial of all the charges imputed to him. And I
remember well that my learned friend said, at the time of the
rule being made absolute, that His Royal Highness appeared
in this court as any other private person would appear; that he
did not take advantage of that exalted rank that belongs to
him; but that he appeared here as any private individual.
And my learned friend boasted of the magnanimity which he
displayed by taking such a course. Now, gentlemen, I own
that I do not see the truth of that observation, provided that
you agree with me that there is indiscretion in these
proceedings at all, provided you agree with me that any
public injury can follow from them, I cannot see what the
magnanimity is of a royal duke employing the greatest
talent, the greatest experience, and the greatest knowledge
at the bar, in order to crush an individual who can afford to
employ none but the humble advocate who now addresses
you. I own that it is a sort of magnanimity of which I
never heard before. I have thought that magnanimity was
a large, a noble quality; that it was one which enabled the
possessor of it to overlook all petty injuries, all minor in-
sults, all attacks upon his character which could not be
believed. And I would ask you, gentlemen, and I will
put it to any man who is at all acquainted with the
world—who is at all acquainted with the circle in which
His Royal Highness moves—I would put it to my learned
friend, because I know that his honourable mind would
not permit him to give me anything but the most direct
answer, and I would join issue with him upon that point
—I would ask him, does he in his conscience believe that
His Royal Highness has suffered one tittle of injury whatever from the publication in question? I own that I cannot
understand how a person of his exalted rank can suffer by
the attack of a man who is almost anonymous; for you will
remember, gentlemen, that these proceedings are against the
printer, they are not against the author; they are not against

either the head that planned, or the hand that wrote this publication; they are merely against the man who used the types with which it was printed. How proceeding against such a person can benefit him, I cannot understand. You heard from my learned friend several observations upon the art with which this publication had been concocted, and you have also heard a great deal of evidence as to the truth of the facts which are stated in that publication.

" Now, gentlemen, I think that I have a right to call upon you to throw from your minds altogether that evidence, and I ask you to do so for this plain reason, that if the falsehood of all these facts had been proved to you to-day, and it was impossible from the length of time that has elapsed to have done that, but if that had been done, it has nothing at all to do with the subject; the truth has nothing at all to do with the subject, for this reason, because if, on the contrary, I had proved that the statements in that book were all true, I should have been told, nevertheless, it is a libel. Therefore I say, gentlemen, that what is sauce for the goose is sauce for the gander; and although it is His Royal Highness who comes into court on the present occasion, I know the character of English jurymen too well not to feel persuaded that they will mete out to him the same measure of justice as they would give to the meanest peasant. And I say, gentlemen, that if I had shown that every syllable which is in that publication were true—it is not necessary for me to admit it is false, but if I had shown that it is true—I should have been told that it was no defence whatever, and therefore I want to know how the thing is aggravated, logically and reasonably speaking; I want to know how the thing is aggravated by its being shown that it is false.

" Now, gentlemen, there is another point, and only one, with which I shall trouble you, and that is just to remember the words of the information in this case, and to consider in your own minds whether it has been proved to you to-day that the words of that information contain a correct description of the charge imputed to the defendant; the words of the information are that this publication has caused a great damage, scandal, disgrace, and infamy to His Royal Highness the Duke of Cumberland. Now I do not remember that we

have heard one single word of evidence tending to prove that
assertion. We have heard evidence relating to matters that
have nothing at all to do with the present prosecution. As
far as relates to the doctrine of the law of libel, we have heard
evidence as to the facts; but it is your duty, gentlemen, to
consider what you have to perform in relation to the law of
libel, because that law involves all those rights and privileges
to which allusion was made by my learned friend; all those
rights and privileges which he said publications like this
were calculated to invade and destroy; nay, he went even
so far as to tell you that if they were permitted to go
unpunished, this would become a beastly nation. Yes,
gentlemen, that may be the case; but I will also take the
liberty of saying that if, as jurymen, you do not do your
duty in expounding the law of libel through your verdict to-
day, and if other jurors should follow your example, the best
safeguard of liberty will be destroyed, and then indeed England would be a beastly nation.

" Gentlemen, it is for you to consider, therefore, whether a
publication like this,—which instead of being an artful publication I think is one of the least artful, one of the most
clumsy, one of the weakest publications that ever issued
from the press; if you think that such a publication as this,—
whose merits have been magnified, of course you know with
what object, by my learned friend; the writer of which has
been called, or almost called—at all events it has been said
that he has concocted a great deal of learning, philosophy,
religion, and morality. Why, gentlemen, the words are there
—the words morality, religion, and so forth, are there—but
I would ask if you have read the publication, and if you have
not, I would beg of you just to cast your eyes over it, and
see whether it is not one of the worst written books that
ever was published. I consider the whole turn of the thing
is so extremely clumsy that no man could believe it for a
moment. There is one expression which struck me, in a
passage which was read by my learned friend, which is characteristic of the style in which the thing is written, and will
show you the extreme want of the power of composition
which whoever wrote it must have possessed; the extreme
want of a common knowledge of the rules of composition. He

talks about serving him with his drink for the night : after
His Royal Highness had retired to bed he was served with
his drink for the night. I never heard that people were
served with drink for the night ; they generally take drink
before they go to bed (a). If he had been talking about the
old troubadour, or some story of the Saxons, that might have
done, but he talks about serving him with his drink for
the night, and then he talks about an indefinable legacy to
every child of humanity, and all kinds of nonsense of that
description, which shows that the thing is one of the very vilest
publications in the way of composition that ever was printed.
So much for all the art which my learned friend has attributed
to it. So much for the inference which I suppose he will
draw from it, because I take it he would draw this inference,
from being artfully written, that it was maliciously written·
Now, I do not see if the malice is to entirely depend upon the
art displayed in the publication, what quantity of malice there
is in it, for art there is none—none whatever.

" Therefore, gentlemen, I shall leave this matter in your
hands, perfectly persuaded that you will exercise a sounder
discretion on the subject than what has been shown by the
prosecutor on the present occasion ; because I am satisfied that
you will agree with me that proceedings like these, instead of
crushing the publication against which they are made, will
give increased strength to it : they spread it in holes and
corners where it never would have arrived at ; they therefore
defeat their object. They cause also other evils to which I have
alluded, and I think you will agree with me that His Royal
Highness would have been more discreet, that his advisers
would have shown more judgment, if they had refrained from
instituting this proceeding. His Royal Highness may rest
assured that there is one safeguard for the character of all
men, which all men of good character, when they are not
misled by a particular sort of indiscretion, like that which
appears to me to have existed in the present case, generally
adopt, and that course is to leave their character to take care
of itself. That is the course which sensible people generally

---

(a) This statement is, however, confirmed by Strickland in his
Information, p. 114.

adopt, and they generally adopt it with the most perfect success. I feel, gentlemen, that you cannot for one moment conceive that the loose, the vague, the childish statements, I had almost said, and facts contained in that publication can for one moment attach a slur on the character of His Royal Highness the Duke of Cumberland; you might as easily believe that a gnat could sting through the hide of an elephant."

The Lord Chief Justice then proceeded to sum up the case to the jury. He said :—" This is an information filed against Josiah Phillips, as the publisher of the book in question, for a libel reflecting strongly on the person of His Royal Highness the Duke of Cumberland. Whether that person is the author of the work we do not know, but it appears that he is the printer and publisher, or at least the publisher, for his name appears in the title-page as the publisher of the book. Nothing has been said about his being the author, and whether he is the author of that work or not, we have no proof before us ; he may or may not be. It is a matter for the discretion of those who feel they are injured by a publication either to require the author to be given up, or to proceed against the printer, as they may seem to think fit; and in cases where the matters stated are within the knowledge of the party stating them, he ought to have an opportunity of being able to prove them, if true. In cases like those, perhaps, it may be more discreet to require the printer to give up his author, for the purpose of proceeding against such party. But that is not at all so in the present case, because there is no person who pretends to know anything upon the subject more than all the public know, except with reference to the witness Jew, who distinctly disproves that part of the statement into which his name has been introduced. The question is, whether you are satisfied that this publication reflects on the conduct of the Duke of Cumberland ; whether it is meant to scandalize and vilify His Royal Highness, and to impute that His Royal Highness was accessory or privy to the commission of the crime of murdering one Joseph Sellis, and to deprive His Royal Highness of his good name and fame.

"Now, then, they set out in the information that which they call the libel, and which has been read to you. In the first place, it says, after a great deal of pomp, 'that an indescribable sensation was excited by the announcement of an attempt to murder His Royal Highness the Duke of Cumberland. It was said to have been the result of malice on the part of the duke's valet : as faithful historians, we give the particulars of these authenticated facts.' So that here is a distinct statement of certain facts, which this person, who, whether he composes well or not, writes in a book that has a plausible appearance, and which many persons would buy, and which many persons, if the statement were left unanswered, would conceive to be of some authority on such a point; and this man thinks proper to publish facts of this kind. He says, ' Early in the morning of June the 1st an inquiry was made in the palace for the apprehension of certain individuals, then presumed to have escaped, in consequence of an attempt to commit a most dreadful and then unaccountable murder, at an early hour after midnight;' and then he states some particulars of what passed on that point; and then he goes on to talk about his own love of truth, and his wish to give an indefinable legacy to every child of humanity, and some language that I think very well warrants the learned counsel for the defendant in his criticisms upon this composition; but then he goes on to say, ' The selection of the jury and the chosen evidence produced considerable disgust in many persons who were acquainted with the more private life and habits of the duke.'—Then Sir Everard Home's declaration is set forth, which certainly goes a great way to disprove the whole of this statement. But then it has been introduced by the language reflecting on the character of His Royal Highness, and is followed by this extraordinary statement :—' An individual then in the service of the duke, who most probably is now alive, information of which fact might be ascertained by application to the King of Belgium, was inclined to give his deposition upon this subject in the following terms, alleging as his reason the very severe pangs of conscience he had endured through the secrecy he had manifested upon this most serious affair.' Then in the book the word ' deposition' is written as a title by itself, and after that follows the supposed statement of that person. And, undoubtedly, whatever want of skill and of art there may be in composing a book, everybody knows that where there is a deposition set forth, and that is followed by quotations, those persons who are not extremely attentive to the particular mode of statement naturally carry with them the proposition that that is a deposition which actually has been made. Some allusion has previously been made to a legal inquiry into that subject; and anybody, I think, would suppose that this deposition had somewhere or other at least been put forward by somebody who was acquainted with the nature of these transactions. It now turns out, on inquiry from the person who alone appears to be alluded to upon that subject as having made any statement in relation to it, that some of the leading facts imputed to him are utterly untrue, to the knowledge of that person who is supposed to have deposed to them. I need not trouble you with the particulars of that deposition, but will merely call your attention to the manner in which it is set out in this work.

"Now, gentlemen, it is set forth as a deposition; it had every appearance of authenticity and every appearance of having been used upon some occasion of that sort. And then that deposition being set forth, stating the facts in a manner that points to such a conclusion as I have adverted to, I will take it up as the learned counsel for the defendant has submitted it to you (not a just criterion by any means in every case), but as putting it in the most favourable way possible for the defendant who stands before you. Supposing, instead of an illustrious member of the Royal Family, this publication had been issued with regard to one of ourselves, or with regard to any individual with whom any one of us was acquainted in society, would it or not have been impossible for that individual to rest silent under such an imputation? And could any man who lives at all in society have escaped some degree of pain, if knowing that such facts were said of him, he had declined the opportunity of denying them upon oath, and proceeding afterwards to bring the criminal to justice? The particular course of proceeding that has been adopted here has this peculiarity in it, that the person that moves for leave to file a criminal information cannot obtain it without distinctly swearing to the falsehood of the acts imputed to him; and the person who makes the charge has the opportunity, in answer to that statement, of denying it upon oath, and of proving any facts which either go to show that the party applying to the court is guilty of the charge that has been made against him in the publication, or to show even that there can be reasonable doubt, and a probable cause for making the imputation that the party publishing such a book has made. It could only have been upon no such counter-affidavit being filed that this rule was made absolute, according to the view of the Court of King's Bench something more than a year ago, when the application was made; and therefore it comes before you in the present stage of the proceedings with the fullest proof that these facts were untrue which are imputed in the publication which you are called here to pronounce upon.

"I submit this case to you, gentlemen, upon the only point that is now before you, namely, is or is not this party guilty of having published a libel strongly reflecting upon the character of His Royal Highness the Duke of Cumberland? If you are of opinion he has, you will say he is guilty; if that appears to you to rest in any reasonable doubt, you will say he is not guilty. But you will not take into your consideration any views of what course it may be most expedient to take upon such occasions, for the question, aye or no, guilty or not guilty of publishing this libel, is the question now submitted to you for your consideration."

The jury immediately returned a verdict of *Guilty* (a).

(a) The contemporary reports of the trial are all silent as to the result of the verdict, but from inspection of the Crown roll preserved at the Public Record Office it appears that on the 2nd day of October in the following year the defendant was outlawed.

The following are copies of some of the depositions made the morning after the attack on the Duke of Cumberland. The principal ones only are inserted :—

MIDDLESEX.—*The Information of His Royal Highness* ERNEST AUGUSTUS, *Duke of* CUMBERLAND,

Who, being upon his oath, saith that before three o'clock this morning, being in bed and asleep, he received two blows upon his head, which awoke him, and upon starting up he received two other blows upon his head, which, being accompanied with a hissing noise, it occurred to him that some bat had flown against him, being between sleeping and waking, and immediately received two other blows ; there was a lamp burning in the room, but he did not see anybody; that there was a night-table standing near the bedside, where a letter lay which was covered with blood. His Royal Highness says he then got up and made for the door, which opens at the head of the bed ; he then received a wound upon his right thigh with a sabre ; he then called out to Neale, his page, and said there was a murderer in his room, and upon returning to his bedroom with Neale, he perceived that the door leading to the yellow room was wide open, which is always locked the last thing when he gets into bed; a naked sword had been dropped, which he supposes must have given the wound in his thigh. The man who gave the blows never spoke a word, and upon Neale returning with His Royal Highness, the man had fled through to the yellow room which leads into the ball-room, through the other yellow room into the armoury, to the summer bedroom through the dressing-room into Sellis's room (the page whom His Royal Highness believes gave him the wounds). His Royal Highness then went downstairs with Neale, and ordered the doors to be secured, that no person might escape out of the apartments. His Royal Highness further states that upon his return into his bedroom, he discovered that the sword which lay upon the floor was his own regimental sword, and in the closet, at the foot of his bed, was found the scabbard, with a pair of slippers belonging to Sellis, and the key of the closet-door, which is usually on the side of the door next the room, was found on the inside of the door next the closet; there was also a dark lantern in the closet, and from these circumstances he has reason to believe, and doth believe, that the blows and wounds he received were given him by the said Joseph Sellis. His Royal Highness further saith that the said Joseph Sellis had not incurred his displeasure, and that he had not any reason to think ill of him.

The mark of ✗ his Royal Highness the Duke of CUMBERLAND.

Sworn before me, the 31st May, 1810.

J. READ.

MIDDLESEX.—*The Information of* CORNELIUS NEALE, *Valet to His Royal Highness the Duke of* CUMBERLAND,

Who, being upon his oath, saith that whilst he was in bed, in a room adjoining the bedroom of His Royal Highness, a little before three o'clock, he heard His Royal Highness call out " Neale! Neale! I am murdered!" upon which he got out of bed and met the Duke of Cumberland at the door. His Royal Highness said the murderer was in his bedroom. Informant says he instantly darted into the bedroom of His Royal Highness and seized the poker, and then perceived that the door leading into the yellow room was wide open, which he immediately ran to, and set his foot upon a naked sword which was lying on the floor, just by the door. He took up the sword, and asked leave of His Royal Highness to pursue the assassin; but His Royal Highness desired he would not, but to call the servants. His Royal Highness then leant upon informant's arm, and they went together into the porter's room, and called the porter, and he was ordered by His Royal Highness not to suffer any person to go out of the house. They then returned upstairs again, and upon going upstairs they met Mrs. Neale, whom His Royal Highness desired to call Sellis. She ran to his bedroom, and came back again and said the door was locked. His Royal Highness then, finding himself faint from loss of blood, lay down upon the bed. His Royal Highness then desired informant

to look after the assassin, and to find out where he could
have been concealed.   Informant opened the door at the foot
of the bed leading to a small room which has three closets;
the water-closet, the closet where informant supposed the
assassin had concealed himself, and another closet for dirty
linen.   In the closet where he supposed the assassin was
concealed, informant found a pair of black leather slippers,
with the name of Sellis written in each slipper, which informant believes to be of the handwriting of Joseph Sellis,
an Italian, one of the valets of His Royal Highness the Duke
of Cumberland; there was also a dark lantern, a bottle of
water, and the scabbard of the sword which was found upon
the floor in the bedroom ; there were also two bolsters, which
are used in the day-time for ornamenting the bed of His
Royal Highness, and the key of the closet was in the inside
of the door, which was not usual, and could have been of no
use but for the purpose of locking the door, where he supposes
the assassin had concealed himself.   Informant saith about
this time a report came to the duke that Sellis was murdered.
Informant saith that he assisted His Royal Highness to go
to bed.   About this time Mr. Home, the surgeon, came, and
this informant assisted him in binding up his wounds.   Informant saith there are several wounds upon his Royal Highness's head, one upon his throat.   That the back of his right
hand is cut across, and that there are wounds upon his left
arm, and a wound upon the back of his right thigh, and he
has reason to believe that all the wounds were given by the
sword found upon the floor in the bedroom, which was very
bloody.   Informant saith that between the duke's room and
informant's room there are three doors, but only a wainscot
partition between the beds.   That he never heard any noise
till the duke called out " Neale ! Neale ! I am murdered !"
Informant saith that he attended His Royal Highness to bed
last night about twelve o'clock ; and after His Royal Highness
had passed the yellow room (which he always does when he
goes to bed) informant shut the door, and is very sure he
locked it, and he afterwards remained in the duke's room
until His Royal Highness got into bed.   No other person
was in the room, and His Royal Highness desired informant
would call him at seven o'clock.   Informant went out by the

doors leading to his own room, and ordered the housemaid
to light His Royal Highness's fire at six o'clock; he then
went to his own room, and went to bed. The doors between
His Royal Highness's bedroom and the bedroom of this informant were shut, but not locked. His bedroom door next
the passage is always open; that he is very wakeful, and if
anyone had come in that way he must either have heard or seen
him; there being no other entrance to His Royal Highness's
bedroom but the door from the yellow room, which he left
locked, this informant verily believes that the said Joseph
Sellis, or some other person who made the assault upon His
Royal Highness, must have concealed himself in the closet
where he found the slippers, the dark lantern, and the scabbard of the sword. Informant saith that the said Joseph
Sellis had taken out His Royal Highness's uniform and the
sword, and brought them into his bedroom for a regiment
inspection which did not take place, and Sellis afterwards
returned the regimentals to the wardrobe, but left the sword
in the bedroom, where informant believes he saw the sword
some time yesterday.

CORNELIUS NEALE.

Sworn before me, May 31, 1810.

    J. READ.

MIDDLESEX.—*The Information of* ANN, *the Wife of* CORNELIUS
    NEALE, *Housekeeper to His Royal Highness the Duke of*
    CUMBERLAND,

Who, being upon oath, saith she was called up this morning, about three o'clock, by her husband, and at the same
time heard His Royal Highness exclaim that he had been
murdered. Upon going into Mr. Neale's room (called the
page's room) she found His Royal Highness bleeding very
much. Mr. Neale was with him. His Royal Highness desired
her to call the servants, and after His Royal Highness had
got back to his bedroom, she went and called Joseph Sellis
at his room door, but no one answered; the door was fast.
The porter was with her, and tried to open it, but could not.
He then knocked very violently at the door, but no one
answered. She then tried to open the door of the yellow

room, leading to the ball-room, but could not open it, and found afterwards that the door was bolted withinside, which she never knew it to be before.   Informant saith that she then returned by the ball-room through the yellow rooms, and through the summer rooms, to get at Sellis's room the other way, and thinks five or six minutes had elapsed since they tried at the first door ; and just as she got to the bed-room door she heard a guggling sort of noise, like water in a man's throat, and heard a dropping on the floor like water, and the porter looked into the room, and exclaimed, " Good God ! Mr. Sellis has cut his throat ;" upon which she became very much frightened, and went away and desired the porter to get assistance.   Informant says that the folding-doors leading from the ball-room into the yellow room were shut, and all the other doors from the ball-room to Sellis's room were open.

ANN NEALE.

Informant further saith that she has known Joseph Sellis for near twelve years, and for the last five years he has lived in His Royal Highness's service : says that he was very obstinate and quarrelsome, and would not bear contradiction, not even from His Royal Highness, and would never acknow-ledge himself in fault.   Had observed nothing particular in his deportment lately.   He had been ill for three weeks or a month, of a violent cold, but was getting better of it.   In-formant says that His Royal Highness had been very kind to him, and about a week or ten days ago had permitted him to go within the carriage, instead of riding on the outside, which he had been accustomed to do.   She has no reason to believe that he had any grudge to His Royal Highness : that during his illness His Royal Highness permitted him to go to bed, instead of sitting up for him, which it was his place to do every third night.   That during the last four or five years His Royal Highness had allowed his wife and family to live in the house, with an allowance of coals and candles.   That (after the birth of the last child) about three months ago, His Royal Highness and the Princess Augusta stood for the christening by proxies, and she has heard Sellis say that the Queen had made him a present of two pieces of

Indian muslin, and that the Princess Augusta had also given him a piece, with several other presents for the child's baptism. Informant saith that the Duke of Cumberland was very partial to Sellis, and always had him to travel with him. He lived very much to himself, and was very distant with the other servants. Informant says that there are a pair of green doors across the gallery which separates His Royal Highness's apartments from the Queen's public rooms, which are always kept locked, of which she has the key; but there was another key, which Sellis had, and which he informed her His Royal Highness had permitted him to get made in order that he might pass from His Royal Highness's apartments to where his wife lived without going out of doors, and that he must have passed that way yesterday. Informant farther says that in passing through the ball-room and the yellow room adjoining, she found the upper part of the window-shutters open in the ball-room, the yellow room adjoining, and one in the spare bedroom, which was usually shut at night.   ANN NEALE.

Sworn before me, May 31, 1810.   J. READ.

MIDDLESEX.—*The Information of* MATTHEW HENRY GRASLIN, *Servant to His Royal Highness the Duke of* CUMBERLAND,

Who, being upon his oath, saith that he was called up this morning about three o'clock by Mrs. Neale, who said, "Get up, get up! the duke is murdered!" Informant says he got up and took a pair of pistols with him; and when he came to the sitting-room next His Royal Highness's bedroom, Mrs. Neale desired him to call Joseph Sellis, but he was not able to find the way to the apartments where Sellis and his wife lived, and came back again; and then the porter went and brought back word that Sellis was sleeping in the duke's house. He then went, in company of Mrs. Neale and the porter to Sellis's room door, where they called and knocked, but no one answered. They then went round by the ball-room and summer apartments, and searched, as they went on, till they came to the other door of Sellis's room, where they heard a noise like water in some man's throat, and the porter cried out, "Sellis is murdered!" The door

I

of the room was open, but neither of them went into the
room ; they went back for further assistance. Informant
says that he saw Sellis last night about eight o'clock in the
porter's room ; he came there, and asked who was for Windsor
to-morrow. Informant says he answered that he was.
Informant further says that in passing through the ball-
room and the summer apartments, two window-shutters of
the ball-room were a little open, and one window-shutter in
each of the other rooms was a little open at the top.

MATTHEW HENRY GRASLIN.

Sworn before me, May 31, 1810.   J. READ.

MIDDLESEX.—*The Information of* THOMAS STRICKLAND, *Under
Butler to His Royal Highness the Duke of* CUMBERLAND,

Who, being upon oath, saith that he saw Joseph Sellis
last night, about ten minutes before eleven o'clock, in His
Royal Highness's bedroom. He was standing by the dress-
ing-table, with what appeared to this informant to be a shirt
in his hand. Nothing passed between us. Informant says
he went there, as it was usual for him to do, to take up His
Royal Highness's cup, which he placed upon the stand by
the bedside. Informant says he was not surprised at seeing
Sellis there, as he did not know but that it was his turn to
be in waiting. Sellis looked earnestly at him, and had a
smile upon his countenance, but did not speak. Sellis had
his coat on, but he did not observe any other part of his
dress, nor did he take notice whether there was or not a sword
in the room. Says he had very little intercourse with Sellis,
but when he had, he always found him to be a very civil man.
He left Sellis in the duke's room, and never saw him afterwards.   THOMAS STRICKLAND.

Sworn before me, May 31, 1810.   J. READ.

THE TRIAL

OF THE CASE

SMYTH *v.* SMYTH

AND OTHERS,

AT THE GLOUCESTER SUMMER ASSIZES,

BEFORE MR. JUSTICE COLERIDGE AND A SPECIAL JURY,

On August 8th, 9th, and 10th, 1853.

Counsel for the Plaintiff: Mr. *Bovill* (now Chief Justice of the Court of Common Pleas), Mr. *Phipson*, and Mr. *Dowdeswell.*

For the Defendants : Sir Frederick *Thesiger*, Q. C., Mr. *Crowder*, Q. C., Mr. *Alexander*, Q. C., Mr. *Gray*, Mr. *Skinner*, and Mr. *Taprell.*

INTRODUCTION.

" *Magna est veritas et prævalebit !*" Seldom has the truth of this maxim been more strikingly exemplified than in the case of the Claimant to the large estates of the Smyth family in Somersetshire and Wiltshire—" Sir Richard Hugh Smyth, Baronet," otherwise " Dr. Smith," otherwise " Thomas Provis." Seldom has exposure been more complete, more overwhelming, or more merited. Since the trial of Alexander Alexander, *soi-disant* Earl of Stirling, at Edinburgh, in the year 1839, for forgery (to which the present case bears in some respects a great resemblance) there has probably been no civil cause in modern days which attracted at the time so much attention as the one now under consideration (*a*).

A short statement showing the pedigree of the Smyth family, and how the claim originated, will perhaps be found

---

(*a*) When this was written the Tichborne Case was only in its infancy, and the trial had not commenced.

I 2

useful for the purpose of following the case attempted to be
set up on the part of the Claimant; but as the whole of the
interest of the trial is derived from the evidence of the
plaintiff himself, from his cross-examination by Sir F. Thesiger,
and from the dramatic *dénouement* and collapse of the whole
case, no further summary or outline will be attempted. The
clear and lucid manner indeed in which the case was opened,
under circumstances of great and unexpected difficulty, by
Mr. Bovill, whose opening statement is preserved in the following report, as far as possible, is in itself far better and
much more intelligible than any outline.

In the year 1800 there died in Gloucestershire a Mr. Thomas
Smyth, a gentleman of ancient family and large landed pro-
perty, known and referred to in the following report as
Thomas Smyth of Stapleton.   He left issue,—

1. Sir Hugh Smyth.
2. Sir John Smyth.
3. Two daughters : one afterwards married to John
    Upton, Esq., and the other to Colonel Way.

Thomas Smyth left also a will, whereby he devised the
Stapleton Estate, in respect of which the action was brought,
to his second son, John, for life, with remainder to his issue
in fee, and in default of such issue to his (testator's) eldest
son, Hugh, in fee.   In default of any issue of Hugh the estate
then went to the daughters above named successively in fee ;
and it was in fact by the son of one of the daughters of
Thomas Smyth that the estate was held at the time of the
action being brought, both Sir John and Sir Hugh Smyth
having died without issue.

On Sir John Smyth's death without issue the estate went,
under the limitations contained in Thomas Smyth's will, to
Sir Hugh Smyth and his issue in fee ; and if the Claimant
could have made out that he was the eldest legitimate son of
Sir Hugh Smyth he would indisputably have been entitled
to the estate.   But, on the other hand, if Sir Hugh left no
issue the defendant would be entitled.   Both parties claimed
under the same will, and the real question in dispute was
whether Sir Hugh Smyth, the eldest son of Thomas Smyth
of Stapleton, had left issue.

Sir Hugh Smyth was twice married, first to a Miss Wilson,

by whom it was admitted by both sides he had no issue, and secondly to a Miss Howell, by whom it was equally admitted he had no legitimate issue. The Claimant could not therefore by any possibility make out his title as heir-at-law to Sir Hugh Smyth by either of these marriages. He set up, however, that Sir Hugh had been thrice married, and that previous to the marriages mentioned above he had married in Ireland a Miss Jane Vandenbergh, and it was this marriage, and the subsequent birth of himself as the issue of it, that the Claimant sought to prove in the present action.

Mr. Bovill, on whom, in consequence of the absence of Sir Fitzroy Kelly and Mr. Keating, the conduct of the case had unexpectedly devolved, after explaining the absence of his two learned leaders, proceeded to give a concise outline of the facts as relied upon by the plaintiff.

" The question at issue," he said, " is whether the plaintiff is entitled, not only to a small estate called the Heath House, and the adjoining park at Stapleton, in this county, but also to an estate at Elmington, in the parishes of Henbury and Compton, near Bristol, and to other larger estates in Somersetshire and Wiltshire belonging to the late Sir Hugh Smyth and to Sir John Smyth, late of Ashton Court, near Bristol. The rentals of these estates amount to upwards of £20,000 a year; but the inquiry now before you relates and will be confined to the two small portions of the property I have mentioned; and the question to be tried by you will have reference to the title to those two properties only.

" The present Claimant is fifty-six years of age, and comes forward at this late period of his life to claim the estates of his ancestors. He became entitled to the Heath House Estate only in 1849, on the death of his uncle, Sir John Smyth, and to the Almington or Elmington Farm on the decease of his father, Sir Hugh, in 1824."

Mr. Bovill then stated at some length the pedigree of the plaintiff, a summary of which has been already given, and proceeded,—

" The question involves as well the title to two baronetcies (*a*). The family of the Smyths is an old one, and the title was granted for some services to the State. The last baronet was Sir John Smyth, of Ashton Court, who survived his brother, Sir Hugh Smyth. The estates are now in the possession of the descendants of the sister of Sir Hugh and of Sir John. The principal defendant is Mr. Greville Smyth, who is under age, and appears by his guardian. The other defendants are trustees having the management of the estates.

" Supposing Sir Hugh to have died without issue, the property would go to the sisters and their descendants; but if he had issue that issue would be entitled to it. We on the part of the plaintiff set up that there was in fact issue of Sir Hugh Smyth, and that that issue is the plaintiff.

" That Sir John was aware that his brother, Sir Hugh, had left issue I shall prove by a document under his own hand, and also that Sir John abstained from marrying lest his son should appear and claim the estates. I shall also prove a remarkable circumstance in strong confirmation of the probability that he did know of this son being in existence—on the very day on which the present Claimant first made his appearance in the presence of his uncle, Sir John, Sir John was so shaken in body and mind that he went home from Ashton Court to Heath House, and there he stated the fact of his having had an interview with the son of his dead brother, and that he was satisfied he was the man whose appearance he had so long expected. I shall show that he was not able to eat his dinner, that he went to bed for the last time, and that it had such an effect upon his mind that that night it killed him.

" The Claimant's history is indeed a remarkable one. It turns out that Sir Hugh Smyth, the eldest son of Thomas of

---

(*a*) This is scarcely correct. The first baronetcy was granted in 1661, but it expired in 1741 for want of male heirs of the third baronet, Sir John Smyth. The estates, however, descended to his sisters, one of whom married a Mr. Jarrit Smyth, of Bristol, who was created a baronet in 1763. This would be the only baronetcy in existence at the time of the trial; and it is obvious that no descendant of Sir Hugh Smyth who could only claim connection with the family of the first baronet through the female line could claim to be entitled to both baronetcies.

Stapleton, was married in Ireland in 1796. In consequence of the position in which he was placed, his father wishing him to marry a Miss Wilson, daughter of the Bishop of Bristol, he had kept his marriage in Ireland a secret. The Smyths had family connections with the family of the Earl of Bandon, and Sir Hugh went over to visit them, and then and there married Miss Jane Vandenbergh, a daughter of Count Vandenbergh, about whom I can give no information, and who was staying with Mrs. Bernard, afterwards the Countess of Bandon.

" The marriage took place on the 19th of May, 1796, at the private residence of the Bandon family at Lismore. The rebellion was then just breaking out in Ireland, and the Countess of Bandon, the Marchioness of Bath, and Jane Smyth, wife of Sir Hugh, came over to England, and took up their abode in Bath, at No. 1, Royal Crescent. In January, 1797, the lady was confined of a child at the house of a carpenter named Provis, at Warminster, where she was sent for the purpose, and a suggestion has been made that the Claimant is the son of Provis, but there is abundant evidence on the part of the plaintiff to prove the contrary. The lady was attended in her confinement by a person named Lydia Reed, but unfortunately died shortly after her son was born, and the child was left in Reed's care. It will be part of my case to identify this child through all the various scenes of its life down to the present day.

" A register of the marriage was made, but not in the form usually followed in this country, because in Ireland at that time, and until a very recent period, marriages did not generally take place in a church, but all persons of any condition in life were married in private houses. The entries of marriages were usually made in a Bible, and I shall produce the Bible in which the entry was made in this case, and signed by the officiating minister, the Rev. Mr. Lovett, of Lismore. I shall prove his signature, that of Sir Hugh Smyth, and the signatures of the attesting witnesses, and also the entry in the same Bible of the register of the baptism of the child by the Rev. Mr. Symes, at No. 1, Royal Crescent, Bath.

" A few months after the death of the plaintiff's mother,

Sir Hugh Smyth married a second time. His second wife was a Miss Wilson, a daughter of the Bishop of Bristol, and as Sir Hugh was still desirous of keeping the first marriage a secret, the plaintiff was left at Provis's until he was sent to school. When inquiries were set on foot respecting the legitimacy of the plaintiff, the first document that turned up, and which had been in possession of the family of Lydia Reed, the nurse, was a letter written by Sir Hugh to his wife, on the day of the Claimant's birth, as follows :—

'Stapleton, Feb. 2, 1797.

' Dear Jane,—The bearer is my old nurse, Lydia Read, in whom I have every confidence as to her skill and attention to you. Dr. Seagrim will attend you. I will endeavour to be over to-morrow, and bring my mother with me. Till then, God bless you, and that you may have a safe deliverance is the prayer of your affectionate husband

'Hugh Smyth.

' To Mrs Smyth, Warminster.'

" The nurse is dead, but I shall produce her niece, who has nursed the Claimant when a child, and who will be able to identify him. It is not that the nurse of a child can also identify the man; but I will go on to trace him through other witnesses, step by step, until no link in the chain be wanting, and of such strength shall that chain be that even the great power and talent of my learned friends will not be able to break it.

" There are two peculiar circumstances which enable the witnesses to identify the Claimant—one is, that his wrist was lacerated at his birth, and the other, that the thumbs of all the Smyth family turn back in a remarkable way, which is peculiar to the Claimant also.

" After the Claimant's childhood he was sent to Lower Court, and thence to the school of Mr. Hill, of Brislington, where he was known as Richard Hugh Smyth. He was next educated at Warminster School as a gentleman, and in the same name, and the Marchioness of Bath, and other persons of distinction more or less connected with his father and mother, visited him there. From thence he went to Winchester College, and there payment for his education was made by one Grace, who was Sir Hugh's butler. The defendants have or ought to have the accounts of the man Grace, which will prove whether this statement is true or false. The Claimant has applied for an inspection of the steward's accounts, but it has been refused.

" It turns out that Grace was a man on whom no reliance could be placed, and on his death in 1821 his remains were turned out of the house and placed in an outhouse. You will naturally ask, what has this to do with the case? but I believe that the fact will turn out to be that this man Grace, in consequence of a severe illness which the Claimant laboured under in 1814, reported him to be dead, and that Grace received the money for the Claimant's education and appropriated it to himself.

" When the Claimant recovered, the Marchioness of Bath sent him abroad, and supplied him with a sum of money, between £1400 and £1500. Sir Hugh believed that his son was dead, probably in consequence of Grace's representations, but in course of time Sir Hugh considered it probable that his son was still living. In 1822, Sir Hugh being seriously ill, and impressed with the idea that his son, who had been abroad since 1814, was still living, executed a document found very recently amongst the papers of Lydia Reed, which declared that his son, if he ever appeared, was entitled to the estates.

" The signature of Sir Hugh to this document at first is difficult of recognition, and no one would at first sight believe that it was the signature of the same person who signed the other documents, but this is accounted for by the fact that Sir Hugh was at that time very ill, and the signature appears to have been written with a very trembling hand. But fortunately it does not rest simply on this evidence, for the document bears the impression of the Smyth coat of arms upon the seal. The defendants have that seal; let them produce it and see whether it fits the wax.

" The deed is attested by the brother of Sir Hugh, whose

signature will be proved by James Abbott, his confidential agent and steward, and by two other persons."

Mr. Bovill then read to the jury the deed in question, of which the following is a copy :—

"*I, Sir Hugh Smyth, of Ashton Park, in the county of Somerset, and of Rockley House, in the county of Wilts, do declare that in the month of May, 1796, I was married at Court Macsherry, in the county of Cork, in Ireland, by the Rev. Verney Lovett, to Jane, the only daughter of Count John Samuel Vandenbergh, by Jane, the only daughter of Major Gookin, of Court Macsherry, and Hesther, his wife. Now my wife, driven from Ireland by the troubles there, came to War-minster, in the county of Wilts, on the 2nd day of February, 1797, gave birth to a son, and she died the same day. The boy was left to the care of my own nurse, Lydia Reed, who can at any time identify my son by marks upon his right hand. The boy was baptized at No. 1, Royal Crescent, Bath, by the Rev. James Symes, curate, by the names of Richard Hugh Smyth, son of Hugh Smyth, and Jane, his wife. From circumstances of a family nature this boy was brought up in private, and through the rascallity of my butler Grace, under whose especial charge my son was, he left England clandestinely, in the year 1813, and I had been assured by Grace that my son had died abroad, but at the death of Grace I became possessed of doubts of my son's demise. Now, under the impression that my son had died, I made or executed a will in the year 1814. That will I now abrogate, annul, and sett asside, by this, my last will and testament, and by this docu-ment do acknowledge Richard Hugh Smyth my legitimate son and heir, and that he must possess, him and his heirs for ever, the vast estates of my ancestors, as secured to him by the will of my late excellent father, Thomas Smyth, of Stapleton ; and here I implore my dearly beloved brother John to use his best endeavours to secure the return of my son, and in case he does return to restore to him his rights, and which I know my brother will do for my sake. Further, I do desire that documents do remain in the custody of my nurse, Lydia Reed, and whom no doubt my son will be sure to seek. In*

security of and in furtherance of the object of this deed, I,
Sir Hugh Smyth, do seal it with my seal, and sign it with
my name, this 27th day of January, in the year of our Lord
1822, in the presence of the parties whose signatures appear.

" HUGH SMYTH. (L. S.)

" JOHN SMYTH,
"WILLIAM EDWARDS,
" JAMES ABBOTT,
"WILLIAM DOBBSON."

" In the following year Sir Hugh, still anxious about his
son, executed another document; he was then in better
health, which will account for the difference between the
two signatures." The document is as follows :—

" *I, Sir Hugh Smyth, of Ashton Park, in the county of*
Somerset, and of Rockley House, in the county of Wilts, do
declare that in the year 1796 I was married, in the county of
Cork, in Ireland, by the Rev. Verney Lovett, to Jane, the
daughter of Count Vandenbergh, by Jane, the daughter of
Major Gookin, of Court Macsherry, near Bandon. Witnesses
thereto—The Countess of Bandon and Consena Lovett. In the
following year, Jane Smyth, my wife, came to England, and
immediately after giving birth to a son, she died on the 2nd
day of February, 1797, and she lies buried in a brick vault in
Warminster churchyard. My son was consigned to the care
of my own nurse, Lydia Reed, who can at any time identify
him by marks upon his right hand, but more especially by the
turning up of both the thumbs, an indelible mark of identity
in our family. My son was afterwards baptized by the Rev.
James Symes, of Midsomer-Norton, by the names of Richard
Hugh Smyth, the sponsors being the Marchioness of Bath
and the Countess of Bandon, who named him Richard, after
her deceased brother, Richard Boyle. Through the rascallity
of my butler Grace, my son left England for the continent,
and was reported to me as having died there, but at the death
of Grace the truth came out that my son was alive, and that
he would soon return to claim his rights. Now, under the
impression of my son's death, I executed a will in 1814. *That*

will I do by this document declare null and void, and to all
intents and purposes sett asside, *in all its arrangements, the*
payment of my just debts, the provision for John, the son of the
late Elizabeth Howell, and to the fulfilment of all matters not
interfering with the rights of my heir-at-law. Now, to give
every assistance to my son, should he ever return, I do declare
him my legitimate son and heir to all the estates of my
ancestors, and which he will find amply secured to him and
his heirs for ever by the will of his grandfather, the late
Thomas Smyth, of Stapleton, Esq., and further by the will of
my uncle, the late Sir John Hugh Smyth, Baronet. Both those
wills so fully arrange for the security of the property in
possession or reversion, that I have now only to appoint and
constitute my beloved brother, John Smyth, Esq., my only
executor for his life, and I do by this deed place the utmost
confidence in my brother that he will at any future time do my
son justice. And I also entreat my son to cause the remains
of his mother to be removed to Ashton, · and buried in the
family vault, close to my side, and to raise a monument to
her memory. Now in furtherance of the object of this deed,
I do seal with my seal, and sign it with my name, and in
the presence of witnesses, this 10*th day of September, in the*
year of our Lord, 1823.

" HUGH SMYTH.   (L. S.)

"WILLIAM EDWARDS,
"WILLIAM DOBBSON,
"JAMES ABBOTT."

" With reference to the paragraph in the above document
as to the burial of Hugh Smyth's wife, it is a curious circumstance in the case that there is a brick vault in Warminster churchyard which no one knew anything about.
An application has been made to the Bishop to allow the
vault to be opened to see if there is any coffin-plate which
would give any information, but permission has been refused.
The custody of the second deed is not so clearly made out as
that of the previous one, but we shall be able to trace the
possession of it to an attorney's clerk. Connecting one
thing with another the document will be found to be of
essential importance.

" From 1814 to 1826 the Claimant was on the continent. He went abroad and travelled with Lord Knox, devoting himself to the subject of education. He learned a system of mnemonics or artificial memory, gave a great deal of attention to the subject of elocution, and lectured about England on his return from the continent as Doctor Smith. He supposed himself to be a son of Sir Hugh, but he was also aware that his appearance would give a good deal of offence to those who were connected with his father, and he abstained from prosecuting his claim. On his return to England in 1826 he found his father was dead, and he then heard that Sir John Smyth was in possession of the estates. There was an illegitimate son named John, and the Claimant was under the impression that this Sir John Smyth was an elder brother and entitled to the estates, and he took no active steps until 1828, when he had stronger notions of his own rights. The case rested dormant until 1849, when he went to Sir John and had that extraordinary interview with him that ended in his being acknowledged as the son of Sir Hugh, and caused Sir John's death that very night.

"The real point for you to determine is whether the plaintiff's father, Sir Hugh Smyth, was married as was alleged in 1796, whether the plaintiff was born in 1797, and whether he was the son of the late Sir Hugh. The defendants have said they will undertake to prove the deeds of 1822 and 1823 to be forgeries. We defy them to the proof. There are five signatures to the one and six to the other, and if they are forged all these signatures must be forged too."

On the conclusion of Mr. Bovill's speech the letter alleged to be Sir Hugh's and written to the nurse Reed, and the two deeds of the 27th January, 1822, and 10th September, 1823, were put in, and also a Bible containing the certificate of the marriage of Sir Hugh and Miss Jane Vandenbergh, and of the baptism of the plaintiff. The Bible was an old-fashioned family Bible, with the name of " *John S. Vandenbergh*" on the title-page. The following are copies of both the certificates :—

" *I certify that Hugh Smyth, Esq., son of Thomas Smyth, Esq., of Stapleton, in the county of Gloucester, in England by Jane, his wife, was this* 19*th day of May,* 1796, *married by me to Jane, the daughter of Count John Samuel Vandenbergh, by Jane, the daughter of Major Gookin and Hesther his wife, of Court Macsherry, county of Cork, Ireland.*

" VERNEY LOVETT, D.D., *Vicar of Lismore.*

" *Signed by* { " HUGH SMYTH,
" JANE VANDENBERGH.

" *Witnesses,*
   " CAROLINE BERNARD,
   " JOHN S. VANDENBERGH,
   " CONSENA LOVETT."

The certificate of baptism was as follows :—

" *Richard Hugh Smyth, son of Hugh Smyth, Esq., and Jane, his wife, born September* 2*nd,* 1797, *baptized September* 10*th,* 1798, *at No.* 1, *Royal Crescent, Bath.*

" J. SYMES, *Clerk.*

   " CAROLINE BERNARD,
   " ISABELLA THYNNE."

Evidence was then called to prove the authenticity of the documents. The Rev. George Turner Seymour, a magistrate of Somersetshire, deposed that he was acquainted with the late Sir Hugh Smyth. He believed the letter written to the nurse to be in Sir Hugh's handwriting, and also the signatures to the certificates in the Bible.

The deeds of the 27th January, 1822, and 10th September, 1823, were then produced, and the witness stated that he could not say the signature to the first was that of Sir H. Smyth, but he believed the one to the deed of 10th September, 1823, to be his.

Mr. Morris, a surgeon of Marlborough, proved that he attended Sir Hugh in 1822 and 1823, the years the deeds were signed. He stated Sir Hugh was always ill, and was considered a nervous patient, but witness thought his illness was imaginary. It was not an illness that would cause tremulousness of hand. He fancied himself ill one day and would be out hunting the next.

Mr. Kingston, of Bandon, deposed to being acquainted with the Rev. Mr. Lovett. Believed the signature "Verney Lovett, D.D., Vicar of Lismore," and also the whole certificate in the Bible produced to be his writing. Had frequently seen Mr. Lovett write.

The Hon. Captain Smyth Bernard, brother to Lord Bandon, spoke to having known the Rev. Mr. Lovett. His grandmother, Mrs. James Bernard, was before her marriage Mrs. Hester Gookin, and her maiden name was Smyth. About the time of the rebellion in Ireland in 1789, the Bandon family went to Bath for protection.

On cross-examination the witness said :—He never knew that any of his family were related to the Smyths of Ashton Court. His mother's name was Catherine Henrietta, and her ordinary mode of signing was C. H. Bandon. Never heard of Major Gookin having a daughter, and never heard the name of Vandenbergh in connection with them, nor before this case. When the signature Caroline Bernard was shown to him he said it could not be his mother's, as her name was not Caroline. The signature in the Bible, Caroline Bernard, was not his mother's, nor was the baptismal entry. Had seen the person calling himself Sir Richard Smyth. He sent in his card, and witness saw him. His visitor wanted to know who his (witness's) mother was. Never heard of the practice of marrying in private houses in Ireland. He was obliged himself to go to church.

John Symes, son of the Rev. James Symes, proved that the signature James Symes in the Bible, appended to the entry of baptism, was his father's. His father was in the habit of baptizing in private houses. On cross-examination he admitted having been in the workhouse for eleven or twelve years. A Mrs. Mattick came and took him out. She said it would be a good day for him if he could come and prove his father's signature. It might be 50*l.* a year to him.

Ann Symes, the granddaughter of the Rev. James Symes, also spoke to her grandfather's signature. The signature in the Bible, "Isabella Thynne," was also deposed to by the Hon. Carolina Boyle, who knew Lady Isabella Thynne very well, as being in Lady Isabella's handwriting, and a clerk in Drummond's Bank gave evidence to the same effect.

Several witnesses were then called to prove the signatures of the different parties who had signed the two deeds of the 27th January, 1822, and 10th September, 1823, either as principal or witnesses, which they did with some considerable amount of certainty. One of them, the widow of Grace the butler, on cross-examination denied the truth of the assertion that her husband's remains were on the occasion of his funeral treated with indignity, and asserted that Grace was not in any way connected with Sir Hugh before 1801, and could not therefore have had the care or in any way have been concerned in the management of a son of Sir Hugh's born in 1797, and two years old in 1799. The signature of Wm. Dobson to the deed of 1822 was, however, not proved by the witnesses called for that purpose, but they both agreed that he did not spell his name "Dobbson" with two b's as in the deed.

In consequence of the extraordinary turn the case took on the cross-examination of the plaintiff, it is quite unnecessary to give the evidence of these witnesses in full. The whole of the first day and part of the second were taken up with the proof of the signatures, before the plaintiff himself, Sir Richard Hugh Smyth, was put into the box. His evidence was listened to with the greatest attention, and at certain parts of the cross-examination the excitement in the crowded court was intense. After some further introductory matter had been given in evidence he was examined in chief by Mr. Bovill, and stated as follows :—

" My first remembrance goes back to the time when I was living at Warminster, at the house of a Mr. Provis, a carpenter. When I was about three years old a woman named Mrs. Reed and a girl Mary Provis were living there at the time. When I left Mrs. Provis, Sir Hugh's butler, Grace, took me away. I did not at that time know whose son I was. I did not know my mother. She died the moment I was born, as I understand.

" Whilst at school at Brislington I visited old Colonel Gore. I also went to Bath to No. 1 in the Royal Crescent, then inhabited by the Earl of Bandon's family. I went there several times, and also to another house called Lidcombe in the neighbourhood. I left Brislington school in about two years. I was taken to Warminster Grammar School by some ladies from Longleat, the Marchioness of Bath's. Many ladies came to see me from Longleat and Bath at times. I have since learnt their names. The Marchioness of Bath was one and Lady Isabella another. I remained at Warminster school about two years. I then went to Winchester College as a commoner under Dr. Goddard. I remained there until 1810, the year Dr. Goddard left. I left Winchester in consequence of what Dr. Goddard said, that my bills had not been paid for the last eighteen months. I went to London by the advice of Dr. Goddard to the Marchioness of Bath and told her what Dr. Goddard had said. She lived in Grosvenor Street. I stayed there some considerable time, until her Ladyship had matured her mind on the subject. I did not hear anything about my family till my last interview with the Marchioness. That was some little time after going to London to see her on this very subject. She said Sir Hugh was my father, and advised me to go to Ashton Court to see him.

" Her Ladyship stated she could not tell me anything respecting my mother, but told me I should get it from the Bandon family. She also told me that in the possession of Mr. Davis, her steward, at Warminster, would be found the Bible of my mother, pictures, and other trinkets, jewellery, and things of that kind belonging to my mother. She also gave me a large sum of money. The possession of the money at that time took away all other thoughts, and I paid no attention to her Ladyship's advice. The money was some hundreds of pounds, 1400*l.* or 1500*l.* It was in notes. I did not go to my father's. I went to pay a visit to a lady at Wycombe Abbey, the seat of Lord Carrington. I received nothing from the Marchioness of Bath except the money. I cannot remember the name of the lady at Wycombe Abbey. I only know the house. I was there some considerable time ; some three or four months ; and on my return to London the Marchioness was not at home ; she had left some little time after I was taken ill at the Marchioness's house in London. My illness was the small-pox. I was ill a length of time; I should say eighteen months. I was removed to Parliament

K

Street to the care of, I think, a Dr. Williams, some time in 1811. I was at that house about eighteen months."

The witness then proceeded to give minute details of what he recollected in his early days, from which it was to be inferred that he had always been treated as a person of position, and continued :—

" I travelled through the whole extent of Europe after the proclamation of peace. I became acquainted with Bell and Lancaster, who at that time were making investigations in Germany and over all the Low Countries. They gave joint lectures. I cannot charge my mind whether they had established their schools in England before that, or whether they did it afterwards. I remember their separating on differing in opinion. They then returned to England in 1826, and I also. On my return to England I made some inquiries about my family. I heard Sir Hugh Smyth, my father, was dead. I should correct myself here a little. I was not then " decisive " that Sir Hugh Smyth was my father. I should say that I heard Sir Hugh Smyth was dead." After relating various details of his life from 1826 to 1835, from which it appeared he had been in the habit of going about lecturing upon education at schools and institutions in England and Scotland, and in that manner earned his livelihood, the witness proceeded :—" I never at that time made any inquiry for the things the Marchioness of Bath told me were with Mr. Davis; I never inquired of Mr. Davis. I learnt in 1838 or 1839 that Davis was dead. I then saw old Mr. Provis, who was living at Frome. I had some words with him for obstinately refusing to give me any information respecting my mother. He said he should say nothing further. I was taken away from his house at so early a period of life that he never troubled himself any further. I had seen him several times before. This was the last interview. He seemed to draw back. I used some harsh expressions, and he struck me with his stick on the head. I told him it was the last time I should call upon him ; he had struck me, and had no right. I put him down in a chair. The words I said were, ' How dare you strike me ?—you could have done no more to your son.' I was going away and he called me back, took me upstairs to his bedroom, opened his bureau and gave me the Bible and the jewellery. The large picture said to be that of my father hung in the room below. He also asked me to pledge my word to him that I would follow his directions. I assured him I would. He then gave into my hands a bundle of papers, sealed up, with directions to take them to Mr. Phelps, an eminent solicitor, at Warminster. I then left him, and never saw him more. I brought the Bible and jewellery away without opening them. That is the Bible (produced), and this the jewellery."

Much interest was caused by the production of the jewellery. The Claimant brought out a new-looking morocco case containing a miniature portrait supposed by him to be his mother's, four gold rings, and two brooches. One ring was marked with the initials " J. B.," suggested to be those of Jane Bernard, and one of the brooches with the words " Jane Gookin " at length. It will be seen as the trial progresses that the production of the latter brooch had a very decisive effect on the Claimant's case. The witness continued:—

" I first saw the writings in the Bible after our first visit to Ireland. We went there at Christmas last. Every year after the year 1838, on coming to Bristol, I made inquiries about my family. I obtained no information. I asked ' How is Sir John—is he married?' ' No.' ' Then there may be a chance for my family.' I had no idea he was the brother of my father, but the son. At that time I had no need, and made no search. In 1849, May the 19th, on a Friday, I called on and saw Sir John at Ashton Court. I went there alone. I saw Sir John himself, and Mrs. Way, his younger sister Mary. They were going into the Court from Heath House. Mrs. Way seemed rather annoyed at my intrusion, and said, ' You had better go away, man ; Sir John is not in a state to be seen.' I said my business was with Sir John, and Sir John I would see. She went away. Sir John took me to the small dining-room, half library and half dining-room. I rather suppose he felt conscious of who it was. We sat down. I told him as much as I could remember of my past life. He appeared excessively agitated, and was thrown into such a dreadful state that it was painful to behold him at that time. I had never seen him before. To calm him I merely said I was not come to take his title or his property ; I

wanted a provision for my family in a suitable manner, and
security after his death.   He made use of this remarkable
expression, my lord—one he was always accustomed to—
' You are indeed the son of my dear brother.'   After considerable conversation it was agreed that I should go to Chester
and fetch my family, and he would make every arrangement;
they should stay at Ashton Court and he would live at Heath
House.   He gave me all the money he had,—a 50*l.* note of
the Bank of England.   He said he would give me a draught
for more if I required it, and I only regret I did not take it.
I imagined several times I heard a movement of some one
listening, and mentioned it to Sir John.   He said, ' Tut, tut,
nonsense.'   I left Bristol by the 5 o'clock train for Birmingham.   On my return with my family in twelve days I called
on Mr. Panton, in High Street, Bristol, and the first news I
heard was that my uncle had been found dead in his bed.
The words Mr. Panton used were ' Sir, you are too late ; your
uncle, if it be so, was found dead in his bed the next morning.'
I made no remark ; I was too much confounded at the extraordinary circumstance.   When I found Sir John was dead I
did the best I could.   I saw no chance then, and took my
family to Bath."

Witness then stated that from 1849 to 1851 he had gained
his living by lecturing and private teaching; and that he
then endeavoured to attract legal firms to take up his case,
but without success, and proceeded,—

" I went to Ireland last Christmas ; that was six months
after I had seen my present attorney, who went with me.   I
had not the most distant idea we should obtain everything we
wanted.   It so happened Providence brought everything to
light.   On my return from Ireland I gave notices to the
tenants.   The notices were issued in March.   I assumed the
title of baronet by the advice of a gentleman in Bristol on
my seeing Mr. Stone.   I had made up my mind to pursue it
with vigour: I was driven to it by circumstances.   I took
up the name and arms and issued cards, expecting if I was
wrong I should be prosecuted and made the defendant.   I
did this fairly and freely.   I got the portrait of my father
(produced) two years after Provis's death, from his daughter,
Mrs. Heath, living at Mere, in Wilts.   I received this (the

letter from Sir Hugh to his wife). I could not be accurate
as to the time without vast recollection. It was in the
autumn in last year. I first saw it in my attorney's hands.
I saw the large parchment first. I never saw the small one
till now. I first saw the large parchment (the deed of 1823)
some time in March last. It came to me by railway from
London. There was a letter inclosed with it. The letter is
dated March the 7th, but I think I did not receive the parcel
till the 17th. I first heard of the small parchment of 1822
when my attorney spoke of it to me. I first saw this parchment (the small one) to-day. I do not know where it came
from. I have a mark on my wrist made at my birth."

Cross-examined by Sir FREDERICK THESIGER.—" Provis's
family consisted of himself only and two boys when I lived
with him. His boys were John and Thomas, but I only
knew Thomas. The boy did not come home at night. I
recollect living in Provis's house at the age of three and a
half. I was treated with the greatest kindness, care, and
respect, and wore red morocco shoes, never being without
them. It may be that I wore the red shoes down to the
time of my leaving the house. I can remember many little
actions of my life when I was at Provis's. I was a mis-
chievous child."

Sir F. THESIGER.—That I can easily believe.

Witness.—" I was termed the little gentleman of the
place, and pulled the people's shutters down, and so on. I
remember the proclamation of the peace."

On being pressed for other incidents in his early life,
plaintiff refused to answer, and appealed to the Judge. On
being told he was bound to answer, he said he knew no more.
A number of questions were then put as to his early school
days, and where he spent his holidays, and some letters of his,
written in 1852, were then produced. In one, addressed to
Lady Caroline Thynne, he stated that immediately after
his being at Winchester, Lady Bath did him " the honour,
and maternal kindness," of adopting him as her *protégé*,
out of the regard she had to his mother. Lady Caroline
Thynne answered the letter, and in a letter from the
Claimant to Lady Caroline in reply, he mentioned he had
received from Lady Bath an obituary ring of his mother's,

with the following inscription, "*In memory of Jane, wife of Hugh Smyth, Esq., married May,* 1796; *died February,* 1797.*" The following scene then ensued :—

Sir F. Thesiger.—Where is that ring?

Plaintiff.—In the box.

Sir F. Thesiger.—Find it, sir.

The plaintiff then took up a case, from which he produced a ring-box, but on opening it no ring was to be seen.

Sir F. Thesiger.—There was not a word said about this ring in the opening.

Witness.—It was in that box.

Sir F. Thesiger.—When did you see it last?

Witness.—I do not remember. It was taken with the other jewels to Ireland.

Sir F. Thesiger.—Did you see it in Ireland?

Witness.—Yes.

Sir F. Thesiger.—Was that the last time you saw it?

Witness.—I have seen it since, I believe, in London.

Sir F. Thesiger.—Where, in London?

Witness.—In my attorney's office. I cannot exactly say when, but I have not seen it for some considerable time.

Sir F. Thesiger then referred to the letter, and asked the plaintiff to spell the word "vicissitudes." This he did as follows, v-i-s-i-c-i-t-u-d-e-s. He was then cross-examined as to his having in some of his correspondence expressed his belief that his mother's name was Lovett, and that she was a companion or lady's-maid to the Marchioness, and that she died at the house of Provis, the carpenter, at Warminster, and was buried at Warminster in a brick vault. In explanation of this, witness replied that he had been once cast away at sea on coming from Scotland, and a tea chest containing all his papers and valuables was lost, amongst which was a sort of license for marriage in Ireland, in which the name of Lovett was mentioned. In another letter he stated that he had an oil likeness of Sir Hugh when young, but admitted the statement to be false, and that he only imagined it. The letters were only feelers. In another letter produced, the witness had said he travelled over the country with Lord "Nox," and in other letters he spelt the name in the same manner, "Nox."

Sir F. Thesiger.—How do you spell " rapid," sir ?

Witness.—I do not see that it is relevant to the inquiry.

Mr. Justice Coleridge.—You must answer the question.

Plaintiff.—R-a-p-p-i-d. Sir, I say there are dictionaries in which the word is spelt in that manner.

Sir F. Thesiger.—No doubt : edited by yourself.

Cross-examination continued.—" I was eighteen in 1815. I was not a prisoner under the Emperor Napoleon." Letter produced, written to Mr. G. Langton, in which he said he met Mr. Kknox (with two k's), and was a prisoner on parol under Napoleon in 1815. On being asked to explain, witness said :—"When the Emperor left to go to Waterloo, I left Paris and went to Belgium, and was at the ball at Brussels before the battle. I was in Paris when the allied armies were there. I did not mean that I was a prisoner. Lord Knox might have talked of his father, and I might have told him who was my father. I do not know whether I did or not. There was a good deal of writing on the oil likeness, as for instance, ' *Hugh Smyth, Esq., son of Thomas Smyth of Stapleton, in Gloucestershire, in England, who married in Ireland in* 1799.' I returned to England in 1826, having been absent about ten or eleven years. The money I took lasted a long time, and I earned a good deal by lecturing. In 1826 I had an idea who my father was."

Sir F. Thesiger.—How do you spell *whom ?*

Witness.—W-h-o-m-e. I could find you dictionaries in which it is so spelt.

Sir F. Thesiger.—How do you spell " set aside ? "

Witness.—S-e-t-t a-s-s-i-d-e.

Sir F. Thesiger.—These words are so spelt four times in your letters.

Witness.—I spelt them with two t's and two s's from a learned commentator. I have authority for so spelling. I prefer spelling aside " asside." That is the way in which I think it ought to be spelt. I did not make any inquiries in 1826 about Grace, or the Marchioness, but I think I did in 1828, of individuals in Bristol, but did not go near anyone who knew me when young. I had not time, as I was engaged with my lecturing, and besides, I considered it useless making inquiries, as I thought Sir John was the elder brother. When Provis handed me the Bible, the jewellery, and the papers, he said they had been given to him by the widow of Mr. Davis. I did not look into the Bible then, but I noticed the inscription on the obituary ring, but it did not strike me."

A letter written to Mrs. Florence Smyth was then put in, in which the witness had stated he was born in 1793 or 1797, and one to Mr. Gore Langton, in which he said he could get a copy at any time of the register of his mother's burial in 1797. On being cross-examined on the latter point, the witness said :—" I went to Warminster in the beginning of this year. I saw an entry of the burial in the register when I first went. When I went the second time the entry was erased. The clergyman showed me the register. I will swear there was an entry of the date of February, 1797, of the burial of Jane Smyth, aged sixteen. I went to another village to inquire, and on my return the entry was erased, and another name substituted. The second time I went with my attorney, and the book was left to us both for an hour together, no one else being present. I knew I was born between 1793 and 1797."

Certain notices were then put in which the witness had written to the tenants in Somersetshire directing them to pay their rents to him, and which notices had been signed by the witness " *Henry Brown, for Mr. Rodham.*" Mr. Rodham, being present, denied the authority, and the plaintiff at last admitted that they had been written in a feigned hand to imitate Mr. Rodham's. In these notices Somersetshire was spelt Sommersetshire. The Bible, portrait of Sir Hugh, letters, jewellery, &c., were then handed up and carefully examined by his lordship and the jury. The letters of the plaintiff showed repeated instances of the wrong doubling of consonants in the middle of words, such as " rascallity," " asside," &c. On the back of the portrait of Sir Hugh was discovered, in the course of examination by the judge, the words " *Born* 14 *May,* 1774; *married* 1796." The cross-examination was then continued on several minor points, in the course of which numerous instances of prevarication were brought out by Sir Frederick, and several direct untruths, as for instance, that the plaintiff had been presented to Her Majesty; and the court adjourned until the following day.

On the opening of the court the next morning

Sir F. Thesiger resumed his cross-examination of the plaintiff. The witness denied that he had said in his examination in chief that he had spent his holidays twice at Lord Carrington's, but on the judge referring to his notes it was found he had done so, though, as his lordship said, it might have been under a mistake. He then proceeded to state his answer to Sir Frederick.

" Early in life I spelt my name Smyth, but I afterwards spelt it ' Smith,' because when I spelt it so I was taken for an Irishman. I signed it Smith as late as July, 1852. I do not know how to spell ' scrutiny.' The motto of the Carrington family was *tenax et fides* (it is really *tenax et fidelis*). I should say *tenax* is firm and *fides* faith, and that the motto means ' *firm in faith,*' though it may be rendered different ways. I have said that the motto of the Smyth family is ' *Qui capit capitur.*' " Witness denied having ever represented himself as Thomas Provis or William Thomas Provis, or that John Provis was his father, or ever called him his father, or was called by him his son. Never took an inventory of John Provis's goods. An inventory was here handed up to the witness, and he was asked if it was in his handwriting. He said he would not swear to it; he thought it was in John Provis's handwriting. On being pressed he said he had helped the old gentleman with his books, and it might be in his (witness's) handwriting. He then recollected he might venture to say he had written it. An entry in it was pointed out, " *Picture of Provis's son John.*" The old man, witness admitted, used to call it the portrait of his son. It was the same painting that now had the writing on the back, " *Hugh Smyth, Esq., son of Thomas Smyth, Esq., of Stapleton, Gloucestershire,* 1796." The picture was produced, and after a request from the plaintiff that all the witnesses who were to depose to anything respecting it should leave the court, which, after some discussion, was acceded to, was put in. The plaintiff then admitted it was the same picture as was mentioned in the inventory as " *Painting of son John,*" but " should not think it was

the picture spoken of in his letters to Mrs. Smyth,
Mrs. Upton, and Mr. Gore Langton as the portrait of his
father." The letters were then read, in which it was stated
that this was the picture, and Sir Frederick pointed out to
the witness that there were two erasures on the back of it,
whereupon he admitted that it *was* the picture he had referred
to, and that there was no other picture of Sir Hugh. The
writing on the back was not in same condition now as it was
at first, as he had put an acid on and had brought it out.
It was tartaric acid he used; he applied it lightly, and it
merely took off the dirt. Had used water with no effect.
That was the reason he had ordered the witnesses out of
court, because he knew they would swear they had never
seen the inscription. He was not sure it was tartaric acid
or soda he used. Tartaric acid, if applied in strong solution
would destroy the writing. This was his first experiment.
He knew of it by reading, as Sir Frederick ought to do.

Sir FREDERICK.—Aye! but I do not want to bring out
writings.

Witness.—But you bring out other things, and with considerable acidity. The acid was found in the back kitchen.
Most people had soda and potash in their houses.

Sir F. THESIGER.—They are not acids.

Witness.—They are pulverized minerals.

Cross-examination resumed :—Had said the inventory was
certainly not in his handwriting, and he had not sworn it
was. Now, however, he looked at it again he would swear
it *was* his handwriting. The words *" Painting of son John"*
referred to the picture. Did not know whose portrait it was,
but knew it could not be his son John who died in his infancy. Witness was a married man, and married in 1841.
Was not married in 1814 at Bath to Mary Ann Whittick.
His present wife's maiden name was Ashton, and he had no
past wife. Slightly knew a person named Charles Ingram.
He did not claim to be a nephew of the plaintiff. Again
repeated his denial that he did not marry Mary Ann
Whittick at St. Michael's, Bath, at a quarter to nine on
Sunday the 9th October, 1814, in the name of William
Thomas Provis. Mary Ann Heath, then a girl of twelve,
was not present. Did not meet Mary Ann Heath twenty

years ago, when she said, "Tom, how are you?" Did not say that he was then Dr. Smith. He took two of Mrs. Heath's children to place out in the world, not to educate. He took them out of kindness, and was treated with downright ingratitude, but it would all come out.

Sir F. THESIGER.—It is coming out now very fast !

The cross-examination was then directed to the purchase of some seals from an engraver in London, named Moring.

"I did not order any seals of Moring, seal engraver of Holborn, in December, 1852. It was in March, 1853. It was not before Christmas. The cards were had on the 21st December." The bill was produced, and in it was found on the same date a charge for engraving a steel seal, but the witness denied it was had at the same time. "I did not on the 19th December call on Mr. Moring and order a steel seal to be made of the pattern and size of the one which I brought, and on which were engraved an elephant's head, crest, and garter, and direct the crest, motto, and garter of the Smyths, of Ashton Court, to be engraved on it. I ordered it afterwards. I got the crest from the letter which was in my possession from Joseph Reed. The letter produced is the one I took. I swear I showed it to him, and he took the impression from it whilst I was looking for the explanation of the motto. I called for the seal in the beginning of March. (The seal was here produced.) I afterwards sent an order for a seal with the arms, crest, and motto of the Smyths, of Ashton Court, upon it. The order was executed, and the seal sent addressed to me at St. Vincent's Priory, Clifton. (The second seal was then produced.) I was living in St. Vincent's Priory when the parchment was sent. I do not know Crane, who wrote the letter accompanying the parchment of 1823. I have since ascertained that my wife opened the parcel, and so a different paper became the wrapper. I discovered an error in the motto of the second seal; that on the first was correct, ' *Qui capit capitur,*' but I did not discover the second was *capitor*. The second seal was taken from the document of 1823, the only one I had. Moring had sent to me a penned resemblance of the shield, and it was in the shape of a heart. I wrote back or sent through Nash the stamp on that document.

When I had the document the seal was whole, but I rubbed a piece of silver paper on it to get a facsimile, and in doing so I broke the seal. The rubbing I sent to Moring some time just before June in this year, or May. I got the seal, I think, the 7th of June. I had correspondence with Mr. Bennett, of Ballinadee, to get specimens of Mr. Verney Lovett's writing. I have two which were given to my attorney." (Note to Mr. Bennett read, stating that he had the certificate of his mother's marriage and wanted specimens of Mr. Lovett's writing. He had several livings on the estates, the incumbents of which were very old, and he would serve Mr. Bennett if he would oblige him with what he required. This was dated 13th March, 1853. Upon the envelope was the motto "*Qui capit capitor*," which was on the seal he said he did not have till 7th June.) In explanation of this, witness said :—" It must be a mistake of the engraver ; he should make out his bill better and not lead me astray with wrong dates. I could not have had the seal long before I wrote to the Rev. Mr. Bennett. After I received the deed on the 17th March, I sent the impression to Mr. Moring. He was not long executing it. I do not know when I made the impression with the silver paper."

Sir F. Thesiger then asked how it was that he sealed a letter, dated the 13th March, with a seal made from a document which he did not see until the 17th. The plaintiff in explanation said Sir Frederick had explained it—he must have received the seal before the 13th. Sir F. Thesiger then asked how he could account for receiving the seal before he received the document ; and the plaintiff replied he could not tell—he could not explain, and asked to be allowed to retire.

Sir FREDERICK.—That cannot be. My lord (addressing the court) I have just had a telegraphic message from London of the greatest importance. Sir Frederick then read from the message to the witness—" Did you on the 19th of January last apply to a person at 361, Oxford Street to engrave the ring with the Bandon crest, and the brooch with the words Jane Gookin ?"

Witness.—" I did, sir."

The excitement in court at this unexpected avowal was

intense. Sir Frederick himself sat down, and was so much affected as to be quite unable to proceed, or even to repeat the question. Mr. Bovill was also deeply moved. Mr. Alexander then repeated to the court, at the request of the judge, the question asked of the witness, Sir Frederick being quite unable to do so. The ring and brooch were then produced, and admitted by the plaintiff to be the ones referred to. Hitherto he had faced all the previous questions; but at this stage of the case he appeared cowed and crestfallen.

Sir F. THESIGER, to witness.—After this exhibition I cannot spare you. You said yesterday that in the year 1811 you were ill for eighteen months with a medical man in Parliament Street—a Dr. Williams.

Plaintiff.—I did not say it was Dr. Williams.

Sir F. THESIGER.—Upon your oath, sir, were you not during that eighteen months in prison under a conviction for horse-stealing ?

Plaintiff.—No, sir.

Sir F. THESIGER.—In Ilchester Gaol ?

Plaintiff.—No, I was not.

Sir F. THESIGER.—Were you not sentenced to death under the name of Thomas Provis for stealing a gelding, the goods and chattels of George Sladden; and was not your sentence commuted to eighteen months' imprisonment, in consideration of your youth ?

Plaintiff.—It was not I; it must be some other person.

Sir F. THESIGER.—Have you got the marks of the king's-evil on your neck, and also on your right hand ?

The witness hesitated, and at last bared neck and hand, and there the marks were apparent. Those on the right hand were the marks which he had said were inflicted in childbirth, and which he represented in the deed as the indelible marks of identity in the Smyth family. The sensation in court was intense.

Sir F. Thesiger then drew attention to the fact that the motto on the deed of 1823 was " *Qui capit capit*or." The jury here examined the deed and intimated that it was so.

His lordship thereupon appealed to Mr. Bovill whether he meant to go on.

Mr. Bovill.—" I must say that the progress of this cause has been the most painful I ever knew. At this moment I can scarcely speak, owing to the emotion I see prevail in every part of the court at this appalling exhibition. I and my learned friends have considered our position most anxiously; first, in reference to the plaintiff; next, in reference to the solicitor who instructed us ; and thirdly, in reference to what is due to ourselves as gentlemen and members of the bar. From the great importance of this case and the extraordinary interest attached to it, we have felt that we could not consistently with our duty interpose during the cross-examination which has taken place. We felt it our duty not to make a single remark till the cross-examination should draw to a close. After this most appalling exhibition, and this exposure so unparalleled in a court of justice, which has come on us all by surprise, it would be impossible for us to appear further in a case of this description."

Application was then made to the court by Sir F. Thesiger that the plaintiff should not be permitted to go at large, and he was accordingly taken into custody on a charge of perjury. The jury then returned a verdict for the defendant, and the extraordinary case came to an end.

Mr. Justice Coleridge, before the court broke up, very gracefully intimated his opinion that the plaintiff had suffered nothing from the absence of Sir F. Kelly or Mr. Keating, who, the learned judge observed, could not possibly have done anything more than what had been done for the Claimant by his present counsel, except that perhaps they might have retired earlier from the case. This intimation of opinion was most cordially joined in by the bar and the audience generally, and seemed to give universal satisfaction. Seldom indeed have counsel been placed in a more unfortunate position than were Mr. Bovill and his learned colleagues on this occasion.

All trinkets, deeds, &c., were then impounded ; and in the course of the day the plaintiff was taken before a magistrate and committed for trial on a charge of forgery.

With the committal of the plaintiff to take his trial for
forgery and perjury ended of course all his pretensions to
the title of " Sir Richard Hugh Smyth, Baronet," and the
Ashton estates; though with singular effrontery he still
continued to assert he was the real man, and even went so
far as to assign over his estates to prevent a forfeiture. The
subsequent proceedings are interesting as disclosing the
manner in which the claim had been concocted, and the nature
of the evidence the defendant would have brought forward if
the case for the Claimant had proceeded further. They form
a fitting sequel to the previous trial.

At the next assizes for Gloucester in April, 1854, the late
plaintiff, still under the assumed name of " Richard Hugh
Smyth," was accordingly indicted for forging a codicil to the
will of Sir Hugh Smyth with intent to defraud, and with
uttering the same knowing it to be forged, to which he
pleaded not guilty.

Mr. Alexander, on the part of the prosecution, stated the
circumstances under which the previous action had been
brought, and its termination in the committal of the plaintiff
to take his trial for perjury and forgery; and the shorthand
notes of the plaintiff's examination in chief and cross-examination having been read, Mr. Moring, a seal engraver of
Holborn, was called. He deposed that in December, 1852
(only a few months before the trial), he had been employed
by the prisoner to engrave a crest, garter, and motto on a
seal, from a pattern which the prisoner furnished him with.
The proper motto was " *Qui capit capitur*," but the " u "
being blotted an error was made in the engraving, and the
motto was made to read " *Qui capit capitor*." He also made
a second seal at the request of the prisoner, with the arms
of the Smyths of Ashton Court, in which the same error
arose. The seal on the document purporting to be the will
of Sir Hugh Smyth was made with this second seal, as also
the seal on the letter from Sir Hugh to his pretended wife.
He further proved that there had been an alteration in the
mode of engraving seals within the last four or five years,
and the seals on the will had been engraved in the new
manner. The prisoner had subsequently called upon him
and desired he would not give any information about the

seals. Another witness, a seal engraver, corroborated the evidence as to the seal on the will having been made with the seal engraved by Mr. Moring, and also as to the new mode of engraving.

Mr. Robert Cox, a jeweller, of No. 351, Oxford Street, London, through whose instrumentality the plaintiff had been so effectually confounded on the third day of the trial, proved that on the 5th January, 1853, the prisoner came to his shop and said he was trustee of some children, and had had the care of some jewels which he had lost; but the jewels had been asked for, and he was desirous of buying some others in their place. As the children had never seen the originals the prisoner said the new ones would do just as well. He also asked for a miniature or miniature frame, which he said he should wish to pass off as that of the mother of the children. He selected two brooches and a wedding and a mourning ring. The engraving on the mourning ring, " *Mary, wife of Sir Hugh Smyth, m.* 1796, *d.* 1797," was done by order of the prisoner. On one of the brooches the name " *Jane Gookin* " was engraved, also by his order, and on the signet ring the Bandon crest. The witness deposed that it was by casually reading a report of the proceedings of the first day's trial in the *Times* newspaper that he had been led to communicate with the defence at the last trial.

A bookseller living next door to Mr. Moring deposed that he purchased the Bible in which the certificates of marriage and baptism were written, and on the title-page of which were the words " John S. Vandenbergh," from a gentleman of that name, and sold it in February, 1853, to the prisoner. Mr. Vandenbergh, who sold the Bible, corroborated this evidence, and stated the Bible was his deceased father's, and the words " John S. Vandenbergh " on the title-page in his father's handwriting.

So much for the authenticity of the documents and jewellery on which the prisoner had founded his claim ! The sister of the prisoner was then called, who deposed he was her brother, that he had been married in 1814, in her presence, to Mary Ann Whittick, at Bath (which the prisoner had denied at the trial), and that the picture put forward by the prisoner as that of Sir Hugh Smyth was the portrait of her brother John !

Mr. Herepath, the celebrated chemist, proved that the ink on the two parchments was not nearly so old as 1822, and the ink in the letter from Sir Hugh to his supposed wife was modern, and had not been made two years. On the Bible being shown him, he said the signature "John S. Vandenbergh" on the title-page was written with old ink, but the certificates with ink of quite a modern date. Mr. Gough, a parchment maker, proved that the parchment on which one of the wills was written was made on a new process, only invented within the last ten or fifteen years, though the larger deed was older.

A witness of the name of Crane then gave some evidence showing an audacity on the part of the prisoner almost incredible. He said he went to call at St. Vincent's Priory about April in the preceding year, where he saw the prisoner, who told him he was the lawful heir to the Smyth family. That the prisoner said to witness, " I want you to write a letter, that is if you can do so convenient. It will put you in business or a situation for life." He then showed witness a will on parchment, and said, " I want you to write a letter stating that a man named Coward lodged in your house, that he was out of his head, and left, and died in an asylum you don't know where." Another person of the name of Mattick was present, and on the witness intimating that he did not know how to put it together, the prisoner said, looking at them both, " Come ! can't you two do it; I have told you what to say." Witness then went down-stairs and wrote the letter, which he gave to the prisoner. He never knew a person called Coward. The witness identified the will as the one the prisoner showed him, only at that time there was no seal on it.

Some further evidence was then given proving the identity of the Claimant with Thomas Provis, and a Bible was produced in which was an entry of the prisoner's marriage with Mary Ann Whittick in his own handwriting. It is quite unnecessary to reproduce all the evidence given on these and other minor points, all tending most conclusively to establish the prisoner's guilt. He cross-examined some of the wit-

L

nesses with considerable smartness and flippancy, and elicited
that the defence had cost the Smyth family between 6000*l.*
and 7000*l.*, which seemed to give him not a little satisfaction.   In his defence he made a long rambling speech,
raising what he deemed to be a point of law that a man
could not be convicted of forging the name of a person who
was dead. This objection the judge, Mr. Russell Gurney, who,
in consequence of the sudden death of Mr. Justice Talfourd,
was presiding at the trial, overruled, and the jury after a few
minutes' deliberation returned a verdict of guilty both of
forgery and of the uttering, and the prisoner then received
the well-merited sentence of twenty years' transportation (*a*).

(*a*) At the same assizes at which the Claimant was tried for forgery,
a person of the name of Castro was also put on his trial, a somewhat
singular coincidence, bearing in mind the *cause célèbre* now pending.

THE TRIAL

OF

THE REV. WILLIAM BAILEY, LL.D.,

FOR FORGERY,

BEFORE MR. JUSTICE WILLIAMS AND MR. JUSTICE MAULE,

AT THE CENTRAL CRIMINAL COURT,

February 1st, 1843.

Counsel for the Prosecution : Mr. *Humfrey*.

For the Prisoner : Mr. *Clarkson* and Mr. *Jones*.

INTRODUCTION.

It has been observed by a learned writer of considerable experience in criminal matters (*a*) "that of late years there has been a marked increase in all crimes requiring superior intelligence rather than brute force for their successful accomplishment, and which can only be effected by the mis-applied union of talent and education. The abolition of the punishment of death for all crimes against property," the writer argues, "may have tempted persons of comparative refinement, of cool head and callous heart, to adventure on forbidden ways of enriching themselves at the expense of their neighbours when failure and detection would not involve their personal safety." Amongst this class of crimes of modern date are to be numbered the case of Alexander Alexander, titular Earl of Stirling; the forgeries arising out of the unclaimed dividends in the Bank of England, a scheme remarkable for its ingenuity in the discovery and punishment

---

(*a*) Mr. Townsend, Q. C., Recorder of Macclesfield, in his "Modern State Trials," vol. 1, p. 404.

L 2

of which, however, one innocent person was unfortunately involved ; the case of Provis, already reported in this volume ; the case of the gold-dust robbery, tried in the year 1857, where Agar with his £3000, and Pierce with his house at Kilburn, both lodging at fashionable watering-places, and journeying up and down the South Eastern Railway with first-class tickets, form a picture of criminal enterprise hardly to be looked for : and the case of the Rev. William Bailey, now under consideration.

The circumstances out of which this latter case arose are the most extraordinary. In the year 1841 there died at No. 12, Great St. Andrew Street, Seven Dials, a man of the name of Robert Smith, a person of the most penurious habits, and so dirty and mean in appearance as to cause him frequently to be taken for a beggar. He was, however, a person of considerable means, though at his death his fortune was greatly exaggerated, as were also several circumstances connected with him, such as, for instance, that he could scarcely write his name, and had left no relations. Probably it was this latter report, coupled with the rumour of his great wealth, that excited the cupidity of Dr. Bailey, then a fashionable preacher of some celebrity, and minister of St. Peter's Chapel, Queen's Square, Westminster. Accordingly, shortly after Smith's death, his administrator received notice of a claim made by Dr. Bailey on behalf of his sister, for moneys alleged to have been paid to Smith for investment, amounting in the whole to 2875l. The administrator could find no trace of any transactions with Dr. Bailey in the deceased's books, and he therefore denied his liability, and left Dr. Bailey to take such steps to recover the amount as he might be advised.

Dr. Bailey, nothing daunted by the rejection of his claim, commenced an action to recover the amount alleged to be due, which came on for trial in the Common Pleas, before Chief Justice Tindal, on the 9th July, 1842. The action was most vigorously fought, and most vigorously defended. Mr. Serjeant Channell and Mr. Hayward were for the plaintiff, and Sir T. Wilde, Mr. Serjeant Talfourd, Mr. Kelly (now Chief Baron of the Exchequer), and Mr. Humfrey, for the defendants. The case opened on behalf of the plaintiff was to the effect that Miss Bailey, the doctor's sister, in November, 1838, sent over from Ireland a sum of money to her brother for investment in English government securities: that Smith, with whom the plaintiff alleged himself to be on intimate terms, advised him not to invest it in the funds, but in the purchase of a rentcharge, and stated that until investment he would himself be Miss Bailey's banker: that Dr. Bailey accordingly gave Smith 550*l.* and other sums which his sister transmitted for investment from time to time, for which Smith gave his I. O. U.: that afterwards, on the 12th August, 1841, on a settlement of accounts between the plaintiff and Smith, Dr. Bailey pressed for some security, and that on that day, in the vestry-room of the chapel in Queen's Square, shortly before evening service, Smith gave the plaintiff an I. O. U. for the whole amount due, 2875*l.* The doctor, it was stated, objected that the security was only an I. O. U., and said nothing about interest; whereupon Smith replied, "Never mind; do you and Mr. Nixon" (a clergyman then officiating for Dr. Bailey, and in the vestry at the time) "put your names to it as witnesses and it will be all right." Dr. Bailey and Mr. Nixon did accordingly sign their names as witnesses, and Mr. Smith then went out of the vestry into the chapel, where he remained all the service.

Such is a short outline of the extraordinary case attempted to be set up by the plaintiff. In addition he asserted that not being satisfied with the I. O. U. he pressed Smith for a mortgage, which the latter positively refused to give, but asked the plaintiff to draw up a promissory note, which he said he would sign, and also a letter to Miss Bailey, promising, if she required it, to give a bond or warrant of attorney as a further security. This note and letter were accordingly drawn up and signed by the deceased.

In support of the plaintiff's case a Mrs. Ellen Grey was called as a witness, who deposed that she happened to be in the vestry-room on the evening of Thursday the 12th of August, and saw Smith hand a piece of paper to Dr. Bailey, who said, "I do not like this." The paper was read over in her presence when she was reading her Prayer Book, but she was not so absorbed in her book as not to hear the words "two thousand and odd pounds," which excited her curiosity, as she thought it strange that Smith, an emaciated, dirty-looking old man, should have so much money. She afterwards was shown into the same pew with Smith, and when the service was concluded went out with him, and on her way home asked what the money meant. Smith said it was Miss Bailey's, and "it was well he had it, as she would have fooled it away." This witness was corroborated by a female servant of the plaintiff, Caroline Laxton, who said that on the 1st January, 1841, whilst she was mending the carpet in the back drawing-room of Dr. Bailey's house, when Smith and Dr. Bailey were in the front room, she heard Smith say, "300*l.* more and it will make up a round sum of 3000*l.* ;" and in cross-examination she even went further, and said she saw through the folding-doors bank notes pass from Dr. Bailey to Smith. The plaintiff himself stepped into the box, and in the boldest manner produced an account book, in which all the loans were entered up, with the dates of the respective advances. No account was, however, given of the manner in which Miss Bailey became possessed of the money, nor was she called as a witness. The plaintiff himself said he had handed the money to Smith in notes as he received it—Irish notes—but it was conclusively shown that Irish notes were subject at that time to an exchange of 1*l.* per cent., which rendered it extremely unlikely that Smith, who was a miserly old fellow, would have accepted the money in that shape. Eventually the case broke down, and the jury returned a verdict for the defendants ; and the notes and documents on which the claim was based were ordered to be impounded. The plaintiff himself was allowed in the first instance to go at large, but ultimately on the 23rd November he was arrested at his dwelling-house, 73, Coleshill Street, Pimlico, on a charge of forgery.

The indictment charged the prisoner with feloniously forging, on the 9th September, 1841, at the parish of St. Margaret, Westminster, a promissory note for the payment of 2875*l.*, with intent to defraud Robert Smith, since deceased. A second count charged the same offence, but with intent to defraud James Smith, the administrator of the deceased, and other counts charged the prisoner with uttering and putting off the notes in question.

Mr. Humfrey opened the case on behalf of the prosecution, and stated the facts in outline as given in the Introduction. Mr. Wheatley, the deputy associate of the Lord Chief Justice, then deposed that he was present at the trial of "*Bailey* v. *Smith*," at the sittings after the previous Trinity Term, when certain documents were ordered to be impounded, which he produced; they consisted of a promissory note for 2875*l.*, an I. O. U. for the same amount, a letter, and a cash book. The shorthand writer's notes of the prisoner's evidence were then verified and read, as follows :—

"I am a member of the Established Church, and a graduate of Trinity College, Dublin. My father resided at Belfast. I knew the late Mr. R. Smith for some years since the year 1832, when I first came to London. He then lent me 60*l.*, which I subsequently repaid. I then left London, and did not return for some years. In 1833 I was employed by my sister to invest a sum of money for her, and I spoke to Mr. Smith on the subject, and he consented to take the amount. I gave him at different times sums amounting to 2875*l.*, for which he was to pay four per cent. The last payment I made to him was for the sum of 175*l.*, on the 12th August, 1841, when a settlement took place according to the account book produced. On that occasion I asked for some security, and he said he would give my sister good security, but he did not do so at the time. He, however, said he should be at my chapel that evening, and would give me the security. On that evening he attended the chapel, and just before service commenced, came to me in the vestry and gave me an I. O. U., at the same time saying he had been disappointed with respect to the security he intended to give. I expressed my disappointment at the document not mentioning the interest to be at four per cent. as agreed upon in the morning, and I think I also felt disappointed that he did not give me the bond as promised. All the conversation took place in my vestry five minutes before the service commenced. Mr. Smith said it would add validity to the security if the gentleman who was to preach for me that evening would add his signature to the document, and that gentleman, the Rev. Mr. Nixon, did so. I also signed it as an attesting witness. A few days after that I again saw Mr. Smith on the subject, and applied for a bond, but he made some excuse at the time, and promised to give me a note of hand for the amount. On the morning of the 9th September, Mr. Smith called at my house and brought a stamp with him upon which the promissory note was drawn, and at his particular desire I added the words 'with interest at the rate of four per cent. per annum for money advanced to me this day.' I signed the note as a witness, and asked Mr. Smith whether I should get some other person to witness it, but he said 'No, I do not wish to have my affairs made public,' and therefore another witness was dispensed with. Subsequently I applied to Mr. Smith for a bond, and he refused to give one, but consented to sign a letter promising to give one if required. I accordingly wrote a letter to that effect, which Mr. Smith signed and addressed to my sister. Mr. Smith was not a constant attendant at my chapel, but only came occasionally. The Rev. Mr. Nixon has since died. I afterwards applied to Mr. Smith for a mortgage, but he became very angry and said he would rather throw up the money than be bothered with a mortgage."

After the reading of the evidence given by Dr. Bailey, Mr. Beilby, a most important witness on the part of the prosecution, was called. He said :—" I am a builder, and reside in Little Queen Street, Holborn. I was acquainted with the late Mr. Robert Smith for about thirty years. Shortly after his death I recollect the prisoner calling at my house. He said, ' You have heard about the death of the miser in St. Giles.' I said I had, and had buried him. The prisoner said he understood he was worth 400,000*l.* and could not write his name. I said that was incorrect, as I had plenty of his handwriting. The prisoner said he should very much like to see the deceased's handwriting, and I showed him a receipt written by him. The prisoner said it was a great curiosity, and he should very much like to show it to a friend, and I allowed him to take it away. The receipt produced is the same. The prisoner kept it two or three days. I do not believe the promissory note to be written by the deceased, nor the I. O. U."

On cross-examination by Mr. Clarkson, the witness said the signature to the promissory note was very much like the writing of the deceased ; but if a cheque were presented to him with such a signature he should not cash it. The signature to the I. O. U. was not in the least like the deceased's handwriting. It was not even an imitation of it further than that the number of letters in the name was the same.

Mr. James Robert Baker, a stock-broker, proved having acted for the deceased for the last nine or ten years of his life, and that he had 15,000l. worth of stock at his death. He did not believe the signatures to the promissory note or I. O. U. to be genuine. The evidence of this witness as to the handwriting was also corroborated by another witness, Mr. J. W. Wilkin.

Mr. William Heirons, a carpenter and builder, proved that on the 12th of August, 1841, which was his (witness's) birthday, the deceased came to some houses witness was building for him in Stanhope Terrace, Mornington Crescent, at about ten minutes to seven in the evening, and remained there until nine o'clock [between these hours the I. O. U. was alleged to have been signed by the deceased in the vestry] ; and during the whole of that time the deceased never left his company.

On cross-examination this witness said he had gone to Stanhope Terrace to meet the deceased, and that his foreman, John Eddy, was also present. The certificate of the witness's marriage was then put in to prove the date, and John Eddy was called to corroborate the evidence as to the deceased having been to the house in Stanhope Terrace at the time mentioned, and that he himself saw him between a quarter before seven and half-past eight in the evening.

Mr. James Smith, a brother of the deceased, after proving that the signature to the promissory note was not in his brother's handwriting, produced a paper which he had received from a person of the name of Kearney : this latter being called gave some most extraordinary evidence. He said : —" My name is Bryan Kearney. I sell fruit in the streets. Some time since, I was selling fruit in Brompton Road; I think about the 1st October last. [This was after the trial of the action " *Bailey* v. *Smith*," but before the prisoner had been apprehended.] The prisoner, who up to that time was a perfect stranger, came up and asked me how I was getting on. I told him I got on the best I could, but bad was the best. He then asked me if I knew anything about law. I told him I did not. He then said he had lately been engaged in a law-suit, which he had lost because the opposite party had three witnesses and he only two. He asked me if I could be a witness for him. I said I would. He gave me a shilling, and told me to call upon him at his house at ten o'clock next morning. I went according to appointment, and he told me that Mr. Smith's counsel would baffle me very much, and that I must be prepared for them. I told him that I did not know what to say. He said he would write it down for me. He then sat down at a table and commenced writing, and afterwards read to me a paper, which he also desired I should read, and told me what I should have to swear to. The paper produced by the last witness is the same the prisoner gave to me, and I subsequently gave it up to the witness. The prisoner then desired me to go to Mr. Hill, his solicitor, in St. Mary Axe, and I did so on the following day. Shortly after I arrived the prisoner came in, and I was then questioned by the solicitor, and what I stated was taken down in writing, but I cannot now recollect what I said. Some time after that the prisoner called at my house and took me as far as Hyde Park Corner, and during our walk he particularly instructed me what I should say. A few days after that the prisoner again called at my house, and desired me to attend the following day at the Exchequer Coffee-house. I went there, and a paper was read over to me, after which I was directed to go before a magistrate and swear to it. A boy was sent with me for that purpose, but I could not swear falsely. My flesh crawled upon my bones, so instead of going to swear the paper I walked home. The prisoner gave me 1s. and promised to give me 30l."

In cross-examination the witness admitted that since the 1st October last he had been living at the expense of the prosecution, and without doing any work. Some attempt was made to damage his character, but without effect. A witness, named Robert Lenney, proved that the paper in question had been written by him at the prisoner's request from a draught in the prisoner's handwriting. The original was afterwards produced by Inspector Pearse, who apprehended the prisoner, and found it in his table drawer. The following is a copy of the paper:—

"I saw the late Robert Smith at Dr. Bailey's chapel on the evening of the 12th August, 1841. Mr. Smith lived at No. 12, Great St. Andrew Street, Seven Dials. The chapel service began at seven, and ended about a quarter past eight. Mr. Smith was just going into chapel before me, and he walked into the vestry. Mr. Smith came out of the vestry just before the service commenced, and after him came out one or two ladies, and then in two or three minutes came the two parsons. Dr. Bailey read prayers and the other strange parson preached. Mr. Smith and the one or two ladies went into the body of the church during the service, but I could see them from the free seats where I sat. I saw Mr. Smith on the stairs as the congregation were passing out, but I took no notice of him afterwards, whether he spoke to any one or whether he walked home with any one. I saw him a few days after in the park, and had a chat with him. Dr. Bailey was in Ireland in June and July, 1841. There had been no Thursday evening service since August, 1841. I never was in any room in Mr. Smith's house but the front parlour. The name Smith was on the door on a brass plate."

Henry Flemming, a cabinet maker, deposed that he unfortunately knew the prisoner, and that on a Sunday in September last the prisoner called upon him, and witness walked out with the prisoner for about an hour. He said his sister had been robbed of about 3000*l.*, and that it would be an act of justice to any one to swear to the fact. He then asked witness to swear that he knew Mr. Smith, where he lived, and that he had seen him at his (prisoner's) house. The witness had never seen Mr. Smith in his life to his knowledge. Prisoner offered the witness 20*l.*, and 10*l.* if he could give evidence for him, saying he only wanted one or two other witnesses and then he could come off victorious. Witness was also instructed to say that he had seen Mr. Smith at his chapel in Queen's Square on the 12th of August, and had afterwards seen him leave with a Mrs. Grey. A paper of instructions was given to him, which he afterwards destroyed at the request of Mrs. Bailey. He should know the contents of the paper if read."

The contents of the paper were then read from the draught in the prisoner's handwriting. It stated with great minuteness what the witness was to say. Witness further deposed that the prisoner afterwards called again upon him at his house, and asked if he could call to mind any particular occurrence which would enable him to recollect the 12th of August. Witness produced a card he had from the Opthalmic Hospital, dated the 12th of August, which the prisoner stated was just the thing. Witness afterwards attended at Westminster Hall and swore an affidavit to the above effect. He had received in all 25*s*. from the prisoner.

Mr. Inspector Pearse proved apprehending the prisoner at his residence in Coleshill Street, and the finding of the documents already produced in the drawer of a writing-table in his study. He also produced a paper in the prisoner's handwriting, containing several initial letters, opposite which were certain sums varying from 10*l*. to 40*l*. The name of " Flemming," written in full, had opposite it " 30*l*.," and " Krny." " 10*l*." Evidence was then given showing that the prisoner had paid money to some of the witnesses, and the books of the deceased were produced to prove that there was no entry in his accounts, which were carefully kept, of any transaction with the prisoner. The case for the prosecution then closed.

Mr. Clarkson then rose to address the jury on behalf of the prisoner. After alluding to the position in life of his client, and the momentous issue involved in the trial, he proceeded :—

" The exhibition which has been made in the course of the trial is indeed most melancholy, and whatever may be the result, it is evident that there are in this country persons who for a paltry sum will jeopardize their souls, and then have the effrontery to get into the witness box and acknowledge it." [Considering that bad as these witnesses might be, it was his client who had suborned them, the justness of these observations on the part of Mr. Clarkson is rather

questionable.] " The gentleman whom I have the honour
to defend is, as his sacred calling will prove, a man of education, who, previous to the institution of these proceedings
has borne a character upon which reproach has never been
breathed, and I would ask you by your verdict to-day to say
that there are no grounds even for the present stigma upon
his character.

" I would ask, are you at all satisfied that the deceased
did not sign the promissory note in his lifetime ? If you are
not, the prisoner is undoubtedly entitled to an acquittal.
Why is it that the prosecution do not indict the prisoner for
forging the I. O. U. instead of the promissory note ? I will
tell you : because that document bears the attestation of the
Rev. Mr. Nixon; but although that gentleman is dead, still
it could have been proved it was his signature, and in fact it
was so proved at the previous trial.

" It has been admitted by the learned counsel for the prosecution that the signature to the I. O. U. and the signature
to the promissory note are in the same handwriting. If,
therefore, I prove to you the attestation of the Rev.
Mr. Nixon, that I apprehend will show the genuineness of
the document, and you will have no hesitation in saying
the promissory note was given by the deceased also."

Mr. Clarkson then laid before the jury an outline of the
evidence he should produce, showing that the deceased was
present in the vestry on the evening of the 12th of August,
when the I. O. U. was signed, from which he submitted it
was to be inferred that the promissory note afterwards prepared for the same amount, and purporting to be signed by
the deceased on a later day, was genuine. He pleaded the
poverty of the prisoner as a reason for not producing his
sister nor the witness Catherine Laxton, who had given
evidence at the trial of the civil action. The following witnesses were then called :—

Susanna Lee, a pew-opener, deposed that she was at the
chapel on the evening of the 12th August last. She knew
Mr. Smith, and remembered him calling and asking for
Mr. Bailey, and she showed him into the vestry. A female
named Young went in at the same time. The Rev.
Mr. Nixon was also there. On cross-examination the witness

admitted she had never seen the deceased before, and did not
know Mrs. Grey by sight.

William C. Tifnell, a warden of the chapel, stated that
on the 12th of August he was at the chapel, and on going
to the vestry he found that Dr. Bailey had some one with
him, and therefore did not go in. He could not say if it
were the deceased or not, as he did not know him. He
knew the Rev. Mr. Nixon, and was acquainted with his
handwriting. He believed the signature to the I. O. U. was
Mr. Nixon's.

Ellen Grey deposed that she knew the late Mr. Robert
Smith, and saw him at the chapel on the evening of the 12th
of August last in the vestry with the Rev. Mr. Nixon and
the prisoner. Witness was present and saw Dr. Bailey read
over a paper which Mr. Smith gave him, and heard Dr. Bailey
make some objections to the paper, to which Mr. Smith
replied that to make it all right the doctor and Mr. Nixon
had better put their signatures to it. Witness then saw both
Dr. Bailey and Mr. Nixon write upon the paper, but could
not say what it was they wrote. After service, Mr. Smith
and witness walked together as far as Birdcage Walk, and in
the course of conversation the deceased told her he had been
to see Dr. Bailey about some money which he had placed in
his hands on behalf of his sister, and that it was a good
thing she had done so as she might have lost it.

On cross-examination the witness admitted she was separated from her husband, and that since the last trial she had
passed by another name. She had walked home with
Mr. Smith, but did not know his name, and had been in his
house with him for two or three minutes to get a volume of
sermons which he promised to lend her. Had lived in
Dr. Bailey's family between four and five months. Dr. Bailey
had been surety for her to a loan society.

The Rev. Mr. Scobell proved receiving notes from Mr.
Nixon, and believed the signature to the I. O. U. to be in his
handwriting, and the Rev. Mr. Hill gave similar evidence.
They both said they had a very good opinion of Dr. Bailey's
character as a moral man; but Mr. Hill, on being pressed
whether he had heard what the Bishop of Winchester had
said of the prisoner at the last trial, admitted he had, and

that since that time he had thought Dr. Bailey's character more questionable. [At the previous trial the Bishop of Winchester was called by the defendant, the administrator of Mr. Smith, and stated that Dr. Bailey's explanation of a signature to a testimonial he had produced to his lordship was not satisfactory to him; at the same time three other witnesses swore they would not believe Dr. Bailey on his oath.]

Sarah Barberry proved that on the morning of the 12th August she saw the deceased at his own home, and he asked whether she would go with him to Dr. Bailey's chapel that night, and witness consented. Deceased said he was going on business respecting some money belonging to Miss Bailey. Witness had on other occasions heard the deceased say he held a large sum of money belonging to Miss Bailey, and when she had been at his house she had seen a book lying on the table, which the deceased said contained the account between them. The book produced was similar to the one she saw at the deceased's house.

On cross-examination the witness admitted she had known the deceased for many years, and that he visited her at her own home. She was by trade a dressmaker.

Catherine Glanville, formerly a servant in Dr. Bailey's family, proved seeing Mr. Smith at the chapel on the night in question in a pew with Mrs. Grey. Was certain it was the 12th of August, as it was the last time she was at chapel. Some further evidence as to character was then given, and the case for the prisoner closed.

Mr. Humfrey, in reply, dwelt with considerable force on the nature of the defence set up by the prisoner, and the character of some of the witnesses called on his behalf. He commented upon the observations made by the prisoner's counsel reflecting on the character of the witnesses who had been bribed to give evidence for Dr. Bailey after the previous trial, which he said (coming as it no doubt did from the instructions of the prisoner, who had himself tempted and suborned these witnesses) was an instance of "Satan reproving Sin." The statement alleged to have been made by the deceased to the witness Barberry was, he submitted, quite inconsistent with his well-known character for closeness. The real weakness of the defence was, however, the absence of Miss Bailey, and of any evidence to show how she had become possessed of the money professed to have been advanced by her to the deceased.

Mr. Justice Williams, in summing up, after alluding to the station in life of the prisoner at the bar, which he said he was quite sure the jury would take into consideration no further than was necessary to lead them to a right conclusion, observed:—"Your attention will not be directed to the fact whether the I. O. U. was a forgery, although that is an important feature in the case, but whether the promissory note which is the subject of the indictment is or is not a forgery. Still, if in considering the case you are of opinion that the I. O. U. is a fiction, then there will certainly be strong grounds for supposing that the promissory note is a forgery, as they are both of the same amount, and the latter is only a confirmation of the former.

"It is most important for your consideration that the sister of the prisoner is not called, for if there had been any truth in the case she could at once have proved it. It is admitted she is living, and no cause whatever is shown for her absence. If you are of opinion the witnesses who speak to the handwriting in the document are correct, then a forgery has undoubtedly been committed; but there is no proof, neither is there any attempt made to show that the prisoner was seen to commit the forgery. If you are satisfied that the promissory note is forged, then there is abundant proof of the uttering of that instrument by the prisoner.

"With respect to the witnesses Kearney and Flemming, nothing whatever can be said in their favour, and very little if any reliance can be placed on what they said, for a man who would deliberately swear to a fact one day and the next swear that his previous statement was a falsehood cannot be believed unless confirmed by other testimony, and very little more can be said of a man who held out a statement for the purpose of its being used as evidence, and then when called upon to swear to it retracted it."

The jury, after a deliberation of only a few minutes, returned a verdict of guilty of uttering the promissory note, knowing it to be forged.

Mr. Jones, on the part of the prisoner, then applied to have the sentence postponed in order to give the counsel for the prisoner the opportunity of moving for arrest of judgment, on the ground that the evidence of the uttering was insufficient.

Mr. Humfrey opposed the application ; and

Mr. Justice Williams remarked that if there were any grounds for such an application it might be made afterwards.

Sentence was then passed on the prisoner of transportation for life (*a*).

(*a*) In the month of April following, Dr. Bailey, in pursuance of his sentence, was transported to Van Diemen's Land in the ship *Gilmore*. The chapel in Queen's Square, Westminster, to which such an unenviable notoriety was given by the proceedings, and of which the prisoner was the minister, enjoying up to the time of the first trial a considerable amount of popularity, and no little reputation as a fashionable preacher, is on the left-hand side of the square, and is now used as a mission room.

THE TRIAL

OF

JOHN TAWELL

FOR THE MURDER OF SARAH HART BY POISON,

AT THE AYLESBURY SPRING ASSIZES,

BEFORE MR. BARON PARKE,

On March 12th, 1845.

Counsel for the Prosecution : Mr. Serjeant *Byles*, and Mr. *Prendergast.*

For the Prisoner : Mr. *Fitzroy Kelly*, Mr. *O'Malley*, and Mr. *Gunning.*

INTRODUCTION.

On the 1st of January, 1845, by means of the electric tele-graph, then quite in its infancy, the departure of John Tawell from Slough, under circumstances of considerable suspicion, was signalled to London. During the whole of that after-noon and evening Tawell was traced to different places in the city, and on the next morning, on the receipt of further intelligence, he was arrested on a charge of murder. He received the announcement of his arrest, and the particu-lars of the charge in a manner thoroughly characteristic of him, denied he had ever been at Slough, and observed, "*My position in life places me above all suspicion.*" It was this character of an outwardly prosperous and highly religious man that Tawell had acted the greater part of his life. Nothing could have been more false.

On the previous day Tawell had been observed coming out of a house in Bath Place, near Slough, in which after his departure the body of a female was discovered lying on the floor dead. This female was a person named Sarah Hart.

A *post mortem* examination assigned the cause of death to prussic acid, administered, according to the prosecution, by Tawell. The case for the defence was, first, that the woman did not die by prussic acid, and secondly (and this was the main point), that if prussic acid were the cause of death it was derived from substances taken by the deceased voluntarily, and evolved by the ordinary process of digestion.

The trial is interesting as raising the peculiar point whether prussic acid could not be obtained from apple-pips contained in apples eaten in the ordinary way as food, sufficient to destroy life ; and it was contended by Mr. Fitzroy Kelly, on behalf of the prisoner, that it was to that cause, and not to prussic acid administered by the prisoner, that the death of the deceased, if caused by poison at all, was to be attributed. The point was contended for with considerable ability on behalf of Tawell, not only by his counsel but also by experienced scientific advisers, amongst others by Mr. Herepath and Dr. Letheby, who doubtless furnished ample materials for the cross-examination of the adverse witnesses ; but Mr. Kelly was unable to satisfy the jury that the death of the deceased proceeded from this cause ; and in fact the defence, though scientific and ingenious, had one fatal defect in it—apple-pips, though undoubtedly containing prussic acid, as do several other substances, such as confectionary, cheese, &c., yet the poison in them cannot be extracted except by distillation. This point was particularly impressed upon the jury by the learned judge in his summing up, and also one other point of importance, that the peculiar smell of prussic acid had been detected in the stomach of the deceased before there was any possibility of its having been set free by distillation.

It is somewhat singular that in this trial, though scientific witnesses of great reputation were employed by the prisoner as advisers, none of them were called upon to give evidence.

The antecedents of Tawell are peculiar. When quite a young man he had involved himself in a crime, the punishment of which in those days was death, and but for a curious coincidence, and the merciful feelings of his prosecutors, he would then have ended his days on the scaffold. Nearly thirty

years previously, dressed as a Quaker, of which body he was
then undoubtedly a member, and representing himself as a
partner in a firm of bankers in the country, he called on an
engraver in the city of London, and produced a bank note.
He pointed to one of the names on the note, said it was his
name, and that he was entrusted by his partners to get a plate
engraved exactly similar to it. The engraver agreed to comply
with the order, and promised to be very careful to make the
plate an exact *facsimile* of the note, about which Tawell professed himself very anxious. In a few days Tawell called and
examined the plate very carefully with the note, and finding
it was correct ordered a quantity of copies to be struck off,
for which he (Tawell) was to send at a time agreed upon. In
the interim, however, the engraver became suspicious, and
communicated with the police. A trap was laid for the
person who was to call for the notes on the day in question,
into which Tawell himself fell. The astonishment of the
police, of the bankers, to all of whom Tawell was well known,
and of the members of the Society of Friends at this discovery
was very great. The bankers felt they were bound to prosecute, and with the evidence in the hands of the police it
would have been quite impossible for Tawell to have escaped.
By a singular accident, however, on searching Tawell there
was found on him a Bank of England note, which on
investigation turned out to be a forgery. There was very
little doubt but that Tawell was quite ignorant of the note
being forged; but advantage was taken of its being found in
his possession to induce the bankers to forego to prosecute for
the forging of their notes, on the condition that the Bank
of England would prosecute Tawell for being in possession
of a forged note of the Bank of England knowing it to be
forged, it being understood that Tawell should plead guilty.

Accordingly, but not without difficulty, the Bank of
England were induced to take up the prosecution, and at the
Old Bailey sessions held in February, 1814, Tawell was
indicted for having in his possession a forged note of the
Bank of England well knowing it to be forged. The case
came on for trial before the Recorder and a London jury,
and Tawell, as arranged, pleaded guilty. The offence not
being capital his life was spared, but he was sentenced to

transportation for fourteen years. By thus pleading guilty
to a crime of which he was innocent, Tawell escaped punishment for an offence of which he was undoubtedly guilty,
and the Society of Friends were saved the humiliation of
seeing one of their own body end his days on the
scaffold.

Tawell's career in Australia was fortunate; he made
money, and after the lapse of several years returned to London
with a competency. He tried hard to get re-admitted into
the Society of Friends, but without effect, and though he
dressed as a Quaker, and always attended their services, and
passed himself off as a member of that body, he was, in fact,
never again admitted or acknowledged by them as a member
of their society.

The facts connected with the present trial will best appear
from the opening statement of Mr. Serjeant Byles, who
conducted the prosecution.

" The prisoner at the bar formerly carried on the business
of a chemist and druggist. He had the misfortune several
years ago to lose his first wife. Shortly before her death the
deceased, Sarah Hart, then a young woman somewhere about
thirty years of age, entered into his service, and I shall show
you by evidence which I need not open in detail the nature
of the acquaintance which subsisted between her and the
prisoner, and that when she left his service she was
pregnant. She lived first after quitting his service at a
place called Crawford Street, London, where I shall show
you that the prisoner was in the habit of visiting her. She
lived afterwards at Paddington Green, thence removed to
Slough, and for some time previous to her death was living
at Bath Place, which consists of four small cottages, forming
one detached building. Bath Place stands upon the Great
Western Road, about a quarter of a mile beyond the Windmill public-house, which is kept by a person named Botham.
In the end house, towards London, lived Mrs. Ashley; in
the next the deceased, Sarah Hart, the mother of two children,
who was living there with them, and who, as it will appear
to you in the course of the case, was entirely dependent on
the prisoner for her support, and whom he was in the habit of

visiting at Bath Place, and supplying with money. The prisoner himself has recently resided at Berkhampstead, in
circumstances of apparent ease and affluence. He married
no long time since a second wife—a lady to whose deep
misfortune no man can allude without feelings of commisera-
tion. I shall show you that notwithstanding the apparent
ease and respectability of his circumstances, he was at the
time this occurrence took place by no means in such circumstances. I shall call his banker's clerk to show you that at
this moment he had overdrawn his account. You will find
that he was in the constant habit of visiting Sarah Hart,
that she was dependent upon him for money, and that he
found himself in this position—that money must be supplied,
or that which would otherwise be secret must become apparent, namely, the nature of his connection with this
person.

" On the 1st of January in the present year I shall show you
that the prisoner was at the Jerusalem Coffee-house, Cornhill, London, the waiter of which he told, about the middle
of the day, that he was going to dine at the west end of the
town, and desired that his great coat should be left for him
on his return about nine o'clock. He did not proceed to the
west end of the town, but to the station of the Great Western
Railway, by the four o'clock train of which railway he proceeded to Slough. On arriving at Slough he went to the
residence of Sarah Hart, at Bath Place; and it will appear
that after he had been a short time with her she went by his
direction to the Windmill public-house for a bottle of porter.
It is important to bear in mind that she was at that moment
perfectly well and in very good spirits. Having bought the
porter, she borrowed a corkscrew, and brought both home
with her to Bath Place. A person spoke to her on her way
back, from whose testimony it appears that she was at
that time perfectly well. Very shortly after her return
Mrs. Ashley, the person who resided in the next house,
being seated at work before a candle, heard a noise in the
room of Sarah Hart. I should observe to you that these
cottages consist each of two very small rooms on the ground-
floor. Mrs. Ashley heard in her neighbour's apartment a
moan or stifled scream. She laid down her work; the noise

continued; she became very much alarmed, and taking up the candle, went to the door, and proceeded down the path leading from the cottage to the road; but before she reached the gate she saw the prisoner approaching the gate which terminated a similar path from the cottage of Sarah Hart. Mrs. Ashley will tell you that at this moment the moans of the deceased were distinctly audible. The prisoner went to the gate; he trembled, appeared greatly agitated, and had much difficulty in opening the gate, which I believe Mrs. Ashley, who had reached it by this time, assisted him in opening, saying, 'What is the matter with my neighbour? I am afraid she is ill;' the moans of Sarah Hart being distinctly audible. The prisoner made no answer, but passed out of the gate and proceeded towards Slough. Mrs. Ashley, in consequence of the noise, went up to Sarah Hart's house, and turning round, saw the prisoner going down the road. She then went into the house, and observed in Sarah Hart's room, just before the fireplace, a small table, and on it a bottle of porter open, and partly drunk, also two tumblers, one of which was next the window, and towards the chair upon which Sarah Hart had apparently been sitting. In one of these tumblers there was some froth, in the other there was porter or porter and water, it is not quite certain which. The deceased, Sarah Hart, was lying on the floor; her cap was off, and her hair hanging down. Her clothes were up to her knees; one stocking was down, and one shoe off. She was still continuing the moaning noise which I have described to you. Mrs. Ashley went up to her and asked her what was the matter, and raised her head up, but the deceased was unable to speak. Mrs. Ashley called in two neighbours, and some water was brought. Eventually Mr. Champneys, a surgeon, was sent for. He felt her pulse, and said he thought he could discover one or two beats. She moved her tongue, or jaw, a little. Mr. Champneys put his hand under her clothes to feel her heart, but he could discover no pulsation. She was clearly dead."

After alluding to the manner in which suspicion was first raised against the prisoner, and how at the railway station a gentleman, the Rev. Mr. Champneys sent to London a message informing the authorities that there was a person

in a first-class carriage who ought to be watched, the learned
serjeant proceeded :—

"A policeman was on the platform, and as soon as
the prisoner got out of the carriage the policeman saw
him get into an omnibus, and putting on a plain coat
over his police dress, he stepped up behind the omnibus
with the conductor. The omnibus proceeded to the Bank,
where the prisoner got out, the policeman taking sixpence
from him. He went forward to the Wellington statue,
turned round, looked back, and then went to the Jerusalem
Coffee-house, in Cornhill, and inquired for the coat which I
have mentioned in the early part of my statement. The
waiter gave him the coat, and he then went from Cornhill
down Gracechurch Street to London Bridge, and over that
to another coffee-house in the Borough, the policeman still
watching him, and taking care, of course, that he should not
be observed. The prisoner stayed there about half an hour.
He then came out, and retraced his steps over London Bridge,
and went down Cannon Street to a lodging-house in Scott's
Yard kept by a person of the name of Hughes, who is, I
believe, a member of the Society of Friends. The policeman,
having waited half an hour, and finding that the prisoner did
not come out of the lodging-house, went away. The next
morning further intelligence was received from Slough, and
the policeman, taking another officer with him, proceeded to
the house in Scott's Yard. He found that the prisoner had
left the house ; and he then went to the Jerusalem Coffee-
house, in Cornhill, where he found the prisoner, and said to
him, 'I believe you were down at Slough yesterday ?' He
denied it. He said he knew nobody at Slough, and had not
been there. 'You must be mistaken,' said he, 'in the
identity; my station in life places me above suspicion.'
The officer, however, took the prisoner into custody, and took
him down to Salthill, where he was handed over to the custody of Perkins, the superintendent of the Eton police."

After detailing the nature of a conversation which took
place between the prisoner and the superintendent of police
at Eton, the substance of which will be given in evidence,
Mr. Serjeant Byles continued :—"By direction of the coroner,
a *post mortem* examination took place the next day, I believe,

after the death of the woman. You will hear what was the nature of that *post mortem* examination more in detail from the surgeons. But it is necessary for me to tell you, in the first place, that the surgeons could not discover any external injury to account for death. They examined the brain; there was no appearance of anything in the brain which could have produced death. In the same manner they examined the lungs, and found nothing but an old adhesion, which, they will tell you, is quite consistent with perfect health, and is very common. It had nothing to do with the death of the deceased. They examined her heart, and found it perfectly healthy; and so were the intestines. There was nothing, so far as they could form an opinion, to show that death had resulted from external injury or from internal causes. In opening the body. one of the surgeons thought he smelt prussic acid, but the other could not discover anything of the kind. Either it did or it did not exist; I will not pretend to say which. Probably the surgeons will not. Certainly when they came to examine the stomach they could discover no smell of prussic acid; but, inasmuch as it appeared to them clearly that the deceased had not died from either external injury or internal causes, they came to the conclusion that she had died by poison of some kind or other; and in order that the contents of the stomach should be known they took them to a scientific chemist in London, who submitted them to a chemical examination. At the time the surgeons conjectured that the woman had died through swallowing oxalic acid. Tests for that poison were applied, and none was discovered. Tests were also applied for sulphuric acid, for opium, for various mineral poisons, and for prussic acid. Sulphate of copper and nitrate of silver were used. I am not competent to describe fully the nature of all the tests that were applied, but the surgeons satisfied themselves upon that occasion that prussic acid had been the cause of death. They found prussic acid in the stomach, and that it produced what they will tell you is an infallible test of its presence, the ' Prussian blue.' Suffice it to say, that after the stomach had been submitted to the examination of Mr. Cooper, the chemist, they came to the conclusion that the deceased had died from the effects of prussic acid.

" Gentlemen, at this time it was not known, and it will be
very important for you to bear this in mind, that the prisoner
had had any prussic acid at all.   There was no reason at that
time to attribute death to the influence of prussic acid, except
what had been found in the stomach.   Subsequently the
remainder of the stomach was taken to Mr. Cooper, and it
was tried by sulphate of iron, nitrate of silver, and cyanide of
silver, and prussic acid was clearly proved to exist. Mr. Cooper
was now able to say, observing the contents of the two portions of the stomach, that in the stomach there were not
fewer than fifty grains of prussic acid, according to the
strength of the prussic acid of the *London Pharmacopœia*.
But, gentlemen, of all poisons this is the most volatile, being
subject to evaporate most rapidly, inhaled while living, and
absorbed by the tissues after death.   The quantity is equal
to one grain of pure prussic acid, which is quite enough to
cause death.   This poison is so subtle and so energetic that
a single drop of the pure acid placed upon the tip of a rod
and put into the mouth of any small creature—a bird or a
dog—would cause almost instant death. About two-thirds of
a grain—a grain and a drop, I am told, are nearly synony-
mous terms—of pure prussic acid has been known to kill as
many as seven adults, one after the other.   Now this acid is
not sold in its pure state.   According to the *London Pharmacopœia*, there are two grains of pure acid to every ninety-
eight grains of water.   But a stronger preparation of it,
called Scheele's prussic acid, is about two and a half times
as strong as that of the *London Pharmacopœia*, consist-
ing of five grains of pure acid to ninety-five grains of
water.

" Owing to the publicity which things of this kind naturally
obtain, it was discovered that on the Wednesday when the
alleged murder was committed the prisoner had been to the
shop of a chemist in Bishopsgate Street and asked for two
drachms of Scheele's prussic acid.   He said he wanted it for
an external injury.   He brought a bottle with him with a
glass stopper, but the shopman gave him another bottle,
which was labelled for him, and he took it away with him on
the day he left London.   I shall show you that he was again
at the chemist's shop on the Thursday, the day after he slept

at the lodging-house; and that he then said he had lost the bottle he had before, and obtained the bottle which he had originally brought and left there.

" Such then is the case against the prisoner. I have stated to you that the prisoner will have the benefit of a full defence by counsel. I think it our duty on the part of the prosecution to make one or two remarks, such as we deem pertinent to the subject, trusting that I shall not make any observation of which any person in the situation of the prisoner can complain. But as the interest of the prisoner is consigned to my learned friend, so on the other hand the interest of the public is placed, under the eye of my lord on the bench, in the hands of the counsel for the prosecution. I wish to call your attention to the first statement made by the prisoner.— He first said he had not been to Slough. That will be proved beyond all question by witnesses who saw him there. It became very soon apparent that that statement could not be true; for Mrs. Ashley, who had a candle at the time, and other persons, could identify him. It will be proved that he was at Slough and at Bath Place. Now the first question you will have to ask is this, did the deceased die by poison? What the poison was is entirely immaterial to the issue before you; although I think it will be proved, beyond any reasonable doubt, what the poison was. But the first question is, did she die by poison? There is no external injury, nor any internal cause sufficient to account for death; and there is more than a fatal dose of prussic acid found in the stomach; and that it is prussic acid results from not positive evidence only, but negative, because tests for other poisons were applied. It will be too clear then that the deceased died by poison, and that the poison is prussic acid. Prussic acid, particularly such a dose as this, is most rapid in its effects. Probably no evidence will be adduced to show that the poor woman bought the poison. But we shall show you that the prisoner had that very morning bought poison. If the deceased did administer it to herself, where is the little phial? It is not to be found. But I shall show you that the prisoner himself had such a phial that morning. Where is it? I shall prove to you that the prisoner went back again to the chemist in Bishopsgate Street, and stated that he had lost that bottle.

Where is it? You will find the prisoner coming out of the house at the time the woman must have been in a dying condition. He is asked what is the matter, but makes no observation. He leaves the woman to herself; and then the next thing that he states is that he never was there."

Mary Ann Ashley, sworn and examined by Mr. Prendergast.—"I am a widow living at Bath-place, Salthill. On the 1st day of January last (Wednesday), a person named Sarah Hart lived next door to me. Between four 'and five o'clock on that day I saw the prisoner go into her house. I heard a stifled sort of scream between six and seven o'clock. The stifled scream seemed to come from Mrs. Hart's house. When I heard it I took a candle off the table and opened my door. I saw the prisoner coming out of Mrs. Hart's house. I found he was agitated, and could not open Mrs. Hart's gate, which is fastened by a small button. I said, directly I got out of my house, 'I am afraid my neighbour's ill.' I was then walking along the path, and I think I spoke loud enough to be heard by the person whom I believe to be the prisoner. He was about six yards off; he made no reply. I then heard the moaning noise in Hart's house. I said nothing more to the prisoner, except observing that the gate was fastened by a little button, and I said, 'Allow me to open it, sir;' he was trying in a hurried manner to open the gate. He appeared to be agitated. The prisoner went out before I went into Mrs. Hart's garden. I saw his face. I had the candle with me, and held it over the inside of the gate where he was. That gave me an opportunity of seeing him so as to say now that he is the same man. I do not recollect having seen him before that time. I found Mrs. Hart's door shut. I have no doubt whatever that the prisoner is the man. The moment I opened the door I found the deceased on the floor, with her head not a great way from the door. She was still making a noise, and her eyes were fixed. She did not move her limbs. I took hold of her hand, and raised her head; I said, 'Oh, Mrs. Hart, what is the matter?' She made no answer. I thought she slightly pressed my hand, but that I cannot positively tell. When I raised her up, a little froth came out of the corner of her mouth. Her eyes appeared to be fixed, and I thought she was dying. When I entered Mrs. Hart's room I saw a porter bottle, with a glass by the side of it, a little more than half full of stout. There was another glass on the opposite side of the table, near the door. It was empty, but there appeared to be something like froth at the bottom of it. A chair was beside Mrs. Hart, and another opposite, away from the door, near the glass that was partly full. I sent for Mr. Champneys, the surgeon, directly. I searched the place almost immediately, but found no small phial or medicine bottle. We suspected that something had been taken by her or given to her. There was a middling-sized fire. I did not look into that."

Cross-examined by Mr. F. Kelly.—" I had never seen the prisoner before that day. It was nearly five o'clock. I saw him go into the house. I heard no voice but hers on the night in question, so that I could not have supposed they were quarrelling. The screams I heard before leaving my house were repeated several times. I cannot say whether or not Mr. Tawell heard the observation I made about my neighbour being ill. The surgeon, Mr. Champneys, on being sent for, put his hand under the clothes of Sarah Hart, and felt her heart. He then bled her. I held the basin for him. Blood flowed from her; about as much as would cover a plate. I believe she was dead before she was bled. I am aware that the deceased had received a present of a box of apples some time before her death. She gave me some of them; when I saw the box it was not full. It would hold about a peck, but I did not see it when she first received it."

Re-examined by Mr. Prendergast.—" Not more than a minute, if so much, elapsed, between the time I heard the screams of the deceased and my going out of the house. It was more than a week before her death that I saw the box of apples. I cannot say how many there were in it; when I spoke of a peck I meant that the box would hold about that quantity, but the box was not full when I first saw it more than a week before her death. I dare say there were about twenty or two dozen apples in it when I first saw it. She gave me three or four. I saw some in the box since deceased's death; there may have been nine or ten."

A Mrs. Barrett then proved that she was sent for by the last witness on the day in question. She brought some water from the next room, which was in a large jug, and poured some of it into the tumbler which had the froth in it.— "I rinsed the tumbler and threw the rinsings into the fire-place. I poured some more into the tumbler and threw it in the face of Mrs. Hart. I thought she was too far gone to give her any to drink. I attempted to put some into her mouth, but I do not think she swallowed any. I then returned to my house, and sent a young person in my service, an apprentice, for Mr. Champneys, who lives about 200 yards from Bath Place."

Cross-examined by Mr. Kelly.—"I think it was about a quarter to seven o'clock when Mrs. Ashley came for me. When I came back again to Mrs. Hart's the surgeon was bleeding her. When pouring the water down the throat of the deceased I fancied that it caused her to foam at the mouth. I did not perceive any foam on her mouth until I tried to pour the water down."

John Kendal, examined by Mr. Prendergast.—"I am the waiter of the Jerusalem Coffee-house. Mr. Tawell is a sub-scriber to it. About three o'clock on the 1st of January he came to the coffee-house, and asked me at what hour we closed the door at night. I told him at eight o'clock, and asked him why, when he told me he was going to the west end to dine, and could not be back until half-past nine o'clock. He left a parcel and great coat with me, and said he would call for them at that hour. He did call between that hour and a quarter to ten o'clock, and I gave them to him."

Witnesses were then called who traced the prisoner from Slough to Eton, and then by rail to London, and proved the sending of a telegraphic message after him. William Williams, a sergeant of police, met the prisoner on the plat-form; put on a plain coat over his uniform and followed him on the steps of the omnibus in which he rode as far as the city. This witness's evidence is a mere repetition of part of the opening statement of the counsel, and need not be repeated. The next witness, William Wiggins, proved taking the prisoner into custody on the 2nd January.—" On seeing him in the Jerusalem Coffee-house, I asked him if he was not Mr. Tawell. He said he was. I then opened my great coat, and showed him by my uniform that I was a police officer, telling him that I should take him into custody, as he was the last person who was seen with a woman who had been found dead at Slough on the previous day. He said, ' I was not at Slough yesterday. I don't know anybody there. I did not leave town all day.' I said he was there, for he had been seen in an omnibus. In reply to that remark he said, 'You must be wrong in the identity. My station in society places me above or beyond suspicion.' I did not observe anything particular in his manner when he made that remark. I took him to Salthill. On arriving there, the coroner's inquest was going on. I searched him, and found on his person 12*l.* 10*s.* in gold, 1*l.* 1*s.* 6*d.* in silver, some halfpence, and a letter addressed to him from his wife."

Cross-examined by Mr. Kelly.—When you first spoke to the prisoner in the coffee-house about a woman found dead at Slough, did he not say that he came from Berkhampstead? —No; but he said that he wished to go to Berkhampstead. Did he not say, in reply to any of your remarks, that he had come from Berkhampstead on the day on which you said he had been at Slough?—Yes; he afterwards said that he had come, not from Slough, but from Berkhampstead.

Samuel Perkins examined.—" I am an officer of police. I received the prisoner into custody on the first day of the inquest. I brought him to Eaton, to my own house. Mr. Williams, prisoner's counsel, had an interview with him next day (Friday). After that interview the prisoner said to me, ' This unfortunate woman lived in my service about two years ago.' Another constable, named Holman, came into the room at that moment, and I told the prisoner that we were police officers, and that what he said I should have to report next day to the coroner. He said he had no objection. He said also that he had been in the habit of sending the deceased money, and that he had been pestered by her writing to him for money; that she was a very good

servant when she was in his service, but that she was a bad
principled woman; that she had written to him to say that
if he did not send her some money she would do something—
would make away with herself; that he went down to her
house, and said he would not allow her any more money;
that she then asked him if he would give her a drop of
porter, and that he sent for a bottle of stout, of which each
had a glass; that she held her hand over her glass, and
said, ' I will, I will;' that she poured something out of a
small phial not much bigger than a thimble; that she drank
a part of it, and that the remainder was thrown in the fire;
that she then began to throw herself about in a manner
which the prisoner imitated by moving his shoulders to
and fro, and that she lay down on the hearth-rug; that he
then went out, and that he did not think she was in earnest,
otherwise he would have called some one."

Cross-examined by Mr. Kelly.—" I have been an officer
about twelve years, and have been seven years connected
with this county. On the morning of the last day of the
coroner's inquest I told the coroner that I had information
to give of the conversation I have detailed, and I understood
him to say that he would not take any more evidence, and
that the examination was closed. I, therefore, was not
examined."

Henry William Champneys, examined by Mr. Prendergast.
—" On the evening of the 1st of January I left my house
about ten minutes before seven o'clock, and ran to the house
of Sarah Hart. On seeing her, I felt her wrist, but could
not say whether there was a pulse or not. I was not certain.
I then put my hand under her clothes to feel her heart, and
while doing so, I thought I observed her jaw move, but I
felt no pulsation at the heart. I considered her dead. I then
bled her in the arm; I did so because I thought it right not
to leave the house without trying every means. About an
ounce of blood flowed from her arm, but I still think she was
dead before I bled her. I put the things that were on the
table into a recess, and returned that evening, and took them
home with me. Next day I examined the body, but did not
find any external injury on it. By direction of the coroner,
on the same day (Thursday) I made a *post mortem* examina-

tion of the body in the presence of Mr. Pickering, another surgeon. On opening it I smelt the odour of prussic acid. I mentioned something about it at the time to Mr. Pickering. I examined the heart, which was quite healthy; I also examined the lungs, and they too were healthy, but their coverings showed adhesions of long standing. The bowels were healthy, and presented nothing that could account for death. I examined the stomach, but did not observe anything on its internal coat worthy of notice. I thought it had more mucus on its surface than is ordinarily perceived. I took out the stomach and its contents, and preserved them. I went next day to London, taking the whole of the contents of the stomach in a bottle, and submitted them to Mr. Cooper, the chemist, in the presence of his son, of Mr. Pickering, and Mr. Nordblad, another surgeon. The contents of the stomach indicated intense acidity. A portion of the stomach was exposed to evaporation in a retort which was first placed in a sand-bath. Sulphate of iron was added to the liquid that came over it. It was a solution of potassia. They remained together for some time. Muriatic acid was added, and the result was Prussian blue. According to my knowledge of pharmacy that could not have resulted without the presence of prussic acid. I should imagine that the prussic acid could not be produced by the decomposition of any portion of the stomach. Mr. Cooper afterwards tried the retort in a water bath, to obtain a lower temperature. It must have been above boiling heat, and distillation took place. The result could not possibly be produced from the decomposition of the stomach. The liquid distilled over was subjected to the same experiment as that produced by the sand-bath, and the result was the same, Prussian blue. Nitrate of silver was applied to the liquid, and cyanide of silver was produced."

With reference to the quantity of prussic acid required to destroy life, the witness stated:—" Less than a grain of real or pure hydrocyanic (prussic) acid would be a fatal dose. Two drachms of Scheele's acid would contain six grains. There are cases on record of persons having died from prussic acid without any smell of the acid being discoverable either in the stomach or other parts of the body. The absence of

N

smell is no proof that a person did not die from the effects of prussic acid. Christison mentions a case of death from prussic acid where no smell could be discovered. The deceased in that case took three and a half drachms of dilute prussic acid. I cannot say positively whether that was the acid of the *London Pharmacopœia* or Scheele's acid. A patient died in an hospital in Paris from seven-tenths of a grain. Prussic acid may be absorbed by the tissues, and the fact of finding fifty grains of the *London Pharmacopœia* acid in the stomach, that is to say, one grain of the pure acid, would not enable me to tell how much may have been there, or how much may have been taken."

Would it be possible for a person who had taken a quantity of prussic acid to leave the house and walk any distance?— Such person might, I think, walk a few yards. On the evening of Thursday, the day after the deceased's death, I put half a drachm of Scheele's acid into a tumbler, and filled the tumbler with Guiness's porter, the smell of the acid was then scarcely perceptible.

Cross-examined by Mr. Kelly.—" I have been in practice four years. I have never examined either internally or externally the body of a person killed by prussic acid. I have tried the effect of the acid on inferior animals in my study during my apprenticeship, but in not more than four cases. The animals were dogs. I helped to dissect them. I have seen dissection of rabbits. I also saw a man who had died through taking prussic acid; but I have no experience in detecting the odour of prussic acid in the human subject. I think that it may be taken without being detected. I should expect that a dead body when seen soon after death exhales a strong odour of prussic acid ; and if death be rapid, all the cavities as well as the blood have the odour."

Do you not believe that there must be something in the mouth or breath to indicate the presence of prussic acid if enough is taken to cause death?—I should always expect it, but there may be exceptions. Did you not smell this woman's mouth, and did you perceive any odour of the kind?—No ; but I did the next day when the body was opened. Neither Mr. Pickering nor Mr. Nordblad did, however. It was not a passing conjecture of mine, I was positive of it. Is it true, after opening the stomach, that you did not think you smelt it there? —I did not smell it there. Is it not the property of prussic acid, as it volatilizes, to emit a very peculiar odour?—Yes. Is it not called by a high authority, a " penetrating, highly diffusive, and peculiar odour? "—Yes. Is it not more likely to be detected when exposed, as this was, to a heat of 212 degrees?—Yes. And did you and those with you try at every heat to catch a smell of prussic acid without doing so?—Yes. When you drew some blood shortly after death, was there any smell there?—I perceived none. Would not epileptic patients be likely to die more quickly from taking prussic acid than other persons?—I am not competent to answer that question. Prussic acid is said to act powerfully upon the nervous system. It is found in a great number of substances, in apples for instance; and probably in many substances in which it has never yet been discovered. I agree with Christison in his opinion, in respect to the formation of this acid. It is made from the blood, bones, and horns of animals. It consists of 62.12 of carbon, fourteen of nitrogen, and one of hydrogen. Those are the elements. They exist and may be obtained from various substances in great quantities. They are in cherry stones, and the stones of various fruits, and in many seeds. They are to be found in the human saliva, but not in the form of prussic acid. When taken it is perceptible in the blood and breath, but most in the stomach. If in apple-pips or other substances the smell would not be given until disengaged by some process for that purpose. Well, then, did Mr. Cooper, Mr. Nordblad, and Mr. Pickering during the experiments for oxalic acid and other poisons fail to perceive any smell at all of them?— Yes. Did not one of you then, having exhausted those processes, come to the conclusion that there must be prussic acid? — Yes. Did not Mr. Cooper then apply a process which would set free prussic acid from apple-pips and other substances? —I believe that is the process, but it was not carried to the full extent. I refer to the heat. When this new process was applied the result was that prussic acid was found. Did you smell it?—No. Did any one else?—I believe not. Beyond the smell I perceived when opening the body I smelt none at all. We did not make any gas and burn it. I went to see the deceased as soon as I was sent for. I first felt the pulse. I fancied I felt a few beats, but I now imagine I was mistaken. It might have been the pulse of my own finger. Is not the analogy between animals and human beings dying of prussic acid considered doubtful by the best authorities?—Yes. The heart would continue to beat for a short time after the pulse receded from the arms. The lungs might be considered as slightly congested. I looked at the gall bladder. The colour was natural. Does not your experience teach you that prussic acid would colour it blue?—Yes. I opened the trachea; but not the bronchial tubes, so that I cannot tell whether there was water in them or not. When I felt the pulse and heart of the deceased I was satisfied she was dead. I saw a slight motion of the jaw just before I was going to feel her pulse, and I apprehend that she died then. I took the stomach from the body eighteen hours after death. The contents were turned into a jug or basin, and afterwards into a bottle. I do not know to what particular purposes the bottle had been previously applied. I did not wash it out, but it was perfectly clean. I tied the neck over with a piece of string. I locked it in the cellaret, and kept the key until I took the bottle to London to Mr. Cooper, with whom I remained experimenting four or five hours. Portions of the contents were taken out to be tested. Mr. Cooper kept them after that. I form my opinion from what I have read as to the action of prussic acid on the whole nervous system. The instance of the seven epileptic patients is the smallest dose I have read of. The exact dose is not determined yet.

Mr. Kelly (reading from *Watson's Lectures on the Practice of Physic*) asked, Do you agree in this—"A blow, a fall, an electric shock, a tea-spoonful of prussic acid may cause death, and leave no vestige on the nervous system?—Yes.

On re-examination by Mr. Serjeant Byles the witness stated, with reference to the smell of prussic acid, that some might perceive it and some not, and it was the proper plan for several to smell together, as some were more susceptible of smell than others.—" All animals, whether human or not, die if they take prussic acid ; there is no difference in the mode of its operation upon men and inferior animals. There was no appearance of disease in the heart of the deceased. Had there been any rupture of the coronary arteries, it would have been apparent. I never knew of such a sudden disease of the spinal marrow as to cause death. I know only of the two cases mentioned by Taylor of the gall bladder having a blue tint. The absence of a blue tint is no proof that a person did not die by taking prussic acid."

Evidence was then given to prove that no bottle containing prussic acid had been found in the deceased's house, notwithstanding a diligent search had been made, and the ashes of the fire-place sifted.

Mr. *John Thomas Cooper* was then called, who stated as follows :—" I am a chemist, and was formerly a lecturer on chemistry and medical jurisprudence. Messrs. Champneys, Pickering, and Nordblad called on me with the contents of a human stomach for examination, and also with a bottle containing porter, a glass, and a piece of a bun. I tested the porter and bun for oxalic and hydrocyanic acid, but did not find either. I tested the contents of the stomach for arsenic, for opium, for sulphuric acid, for oxalic acid, for the mercurial salts, and other metallic poisons, but did not detect any. I then tested them for prussic acid, through the agency of sulphate of iron and a solution of potash, put into a retort, which I placed in a sand-bath. When dissolved and well stirred up I added some muriatic acid. The effect of adding muriatic acid produced Prussian blue immediately. That is a proof of the presence of prussic acid. I do not think the sand-bath was of sufficient heat to decompose animal matter. It is quite consistent that it should have been of sufficient heat to cause these things to dissolve, and yet not of sufficient heat to decompose animal matter. It would require

between 600 and 700 degrees of Fahrenheit to decompose
animal matter. If fluid were not present I think it quite
possible that the sand-bath would decompose animal matter.
I also put some of the contents of the stomach (in a retort)
into a water-bath, and put into the water some salt, in order
to raise the temperature. By that means we can, instead of
212, obtain a temperature to 226. I used an adapter between
the retort and receiver, and had the receiver surrounded with
litmus paper, in order to keep it cool. The distillation was
conducted very slowly. I distilled off the first day about an
ounce of liquid. I could not discover the smell of cyanogen
in it. The contents of the stomach smelt strongly of beer,
of food, and the process of digestion. I applied the same
test to the clear liquid I distilled in this way as in the former
experiment, and it produced Prussian blue. The bottle which
contained the Prussian blue I produced from the sand-bath has
unfortunately been broken, but the blue which I produced from
the water-bath I have. As I was obliged to leave town next
day, I added nitrate of silver to a portion of the distilled liquid
from the water-bath, and about the same quantity was precipitated. The product was therefore cyanide of silver, and
on my return to town I put it into a small retort, added a
very small quantity of muriatic acid, and carefully distilled
it over into a very cool receiver. About a drachm or a
little more distilled over. That liquid smelt of prussic acid.
It was in fact diluted prussic acid. Therefore, from the
cyanide of silver I got prussic acid, and I precipitated the
acid again with nitrate of silver, and formed cyanide of
silver again. I observed in the contents of the stomach
pieces of undigested apple. Prussic acid may be obtained from
apple-pips. I took the pips of about fifteen apples to obtain
prussic acid from. The result was the production of this
Prussian blue (showing an ounce bottle with a pale blue
liquid.) The quantity of prussic acid contained in it is
inappreciable. I do not think any chemist could estimate
the quantity, it is so small. The same degree of heat was
applied to distil the pips as in the other cases, but the distillation was conducted by means of a lamp, and not of a
bath. The contents of the stomach I conceive, from the
results of the tests I applied, to have contained about one

grain of prussic acid, that is to say, fifty grains of the *London Pharmacopœia*, or twenty grains of Scheele's acid."

Cross-examined by Mr. Kelly.—" Until this case I have never examined the contents of a human stomach when a person has been killed, or of a human stomach containing prussic acid. Respecting the effect of prussic acid upon the stomach or tissues of the body, my knowledge is only theoretical. Prussic acid, which I have smelt from its most concentrated to its weakest state, has a peculiar smell. It affects different persons differently. When I smell it, for instance, it affects spasmodically the back of my throat. But it loses its smell in combinations. I am not aware of what quantity of prussic acid destroys life. I have no practical knowledge on the subject. I began my investigation in this case with the view of seeing if oxalic acid was present. I took various portions of the contents of the stomach from the bottle to test them. When I first opened the bottle I dipped into it some litmus paper, which instantly became red, showing the presence of some strong acid, from which circumstance I was led to expect the presence of oxalic acid. That was the reason I applied the tests for oxalic acid. Not finding that, I tried for sulphuric acid. Not finding that, I gave up searching for the acids, and tried for opium, &c. I recognized the odour of beer more strongly in the contents of the stomach than anything else. I did not trace the smell of prussic acid in them, nor feel any spasmodic affection in the throat on smelling them. I did not come to the conclusion, after trying for those acids and mercurial poisons which I did not discover, that there was prussic acid in the contents of the stomach, but I remarked to those present at the time, ' Well, if this woman has taken poison, it can be no other than prussic acid.' I found, also, undigested flesh meat, some portions of apple, and a pulpy sort of mass of which I could make nothing. Digestion had proceeded to a certain point. I did not observe with the apple any pips, either partially masticated or otherwise. I am not able to say if the pips of one kind of apple contain more prussic acid than another. There is a great difference between bitter and sweet almonds—the bitter contain a great deal of prussic acid, and the sweet I believe none at all."

Are there not an immense number of substances which contain prussic acid?—That is a question I feel some difficulty in answering, because strictly speaking, I do not think prussic acid exists in any substance—not even in bitter almonds. I wish to explain what I mean, and it is this, that prussic acid in a free state is so extremely volatile, that it cannot possibly exist, unless in combination with some other substance. It is my opinion that prussic acid is a "product," and not an "aduct," that is to say, that in consequence of its great volatility it cannot exist by itself. You liberate it by combination or change. The elements of it exist in a great many substances. Those elements on taking new arrangements may produce prussic acid; therefore do I feel that it is always a product, and that it does not exist in any substance in a free state; because if it did it must be continually evaporating from that substance. Are not the substances which are already known to contain the elements of prussic acid, and from which it may be produced, very numerous?—They are very numerous, certainly; because all those compounds which contain carbon, nitrogen, oxygen, and hydrogen may in my opinion, by new changes, be made to afford prussic acid. All animal substances, of whatever kind, contain those elements in which are comprised the elements of prussic acid. I will ask you one question more—whether you agree with Taylor in his *Medical Jurisprudence*, that "the odour of prussic acid, which is said to be peculiar, may be found when all other tests fail to prove the presence of that acid?"—I do not believe it. As far as my experience goes, it would lead me to the contrary conclusion. But if I understand rightly, you do not smell prussic acid at all, but feel its effects in another way?—Sometimes it has produced a spasmodic constriction about my throat, without my smelling the odour. At other times I have distinctly perceived the odour of it. It depends, I think, very much upon the state of the nasal organ at the moment.

By Mr. Serjeant Byles.—The same peculiar sensation I feel in the nostrils and back of the throat is, I think, also felt by many on putting prussic acid to the nose

I shall ask you but one more question. Did you some

time before this trial communicate to the prisoner's solicitor the nature of the evidence you were to give?—I did, about a fortnight ago.

By the Judge.—Have you or have you not a doubt upon your mind, from the result of your experiments, as to the existence of prussic acid in the contents of the stomach which you examined?—None whatever, my lord.   Have you or have you not any doubt that prussic acid may exist without being smelt?—I have no doubt whatever upon the subject.   If there was an absence of smell, would you suppose that prussic acid was present in the shape of a salt, and that therefore you did not smell it?—Absence of smell may arise from dilution; it may also arise from being covered by the smell of other substances.   Do you in this particular case ascribe the absence of smell to the circumstance of its being in the shape of a salt?—No; because it could not exist in the stomach as a cyanide of potassium, which is a salt, or as a cyanide of soda, which is a salt, when another and more powerful acid was present; as, for instance, muriatic acid, which in this case was found in a considerable quantity, it being an acid generated by the process of digestion.   Do you not believe that there was also acetic acid present, and is not that a strong acid?—I have no doubt that there was acetic acid present, and it would have a greater affinity for soda or potash than prussic acid.   Are you of opinion that prussic acid would be formed by the putrefaction of the contents of the stomach?— I think not.

Charlotte Howard, a young woman who had lodged at the deceased's house, proved that Tawell was in the habit of coming to see the deceased, and that on one occasion deceased had been affected by illness after his visit, and stated it had arisen from drinking a glass of porter.   Witness had seen thirteen sovereigns on the table after one of the prisoner's visits.

Edward Weston Nordblad, a surgeon, who had been called in on the day in question to the deceased's house, corroborated the evidence of Mr. Champneys and Mr. Cooper as to the finding of the prussic acid in the stomach, and the nature and properties of the acid generally.   He had experimented on dogs with prussic acid, and had found no smell on opening their bodies eighteen hours after death, nor in their mouths. A paper having been handed to the witness, he stated it was a proper prescription for varicose veins, and thought prussic acid might be used successfully for skin diseases to alleviate pain. Rupture of the coronary arteries would be sufficient to produce death; also forcing water down the throat of a person in a state of syncope might cause suffocation and sudden death.

As the evidence of Mr. Champneys and Mr. Cooper has been given at some length, it is not necessary to state more of this witness's evidence, nor of that of the next one called, Mr. Pickering, another surgeon, as they both confirm the testimony of Mr. Champneys and Mr. Cooper in all material particulars, and were both of opinion that the death of the deceased had been caused by prussic acid.

Henry Thomas, sworn and examined by Mr. Serjeant Byles.—" In the beginning of this year I was shopman to Mr. Hughes, a chemist, 89, Bishopsgate Street. Mr. Hughes is since dead. I remember the 1st of January perfectly well. I saw the prisoner on that day; he came between the hours of twelve and two o'clock. He was dressed in a great coat, and wore the usual garb of a Quaker. He asked for two drachms of Scheele's prussic acid. He brought a small half-ounce phial, which had a regular label, ' Scheele's prussic acid.' He gave me that bottle to put the prussic acid in; it had a glass stopper, which I could not at the time get out, in consequence of which I gave him a bottle of our own. I believe that when I was about to put a label on it he said, ' You need not put a label on it;' but I will not swear that he did so. He said he required it for an external application, and he mentioned varicose veins. He paid me fourpence, and I entered it in the book at the time. He came again the next day between the hours of ten and twelve o'clock in the morning, and asked for two drachms more. He said he had had the misfortune to break the other bottle. He took the same quantity in the bottle he originally brought. I have frequently seen him before in the shop, and sold him articles. I might have sold him prussic acid before, but not to my recollection. He had told me that he had been a chemist and apothecary abroad."

Cross-examined by Mr. Kelly.—" The prisoner told me he was suffering from varicose veins, and I judged that he was, from the medicines I sold him. He rubbed his leg. (A paper was shown to the witness.) That would be a good external application for the irritation produced by varicose veins."

Mr. Baron PARKE.—What is that?

Mr. KELLY.—Scheele's prussic acid.

Witness.—" That prescription is in the handwriting of Dr. Addison. I do not believe that Scheele's prussic acid could be mixed with a drink and taken as a poison, and not be smelt after death. I do not think porter would disguise it. I have tried prussic acid on a parrot, which, being ill, a lady wished to have killed. I put about thirty drops of Scheele's prussic acid, and injected them down the throat of the bird by a glass syringe. There were three women present, and they were compelled to leave the room, the scent was so strong and suffocating. The bird was afterwards stuffed. On another occasion I mixed thirty drops of the acid with eleven ounces of porter, and found the odour of the acid slightly perceptible. I did not particularly observe the difference between the time when the froth was on, and when there was none. It is the property of this acid to give out a smell while volatilizing. Apple-pips contain prussic acid. I have assisted in extracting it from the pips of fifteen small apples. Two grains and a quarter of cyanide of silver were obtained. Then one and two tenths of a grain of pure hydrocyanic acid were produced."

Re-examined by Mr. Serjeant Byles.—" I made the first of these experiments on the 9th of this month at the London Hospital, at the request of Mr. Bevan, solicitor to the prisoner. I had never before produced prussic acid from apples."

Henry Smythe, clerk to Messrs. Barnett, Hoare, & Co., bankers, sworn, and examined by Mr. Serjeant Byles.—" I remember seeing the prisoner, who had an account with us, on Wednesday, between two and three o'clock, at the banking-house. He drew a check for 14*l.*, which I paid him in gold—

in money, however. His account was that day overdrawn" (a).

Cross-examined by Mr. Kelly.—"The account was overdrawn 56l. We discounted a bill on the Australasia Bank
for him on the 10th of January; the amount was 682l.,
which was placed to his credit. The account was overdrawn
on the 13th of December, when he drew a check of 100l. He
said he had permission to overdraw from Mr. Gurney Hoare,
one of the partners."

Sarah Bateman examined.—"About five years ago deceased
told me she was pregnant. I remember on one occasion taking
tea at her lodgings with the prisoner. Sarah brought in the
tea and took the things away again. She then came in and sat
down by my side. I said, ' I know, Sarah, what you are
going to speak about, and we had better begin.' She got up
and seemed to put herself very much out of the way, and
showed a disposition to vindicate her master, saying it was
not the case. He said he was about to get married to Sarah
Cutforth (his present wife), and if those things were rumoured
about it would make a very great difference. I said, if I had
said more than what was right the law was open, and
Mr. Tawell might punish me. He laughed, and begged of
Sarah not to excite herself so much; he said he was about to
be admitted as a Friend, and should not like such things to
be talked about—that was her pregnancy. She said she
would be dead to the world from that time; that no one
should know what became of her, not even her own mother."

Mr. F. Kelly then commenced his speech in defence of the
prisoner.—Although the honourable care and caution of his

(a) In the recent case of Thomas Hartley Montgomery, who was tried
for the murder of Mr. Glass, the cashier of the Northern Bank in New-
town Stewart, Ireland, in which it was proved that the murderer carried
away with him several hundred pounds of bank notes on his person,
evidence as to the pecuniary position of the accused, in order to show
a motive, was rejected by the judge who presided at the trial ; yet in
the case of Tawell, where pecuniary motives were perhaps not so evident, it was admitted. The attention of the Crown prosecutor was afterwards called in Montgomery's case (the jury being unable to agree in the
first trial, and in consequence discharged) to the case of Tawell ; and on
the second trial, after some argument, evidence of pecuniary embarrass-
ment was admitted. But on the second trial the jury again did not
agree, and the case is still undecided.

learned friend had led him to abstain from anything that might press unfairly against the accused, the jury must have learned from the public newspapers that he had committed in early life an offence against the laws ; but since that, he had atoned for his offence by a life of industry, kindness, and bounty. That fact was the key to many of the subterfuges and evasions which had marked his conduct in connection with this charge. Having been banished from his country for his early offence, he had recovered his standing in society, and down to the present moment enjoyed the respect and esteem of many friends, while he had acquired some amount of worldly wealth. He (Mr. Kelly) would show that the alleged motive for committing the crime of murder, that of embarrassed circumstances and inability to continue a pecuniary payment, did not exist. He would show also that witnesses for the prosecution came prepared to support mere matters of theory, speculation, and opinion, and that their evidence, although given under the sanction of an oath, was not of any weight. He would show, too, that the indefensible language and conduct of the accused in connection with this case might be accounted for on other grounds than that of his having been guilty of murder.

Before the prosecution could call upon the jury to condemn the prisoner to death it must be proved that the deceased died of poison, and that that poison was prussic acid taken into the stomach. He quite agreed with his learned friend that direct evidence could not always be expected to prove a charge of murder; but upon the question that the woman died of poison the jury were bound to demand positive and direct evidence. It was the duty of the prosecution not only to prove the death, but the cause of the death, in a case of this kind ; and upon that principle he called upon the jury to have, before they sent the prisoner to a horrid and ignominious death, evidence that the woman died of taking prussic acid.

What were the jury called upon to believe ? A woman in health, as it appeared, had died suddenly, and the prosecutor asked the jury to take away the life of the prisoner on the supposition that she had died from prussic acid, and not from any one of the numerous causes of sudden death. If

ever there was a case in which the blessed principle of our
law should be regarded, that there should be positive proof of
guilt, this was the case.   Suppose it were stated that a person
was poisoned by laudanum, would the jury convict, or the
judge suffer the case to go to the jury, when they heard from
the witness for the prosecution, " I never knew a case of a
person dying from taking that drug ?"   No, they would ask
for some one who could speak of the effects of laudanum upon
the human system of his own knowledge, and not from what
he had read in books.   Those witnesses were irresponsible ;
yet they called upon the jury to sacrifice that man upon the
ground only of what they had read in books, and not upon
that of actual experience.   Unhappily this country was not
without experience on this subject. It appeared that of thirty-
nine cases, in no great length of time, poisoned by prussic acid,
only two had been charged with murder, and of all the medical
men who had seen and examined all those cases the prosecution had brought one.   There were many of such witnesses
who could have deposed to whether there was a smell or
not a smell after death, or whether there was a scream or no
scream, or gorged lungs or not, instead of being left to the
uncertain opinions of Mr. Champneys, Mr. Nordblad, and
Mr. Pickering, three very young and inexperienced men, of
little practice, whose opinions did not agree with each other,
and who never saw man, woman, or child who had been
poisoned by prussic acid.

It appeared from their evidence that there were doubts,
only doubts, as to the quantity of prussic acid necessary to
cause death, and as to all the effects and operation of the
poison, the opinions of the witnesses not being derived from
experience, but being founded on books containing con-
flicting opinions and partially reported experiments.   There
was no positive evidence of the quantity of poison in the
stomach of the deceased, nor of the source whence it was
derived.   What was the quantity sufficient to cause death ?
That was a question upon which the jury had to make up
their minds at the very outset.   According to the published
statistics the number of sudden deaths was 1 in 99 ; so that
there were about 3000 sudden deaths in the course of a year.
Here was a woman who had died suddenly, and it was said of

prussic acid. How much was there in the stomach? Witnesses could prove the quantity of arsenic or opium sufficient to cause death; but science was in the dark with regard to prussic acid. Would that jury be the first to decide such a question in the absence of positive evidence, and resting only upon the opinions of persons who had formed them from reading books, and knew no more than the jury might learn in half an hour by reading? Those books were written by persons now living; why were they, or some of them, not called to give positive evidence? The witnesses had said at least a grain of prussic acid existed in the woman's stomach, but they had not proved upon their own knowledge and experience that a grain was sufficient to cause death. They mentioned one case in which so small a quantity had killed a person; but that case they read in *Taylor*, who copied it into his book from some other quarter, and the statement of the case was full of errors.

He would call their particular attention to the part of the book referred to by Mr. Champneys, who had no more practical knowledge of the quantity of prussic acid that would cause death than any one else in court, and with whom, as with the other medical witnesses, it was nothing but guesswork. The part of this work on medical jurisprudence by Mr. Taylor referred to, stated that a person having taken diluted prussic acid by mistake to the amount of one and a half drachm of Scheele's acid, spasms and tetanus were produced, from which the patient did not wholly recover for thirteen days. It also stated, that "admitting the strength of the acid to be as represented, this is the largest dose known to have been taken without causing death." Would it be just on the supposed validity of an opinion such as that, found in a book respecting which he had not the power of putting a single question, to ascertain whether or not there was any error in it—would it be just on such testimony, the book itself saying, "If the strength of the acid be correctly represented," to condemn a man to death? If the strength of the acid were not correctly represented, the deduction was incorrect, and that being incorrect, the whole basis of the medical testimony tumbled down. They had therefore no sworn evidence whatever to clear up the doubts which

existed upon the question of what quantity of prussic acid
would cause death; they had nothing but a reference to
these books, which contained nothing but speculative
opinions. If he had the authors of them on the table to
examine, he might perhaps be able to arrive at some more
definite conclusion; but without that, he maintained that
the whole basis of the medical evidence fell to the ground.
Then with regard to the question of smell, the learned
counsel contrasted the evidence of the medical men, showing
in it great discrepancy. Mr. Champneys fancied in one case
and proved in another the existence of the smell of prussic
acid from the contents of the stomach, while Mr. Nordblad,
notwithstanding his acute powers of smell, could not discover
it at any period.

The learned gentleman then applied himself to the evidence
of Mr. Cooper, respecting his examination of the contents of
the stomach, which examination he had admitted to have
been incomplete, and also to his analysis of apple-pips, which
he also admitted to have been incomplete, as he was not able
to say how much prussic acid he had obtained from the pips
of fifteen apples. He wished to impress upon the jury this,
that next to bitter almonds there was no substance which
contained more prussic acid than the pips of apples, the
quantity differing according to the nature of the apple;
some descriptions of apples containing it in a great quantity,
and in such a form as, in the human stomach particularly, if
swallowed whole, or but slightly masticated, would render
its smell imperceptible. Mr. Cooper concluded, that because
he extracted one-fourth of a grain from a portion of the contents, the rest of the contents contained it in the same ratio,
that the acid was equally diffused through the whole, and
that if he was right in his recollection of the quantity he
had used in the former experiments, a fourth of a grain
would prove the existence of an entire grain in the entire
contents. Now, seeing that he only spoke from recollection
of the quantity, and seeing also that he had admitted in his
evidence that he found very little of the acid the first time,
more the next, and still more the third, thus showing that
as he got nearer to the bottom of the contents he got more
of the solids, and of those portions of the contents that would

produce prussic acid,—observing these things, which he (Mr. Kelly) begged of the jury calmly to do, he did think it was not evidence upon which they could agree to take away the life of a fellow-creature.

In opposition to this evidence the learned counsel replied on that given by Mr. Thomas, in which that witness admitted that he had extracted half a grain of prussic acid from the pips of fifteen apples, and on the possibility of accounting for the presence of prussic acid in the contents of deceased's stomach by the fact of apple and other substances containing prussic acid having been found in those contents. Supposing that the pips of the apples produced a fourth of a grain; suppose there was some little in the cake which she had eaten; suppose there was some in the saliva which she must have swallowed in a large quantity when masticating the apples, and which was known to contain much prussic acid; suppose there was some in the animal substances, and although it was stated that they would not yield prussic acid without being subjected to a greater heat than they had been subjected to, yet it was known that when undergoing decomposition prussic acid was constantly being evolved; suppose these things, put together all these probabilities, keeping in mind that they had positive evidence that the pips of fifteen apples produced half a grain of prussic acid, and he asked them how they could, if they did not wish to commit murder themselves, convict the prisoner of that crime? Again, there was the fact that the woman was in a state of syncope, and that she was choked by her neighbour pouring water down her throat. Again, how many causes of sudden death were there? The late Serjeant Andrews, in a moment of aberration of mind, cut his throat. The wound was sewn up, but a few days afterwards it burst out afresh, and he died. Who could doubt that the cause of his death was the cutting of his throat? But on investigation it turned out that the cause of death was the rupture of a blood-vessel. Suppose a person had been tried for inflicting that wound, and the coincident fact had not been revealed, would not the person have been in danger of being convicted of murder? Therefore, the jury should be cautious, and take into consideration all the coincidences of this case. His learned friend had imputed to the prisoner a motive for committing murder. Now he would not deny that by the deceased woman he had two children. That was an act of immorality, and if the prisoner had not bitterly repented it, he had at least bitterly suffered for it already. He allowed that woman about 1*l.* a week. Would the saving of that sum be a sufficient reason with a person in his circumstances to commit murder? And would it be politic in him to destroy her, and bring upon himself the care of bringing up his children, and of introducing them perhaps into the family of his present wife? Then as to his circumstances, the evidence of the banker's clerk had shown that they were not embarrassed.

Mr. Kelly then proceeded to contend that the prisoner supposed the deceased to be acting when he left, and that to alarm him she might have pretended to put something in the stout, camphor, for instance, of which one of the phials found in the house smelt. Not that he meant to imply that the woman had poisoned herself; for he did not believe she had died of poison at all, but from some one of the many causes of sudden death. As to other circumstances, true he evaded, and when he did not evade he told a direct untruth. But was that evidence against him of having committed murder? He had an affectionate wife at Berkhampstead, with whom and his children he was living happily, when the police officer challenged him, and he for the first time heard of the death of the woman, and it was natural for him, coupling the recollection of his former life with it, a life upon which he could not fall back, to deny any knowledge of the deceased. In common justice, while they could not justify his departure from truth, it would be uncharitable to conclude on that account that he was guilty of murder. True he bought Scheele's acid. Why? He suffered from varicose veins in the leg, and it was prescribed for him. Besides, he had been in the habit of purchasing it at the same shop for more than a year. There was no proof that he had that prussic acid at Slough. If the prisoner had evaded and departed from the truth, he hoped the jury would not on that ground conclude he had committed murder. A man might commit an offence in early life and retrieve himself; he might under painful circumstances be guilty of subterfuge; but he rested the defence of the prisoner mainly upon these confident grounds, that there was neither motive nor temptation to so horrible a crime, and that the jury would not be the first to break through that great and blessed principle of justice, that where there was a doubt the accused should always have the benefit of it. Looking to the nature of the case, and the doubts and uncertainties with which it was surrounded, he did confidently expect a verdict of acquittal.

Witnesses to character were then called, and the court adjourned.

On the meeting of the court the next morning Mr. Baron Parke commenced his charge. The summing up of the learned judge is often referred to as one of the most concise, and at the same time masterly and exhaustive expositions of the duties of a jury in criminal cases that have been delivered. It is given, the principal parts at least, nearly verbatim.

The learned judge proceeded to say that it now became their duty to give their deliberate consideration to the merits of this important case, and to pronounce upon the guilt or innocence of the prisoner, who stood charged with a crime which he might say was unparalleled in the history of human wickedness. The question was one of fact and entirely for their consideration, because, as they were aware, they were alone the judges upon all questions of fact. He would state to them such questions of law as were necessarily connected with the decision of the case; and it would be their duty to receive and act upon the propositions he would lay before them in that respect. He hoped, and he was sure he was not wrong in believing, that they would dismiss from their minds every impression that might have been created upon them out of doors, either from what they had heard in conversation or read in newspapers in reference to this case. He also felt it his duty to warn them against the impressions sought to be made upon them yesterday by the able and ingenious speech by the prisoner's counsel. They were aware that the law respecting criminal trials had been recently altered. So far back as the history of the law went, and during the greater portion of his (Mr. Baron Parke's) professional career, which was not a short one, the practice had been this—the counsel for the prosecution simply stated the

case, but without drawing any inferences, in order that the
jury and the prisoner might be informed of the facts to be
given in evidence against him, thus abstaining from any
observations that could influence the mind of the jury one
way or the other; the counsel for the prisoner was at liberty
to cross-examine the witnesses and raise objections in point
of law : the result of which mode of trial was, that the minds
of the jury were brought to the consideration of the case
uninfluenced by any observations not absolutely called for
by its merits.   It had pleased the legislature to alter that
mode of conducting proceedings in criminal cases, and he
was far from objecting to the alteration, which he thought a
wise one.   By that alteration counsel for the prisoner were
now at liberty to address to the jury such observations as
they pleased on behalf of the accused; the result of which
was to throw an additional and a difficult duty upon the
judge, for whom it became necessary to assume a line calculated to dissipate the effects which those observations as far
as they appealed merely to the feelings of the jury, might
have produced upon their minds.

Having said so much respecting the nature of their duty
he would tell them what the case was, and how it was to be
proved.   It was to be proved by circumstantial evidence—
the only evidence, as they had been told, which in cases of
this kind could possibly lead to the discovery of the truth.
The crime was one which no human eye observed, and which,
like most atrocious crimes, was committed in secret.   The
law had therefore wisely provided that direct proof was not
necessary.   On the other hand, it was equally true that the
circumstantial evidence should be so clearly proved, and so
closely connected together, as to satisfy the mind of a jury
as much as if they had positive evidence of the fact.   This
being the case, he would recommend them to act upon the
rule which he always laid down, viz., first to consider the
facts which had been distinctly proved, and then to consider whether all those facts were consistent with the
supposition that the prisoner was guilty of the offence
charged.   If they thought those facts all consistent with
that supposition—if they thought at the same time that there
was nothing inconsistent with it, and he could offer nothing

for their consideration, except the previous character of the
prisoner, and the supposition that no man could be guilty of
so atrocious a crime, which should weigh but little, as they
knew that such crimes were committed—then must they see
whether those facts were inconsistent with the prisoner's
innocence, taking care to remember that the existence of the
crime was not inconsistent with the other facts of the case.

The prisoner's counsel admitted those facts, but insisted
that it was a rule of law that there should be positive proof
of death having been caused by poison, and of the presence
in the stomach of a sufficient quantity of poison to produce
death. That was not true. It was not necessary to give
direct and positive evidence in every step of the case; because
between such and circumstantial evidence there was no difference, if the latter satisfied the jury that death was
occasioned by poison. It was not necessary to prove what
quantity of prussic acid would destroy life by the testimony
of a person who had actually seen a human life destroyed by
it; neither was it necessary to prove that such a quantity as
would destroy life had been found in the stomach. The jury
should consider all the facts of the case together, and decide
in their own minds whether the prisoner had or had not
administered poison to the deceased, and whether she had
died from its effects. The only fact required to be positively
proved was the finding of the body, when such was possible—
he said possible, because in the case of a man being thrown
overboard at sea, the body could not be found.

The learned judge next addressed himself to the facts of
the case. The prisoner at the bar, he said, stood charged
with the crime of murder by administering prussic acid. It
was not necessary in point of law that proof should be given
that the precise poison named had destroyed life. The
inquiry was the same whether the prisoner was charged with
destroying life by poison or by prussic acid. He agreed with
the learned counsel for the prisoner that it was necessary to
prove that poison had been administered; and then came the
question whether it had been administered by the prisoner
or the deceased herself. The only allegation that she had
administered it was made by the prisoner, and if the jury
thought his extraordinary story of the matter true they

would give him the benefit of such belief. If, on the other hand, they thought his story untrue, then they would have to see whether upon the whole facts of the case they could come to the conclusion that he had administered the poison himself.

The learned judge then referred to the testimony of Mrs. Ashley and other witnesses, showing that the deceased was in good health previous to the discovery of her lifeless body, and also to the testimony of Mr. Champneys, from which it might fairly be inferred that her death was not the result of any internal disease or any natural causes. Supposing it occurred from prussic acid (and the learned judge quoted the evidence upon the point), they had the statement of the counsel to deal with that it might have been generated in the stomach. Let them see what was opposed to that. They had the evidence of two witnesses, Messrs. Champneys and Pickering, to the effect that they had observed the smell of prussic acid in the stomach of the deceased the day after her death. They had the evidence of Mr. Cooper to show that on the next day, by the application of an infallible test, he discovered the presence of prussic acid in the contents of the stomach. They had also evidence to show that the quantity of apples he found therein was very small, that he discovered no pips amongst it, that it was in the pips only that prussic acid was contained, and that prussic acid could only be obtained from them when subjected to the process of distillation. This was very strong evidence to show that prussic acid could not have been produced in the stomach by the distillation of apples—prussic acid having been smelt by two medical men before it was possible for it to have been produced from distillation.

The jury should also look to the moral evidence of the fact that prussic acid was found very soon after a sudden death for which the presence of prussic acid would account. They must, moreover, in considering this part of the case put all the facts of it together; they must look to the previous conduct of the prisoner, and to the circumstance of prussic acid having been in his possession on the day of deceased's death, and not in his possession on the following day. With regard to the alleged differences of opinion as to whether the smell of prussic acid was a test or not of its presence, he thought they could come to no other conclusion after the evidence they had heard than this—that smell was a proof of its presence, but that the absence of smell was no proof of its absence. Mr. Champneys could not smell it when the froth was on the porter, but could when the froth was removed. Mr. Nordblad poisoned two dogs, one with three the other with twelve grains of prussic acid; put his nose to their mouths after death, but did not perceive any peculiar smell. Mr. Champneys put his nose to the mouth of the deceased, but did not discover the smell of prussic acid, which he afterwards did discover in the contents of the stomach.

They had been told that they must have proof of that fact from persons who had had practical experience upon the subject, and who had absolutely witnessed deaths from prussic acid. They had also been told that they must have direct proof of the presence of such a quantity of prussic acid in the stomach as would cause death. But the law did not require any such proofs. The jury had heard the evidence of several scientific men—of men who had read the most authentic works upon the subject, and some of whom had tested the opinions contained in those works by experiments on animals; and it was for the jury to say whether they were satisfied with that evidence, because, if they were, it was in conformity with the law. Those gentlemen were of opinion that a very small quantity of prussic acid—a grain, or even less than a grain—where taken into the stomach, was sufficient to cause death. Then they had Mr. Cooper stating in evidence that from the experiments which he had made he had not the slightest doubt that the stomach of the deceased contained at least a grain, if not more, of pure prussic acid. On the 8th of February, after previous experiments on portions of the contents of the stomach in which he discovered prussic acid, he made further experiments upon the remaining contents of the stomach, and found in them also prussic acid, the precise quantity of which he ascertained. Adding to this evidence the fact, which they all knew from persons who had tried experiments, that a very small portion indeed of prussic acid was sufficient to destroy the life of animals, and suddenly; then coupling with that fact the circumstance of prussic acid having been taken by the deceased before seven o'clock on the evening of the 1st day of January; then adding to all the entire conduct of the prisoner throughout the transaction, it would be for the jury to say whether they had any doubt upon their minds that the poison had been administered by him, or whether they believed that it had been taken by the deceased herself.

The learned judge then reminded the jury what the entire conduct of the prisoner had been, beginning at his first interview with the waiter at the Jerusalem Coffee-house, succinctly tracing his movements to the close. When coming out of the house in Bath Place on Wednesday evening, immediately before the deceased's death, he was seen and met by Mrs. Ashley, who said he was much agitated. When he got from that to the railway station at Slough he returned in an omnibus as far as the turn to Herschel-house under the excuse of going there, but to which he did not go, having come back to the station in time for the quarter to eight o'clock train. When taken into custody next day he made a false representation for some purpose or another. Whether his object in doing so was merely to keep from his wife the knowledge of his visits to Bath Place, or whether he was desirous of concealing from every one the fact of his having gone there on the particular day in question, was for the jury to determine. When taken into custody he denied that he was known to any one at Slough. That might have been true to the letter, because it was not at Slough, but near it, that the deceased had resided; but then why did he tell a deliberate falsehood in stating that he had not left London that day at all? It was for the jury to consider whether his doing so did not show that he had been guilty of some act which required concealment. It might be quite true that he did not wish to have his visits to a woman who doubtless had formerly been his mistress known to his wife, or even to anybody else; but if he had been a perfectly innocent man and present at the death of the deceased, one would think that he would have replied at once to the remark "that he had been seen at Slough, and that a dead woman had been found there," by saying that he happened to have been there when her death took place.

He, however, stated that he had not been there at all, although by his subsequent story to the police-officer Perkins, he admitted having been at her house immediately before her death, and even said he had seen her pour something from a small phial into her glass as if she intended to poison herself. It was to be observed that he mentioned nothing of this extraordinary statement until after he had been brought to Slough and had had a consultation with his counsel. If the story were true, one would suppose that instead of walking away from the house and denying he had been there at all, he would have waited to see if the deceased really had taken poison, and be the first to call for assistance.

It had been said that he was in the habit of purchasing prussic acid from Mr. Thomas, the chemist, for varicose veins in the leg, and that his having purchased it on the 1st of January was no evidence of his having administered it to the deceased. True it was that he might have varicose veins in the leg, although they had received no evidence of the fact, and that prussic acid might, as stated by Mr. Thomas, allay the irritation produced by varicose veins, although it was no remedy for the disease itself; but from the evidence it appeared that on the day the deceased was poisoned, poison was in the possession of the prisoner, and that on the next day he had none. With regard to motives, no motive could justify or palliate such a crime as that with which the prisoner was charged, nor was it necessary for a jury to discover the motive which might have led to its commission. The jury, however, might consider how far such motives as were alleged in this case could have influenced the mind of the prisoner. It was stated in evidence that the deceased had been in the service of the prisoner during the lifetime of his former wife, whom she had nursed in her illness; that after her mistress's death the deceased became pregnant and bore a child to the prisoner; that the connection continuing she became pregnant again, and that during that pregnancy a very remarkable scene occurred which showed the attachment of this unfortunate woman to the prisoner. As described by a witness who was present at the interview, the prisoner, sitting down beside the deceased, told her it was of the utmost importance to him that her pregnancy should not be known, as he was desirous of being married to the lady who was at present his wife, and that he was further desirous of becoming a member of the Society of Friends, whose dress he wore. She at once consented, adding that in order to effect his wish more completely she would remain out of the world altogether, and that she would conceal her future place of residence even from her own mother, who absolutely did not know where her daughter lived at the period of her death.

She went to reside in Crawford Street and was there delivered of a second child. It then appeared that the prisoner made her an allowance of 13*l.* a quarter, and was in the habit of paying it, and that he paid it on the 30th of last September at Bath Place, where she had removed from Crawford Street, but that he had since overdrawn his account at his banker's, and that on the 1st of January he did not pay the 13*l.*, the motive suggested being that he was under pecuniary embarrassments. But a few days after he had overdrawn his account at his banker's he had a bill for 600*l.* discounted, which restored his credit. Besides, who could say what his feelings were on the 30th of September or on the 1st of January, when he went to Bath Place? He might have gone there with the mixed feeling partly of being prepared to pay the money, and partly, if the opportunity occurred, to commit the crime and not pay the money. On the 1st of January he might even have gone down with the intention of paying the deceased her quarter's allowance; and they knew that when taken into custody he had 12*l.* 10*s.* in his pocket, besides some silver.

The learned judge then read his notes of the evidence to the jury. As his lordship proceeded he remarked, with regard to the suggestion made by the prisoner's counsel, that the deceased might have been suffocated by the pouring of water down her throat while in a state of syncope—that such an hypothesis could not be entertained after the evidence of Mrs. Ashley and Mrs. Barrett.

Upon the evidence of the witness as to the experiments he made to obtain prussic acid from apple-pips, the learned judge remarked that it was of no weight, inasmuch as prussic acid was proved to be in the stomach before it could have been created by apple-pips, if there were any such present. The sudden death of the woman put that point out of the question. As to the suggestion of the deceased having died from a sudden emotion of the mind, or from any other cause of sudden death, surely the jury could not entertain it while there was evidence before them of an agent sufficient of itself to cause death.

The learned judge next read the evidence respecting the alleged motive for the commission of the crime, and the history of the connection of the prisoner with the deceased, and then concluded by saying :—" That, gentlemen, is the whole of the case. I have read to you all the material evidence; and now it is for you to form your conscientious opinion, as reasonable men holding the scales of justice evenly between the public and the prisoner. If the evidence leaves any rational doubt on your minds, any doubts which as sensible men you ought to entertain, not a trivial doubt, not a doubt resting only on speculative ingenuity, but a rational doubt, you are bound to give the prisoner the benefit of it. You must have respect to all the circumstances of the case, and particularly to the presence of the prisoner just before the death of the deceased, and the presence of prussic acid in her stomach. You must consider the conduct of the prisoner both before and after the death of the woman ; and if all this evidence leaves any rational doubt on your minds, God forbid that you should not give the prisoner the benefit of it ! It is your duty to do so ; for you are not bound to convict any one except upon evidence which leaves no rational doubt of the guilt of the party upon your minds. But if you think you cannot explain all the circumstances of the case, if you cannot explain the presence of prussic acid and the conduct of the prisoner, and if you think his explanation unworthy of credit—if you believe in your conscience that the prisoner is guilty of the offence with which he is charged—it will be your duty, for the sake of public justice, that the administration of public justice may not be disparaged, and that the confidence of the public in that administration may not be shaken by a person not being convicted upon evidence which, upon due deliberation, is calculated to produce an impression that he was guilty."

Mr. Gunning (one of the prisoner's counsel) reminded his lordship that the prisoner had received a good character for humanity of disposition from several witnesses.

Mr. Baron PARKE.—Yes, gentlemen, there is one circumstance to which I have adverted in a general way before, the good character the prisoner has had. It is evidence in a case of this kind, because it goes to show the impression which the habits of a man have made upon the minds of those about him as to his disposition. The prisoner is reputed to have been a benevolent person. It is admitted by the learned counsel who defended him that he was formerly convicted and transported for some offence; what that was we have not been told, but it is said that it was not one which would affect his character for kindness of disposition (a).

The jury then retired for consultation, and in half an hour returned into court with a verdict of GUILTY. Sentence of death was then passed. The prisoner remained almost unmoved. The verdict generally was considered just, and was confirmed afterwards by the confession of the prisoner.

On the 28th of March, 1845, John Tawell, according to contemporary reports, was suddenly thrust out on to the scaffold in front of the Aylesbury County Hall, and there executed, twenty minutes before the proper time, so suddenly and quietly that some little time elapsed before the greater portion of the multitude was aware that the operation had commenced. He left a confession in writing—" Not to be made public in any way, but the purport to be disclosed."

(a) It has been shown in the Introduction what this offence really was.

THE TRIAL

OF

LOUIS BONAFOUS,

IN RELIGION

FRERE LEOTADE,

FOR THE MURDER OF CECILE COMBETTES,

AT THE ASSIZES AT TOULOUSE (HAUTE GARONNE),

BEFORE M. DE LABAUME, PRESIDENT,

On February 7th, 1848, and following days.

Counsel for the Prosecution: M. *D'Oms* and M. *Delquie.*

For the Plaintiff in the civil action seeking damages (*partie civile*):
M. *Joly* and M. *Rumeau.*

For the Prisoner: M. *Gasc* and M. *Saint-Gresse.*

INTRODUCTION.

THE case of Leotade is generally considered an instance of one of those judicial errors which are to be met with occasionally in our own, but more frequently in French criminal history. It is very little if at all known in this country. The trial is inserted with a view more especially of affording a comparison between the French and English systems of procedure in criminal cases, and also with a view of rendering the case of Leotade more generally known to English readers. As an instance of curious circumstantial evidence, the trial possesses in itself a considerable amount of interest, and is besides remarkable for having given rise to more controversy than any criminal trial that has taken place in France since the trials of *Calas* and *Lesurques.*

In the following Report much that is irrelevant to the real point in dispute—the guilt or innocence of *Leotade,* and not the merits or demerits of the religious community to which he belonged—has been omitted altogether. The evidence, which is very voluminous, has been sifted and condensed, and the order in which the witnesses were called has been slightly altered. The published reports of the trial are very perplexing. Witnesses proving facts against Leotade and witnesses proving facts in his favour seem to have been called indiscriminately, without order or method. For instance, two or three witnesses would be called in succession to depose against the character or habits of another witness who had given evidence against Leotade : which would be followed up by an inquiry whether or not Léotade was exempted from a certain duty which he particularized in accounting for the employment of his time on the day in question : which again would be followed up by another inquiry whether the doctrine of passive obedience held by the members of the community to which he belonged would require or justify the giving of false evidence. All this has been omitted; and as far as possible the pith only of the evidence affecting Leotade given by each witness has been inserted, first the witnesses for the prosecution, and then the witnesses for the defence, entirely ignoring all collateral issues.

The facts of the case are rather intricate, but some care has been taken in order to make them in the following outline as clear and intelligible as possible.

On the morning of the 16th April, 1847, at about six o'clock, the body of a young girl was found lying in the Cemetery St. Aubin, at Toulouse, in the angle formed by the meeting of two walls. One of these walls belonged to the garden of a religious corporation, which will be referred to in the following Report as the Institute, and the other separated the cemetery fron the Rue Riquet. Both the walls were about the same height, and met at nearly a right angle.

The body, on examination, was found to be lying in a kneeling posture, on its face, supported by the elbows and knees. The feet were in the direction of the garden wall of the Institute, and the head was towards the wall separating the cemetery

from the street.   On further examination the body was identified as that of Cécile Combettes, an apprentice to a bookbinder named Conte.   A *post mortem* disclosed that the
deceased had been subjected to a brutal assault during
lifetime, and that the cause of death was fracture of the
skull.

In the hair of the deceased were found some leaves of
cypress, a few small shreds of tow or oakum, about four
inches in length, apparently frayed or cut from off the end
of a rope, and the petal of a geranium in full bloom.   The
summit of the wall separating the cemetery from the Rue
Riquet was constructed of a layer of branches of cypress,
which overhung the wall about ten inches.   A body thrown
into the cemetery so as to fall in the position in which the
deceased was found would come in contact with these
branches in its descent, and on examination it was found that
the cypress boughs had in fact been pressed down by some
falling body, and the end of one of them had scraped against
the outer surface of the garden wall of the Institute.   It was
thought from this to show that the body must have been
thrown from the garden, and not from the street, but in all
probability the cypress boughs would have been disturbed
by a body being thrown from the Rue Riquet as well as from
the garden, and therefore their having been pressed down is
not of much moment.   The fact of the leaves of cypress
being in the hair is, however, important as tending to show
that the body had been *thrown* over one of the two walls and
not *carried* into the cemetery.   This inference is, however,
rather weakened by the fact that the clothes of the deceased
were found carefully, and indeed neatly, packed between the
knees, in a way not likely to happen if the body had been
thrown ; and also by the fact that though the soil of the
cemetery was soft, it having rained heavily for several days
previously, there was not the slightest indentation or impress
made in it by the body.   On the other hand there were found
no traces of any footmarks, which there would have been if
the body had been carried.   Whether the body was carried
in or thrown over is one of the principal points of con-
tention and difficulty in the case.

On the top of the wall of the garden of the Institute were

found growing several plants of geranium, and one of these
plants was in full bloom, and had lost a petal. No geraniums
were found growing on the wall adjoining the Rue Riquet.
It was contended by the prosecution, and it must be admitted
with much reason, that a petal of geranium being found
wanting in one of the plants on the top of the garden wall,
and a petal of geranium of precisely similar character being
found in the deceased's hair, rendered it extremely probable
that the deceased had been thrown from the garden of the
Institute and not from the street. The feet of the deceased
were found pointing towards the wall of the garden, and the
head towards the Rue Riquet, which made it very unlikely
that if the body had been thrown over the wall from the *street*,
the hair could have caught a flower growing on the top of
the wall of the *garden*.

Immediately on the body being found an examination was
made of the interior of the Institute. At the foot of one of
the garden walls, within a short distance of the spot where
the body was discovered, were noticed traces as of a ladder
having been placed; and a ladder was subsequently found
in the garden which coincided with sufficient accuracy with
the impress on the soil; footmarks were also found on the
flower bed, of which at the time no explanation was given,
though a few days after the gardener admitted they were
made by him : and not far from the footmarks a piece of
rope. This rope was in colour similar to the pieces of tow
or oakum found in the deceased's hair.

On the previous day, the 15th April, at about a quarter
past nine in the morning, the deceased, in company with
her master, Conte, and another workwoman named Marion,
went to the Institute to deliver two baskets of books which
Conte had been binding. On being admitted by the porter
and the books taken inside, Marion was sent back to the
workshop, and Conte ordered the deceased to remain in
the vestibule to carry back the baskets. He himself, after
giving his umbrella to the deceased to hold, went into the
library with the books. On his return from the library the
girl was no longer to be found in the vestibule, though the
umbrella she had had left with her was standing against the
wall. The porter on being asked by Conte where she was,

said that very likely she had gone out whilst he was talking
to some one, or had gone to the *Pensionnat*, another part of
the same institution. He afterwards explained as a reason
for not taking more notice of the deceased that it was a
busy morning, being a fair day, and that the bell was constantly ringing.

At the time of the arrival of the deceased in the vestibule
there were five persons in the adjoining parlour. These persons were Frères Navarre, Laphien, and Janissien, and two
visitors, Rudel and Vidal. Frère Navarre afterwards stated
that he was standing in the doorway of the parlour with his
back to the vestibule, talking with the other *frères* and the
two visitors who were inside, when there came a ring at the
front door. He turned round and saw Conte enter with the
deceased and Marion into the vestibule. " Without changing
my place," he said, " and by merely turning my head over
my shoulder, I saw in the vestibule two females, one tall, the
other of shorter stature. I saw on the ground a basket of
books, which Conte was handling. I turned my head to
answer a remark of one of the *frères* in the parlour, and I saw
Conte enter into the court of the *Noviciat*, carrying a basket
with him. I happened to look into the vestibule at the same
time, and I no longer saw there the two persons who entered
with Conte, nor the porter, nor anyone."

The effect of Navarre's statement, therefore, is to show
that the deceased disappeared almost at the same instant
that Conte went up to the library with the books. Marion
undoubtedly went out immediately after her arrival into the
street; and it is quite certain that Cécile did not go out
with her. The porter stated that he locked the door on
Marion's departure, and then assisted Conte to carry up the
books into the library, taking the key of the door with him.
The deceased could not therefore during his temporary
absence have gone out of the vestibule into the street, though
it was possible for her to have entered into other parts of
the Institute.

From the time of the girl's admission into the vestibule
in company with Conte she was never afterwards seen alive,
except by her murderer, as far as either the prosecution or the
defence were able to show   Whether she went out when the

porter was engaged, or went to the *Pensionnat,* or where she went to, is a matter of conjecture. All that is known for certain is that she was never again seen outside the Institute alive. As far, therefore, as the evidence goes it certainly tends to localize the crime within the walls of the Institute, as the deceased undoubtedly was last seen alive in the vestibule, and it would therefore be imperative on the Institute to account for her, unless they could show she was afterwards seen to go out. This they endeavoured to do, and failed ; and to the injudicious and ill-advised attempts made on behalf of the Institute to prove that the deceased was seen to leave the establishment, the condemnation of Léotade may in a great measure be attributed.

In the first place, however, suspicion did not fall upon the members of the Institute, but upon Conte, a man whose character was notorious for depravity. He was arrested a few days after the discovery of the body, when he gave it as his opinion that the girl had been enticed into some disreputable place and murdered. On the next day, however, he sent for the magistrate, and then for the first time deposed that on his arrival at the Institute with the deceased he saw two of the brethren, Jubrien and Léotade, in the vestibule. On being confronted with Conte the two *frères* denied having been in the vestibule. They were however arrested, as was also Conte's other workwoman Marion, who, it must be noticed, on examination stated that neither Jubrien nor Léotade was in the vestibule when Conte and the deceased entered with the books.

The time of this arrival with the books, a matter of great importance, is fixed with some certainty, not only by the statements of Conte and Marion, but by independent evidence obtained inside the Institute. Navarre stated he left the hall to go to the parlour at five minutes to nine by the clock, and returned finally at twenty minutes past nine. During that time, however, he went, according to the *acte d'accusation,* twice to the parlour, first to see Vidal and Rudel, and afterwards with Laphien and Janissien, for whom the two visitors had asked when about to take their leave after the first interview. As this first interview, which is stated to have lasted a quarter of an hour, and to have commenced at five minutes to nine, would consequently have ended at ten minutes past nine, and then Laphien and Janissien had to be found and brought to the parlour, the second one would not commence until a quarter past. It was undoubtedly during this second interview that the deceased arrived in the vestibule, and as it was over at twenty minutes past nine, according to Navarre's statement, the time of her arrival is fixed, within the compass of five minutes, between a quarter and twenty minutes past nine. The time being thus ascertained, an important question arises, Where was Léotade at that moment? The prosecution asserted, in the vestibule ; Léotade himself that he was in the *Pensionnat*, occupied with the performance of his customary duties the whole of that morning, and was never in the *Noviciat* at all in the course of the day. Some discrepancy will, however, be noticed between Navarre's evidence as given at the trial and his original statement embodied in the *acte d'accusation*, rendering it extremely difficult to sift out what were really the true facts. The prosecution always averred that from the very commencement of the inquiries in the Institute they were surrounded by such an atmosphere of dissimulation and passive opposition on the part of the *frères* as to render the efforts they made to discover the truth almost abortive.

In order to show how the prosecution sought to bring the crime home to Léotade, it is requisite that some description of the interior of the premises should be given.

The Institute is divided into two portions, the *Noviciat* and the *Pensionnat,* each under a separate director. The two establishments are quite distinct, being separated one from another by a street, the Rue Caraman. The main entrance, and the one most frequently used, was in the *Noviciat,* from the Rue Riquet, by which Conte and the deceased had entered on the morning in question. From the *Noviciat* a tunnel runs under the Rue Caraman, affording a means of communication between both buildings. Assuming, therefore, the deceased once inside the vestibule of the *Noviciat,* it would be possible for her by means of the tunnel to pass from the *Noviciat* to the *Pensionnat.* On issuing from the

tunnel on the *Pensionnat* side of the Rue Caraman, a long
corridor is entered which leads into the garden, and immediately on reaching the garden, on the left hand, is an out-
building used partly as a stable, and partly as a sleeping
chamber for servants. To get to the stable part of the out-
building it is necessary to pass through the sleeping apartment of the servants. From one corner of the stable a
ladder leads to an upper chamber in which hay and straw
were kept. The theory of the prosecution was that Léotade,
having met the deceased in the vestibule of the *Noviciat*,
enticed her on some pretext or other into the tunnel, from
thence to the *Pensionnat*, and then along the corridor to the
stable; and that there in the hay-loft above the crime was
committed.

In support of this theory the prosecution gave in evidence
that on the body of the deceased being examined there
were found between the dress and the skin some straws of
wheat, on which there were signs of blood, and a feather.
Some particles of hay also adhered to the dress of the
deceased, and to her shoes, which on examination were
found to consist of or to contain clover. Now there were
wheat, straw, and clover in the loft over the stables, and
it was sought to be inferred from this that it was in
the stable the murder had been committed. In addition
there were found on the deceased's clothes, incrusted in
other matter, certain grains, which on investigation turned
out to be grains of fig, and on a shirt found in the *Noviciat*
were also found traces of grains of fig, similar in character
to those found on the deceased, and it was therefore assumed
the two articles of dress had been in contact. The shirt
in question was numbered 562, and was found in the *Noviciat*,
Léotade himself belonging to the *Pensionnat*, but amongst
the keys found in Léotade's possession was one which it was
discovered would open the door of the room where the clothes
were kept in the *Noviciat*.

Assuming the stable to have been the place of the murder,
the body would have to be left in the hay-loft above for the
remainder of the day, and in the night-time Léotade would
have had to descend from the dormitory where he slept into

the garden, and without being heard or seen by the servants who occupied a room communicating with the hay-loft, to have carried the body away and thrown it over the wall into the cemetery. It is a fact of some moment in considering the question of the guilt or innocence of Léotade, that on the 24th of April, about nine days after the commission of the crime, the *juge d'instruction*, in the course of his investigations in the interior of the Institute, asked Léotade to point out the room in which he slept. This Léotade did, and the result was to convince the *juge d'instruction* that it was not possible for Léotade in the night to have left the room without being seen, in order to go to the stable to dispose of the body. Later on, Léotade was asked to point out the room in which he slept on the *night of the murder*, when it appeared he then occupied a room from which it was *possible* to obtain access to the garden by opening two doors which were fastened by locks having the same key. Amongst the keys afterwards found in Léotade's possession, or under his control, was one which opened both these locks. The change of rooms took place on the 17th, two days after the murder. The reason assigned for it was that Frère Luc, who at the time of the murder occupied a room alone, had complained that he felt uneasy at sleeping in a room by himself, and that the director accordingly made him take Léotade's place, who was sent to sleep in another dormitory. The change of rooms appeared to have originated spontaneously with the director, Frère Irlide, and may have been done quite innocently. But the prosecution laid great stress upon it, and it probably pressed harder against Léotade than any other piece of evidence adduced against him in the whole course of the trial.

The inference drawn by the prosecution from all these facts was that Léotade, and Léotade alone, was guilty of the crime. It will be borne in mind that assuming the murder to have been committed in the Institute, the evidence pointed as strongly to Jubrien as it did to Léotade, both of them, according to Conte's statement, having been in the vestibule of the *Noviciat* when the deceased entered with the books. The prosecution, however, after arresting and examining

Jubrien, ultimately discharged him, as also Conte and the workwoman Marion, and thenceforward brought all the means in their power to bear upon Léotade.

The system adopted in the French courts of interrogating the prisoner for the purpose of obtaining a confession is one of the main features distinguishing the practice sanctioned in that country from the practice followed in England. The hardship and unfairness of it to the prisoner are particularly exemplified in the case of Léotade. There was scarcely a particle of evidence disclosed by the depositions taken before the magistrates in the first instance which affected Léotade, beyond the fact that he was one of two of the members of the Institute alleged by Conte to have been in the vestibule when the deceased arrived. In England it is very doubtful indeed whether he would have been committed for trial on such evidence. But in France, where a prisoner can be questioned and cross-examined day by day by an experienced magistrate, direct evidence against him is not a matter of such moment as it is with us. It is interesting to follow the course adopted in Léotade's case, and compare it with the English system.

On the 6th of August, after a long and tedious preliminary investigation, Léotade was committed for trial at the next assizes to be held at Toulouse. In the course of this investigation, and after his committal, he was subjected to close solitary confinement for upwards of 100 days, and not allowed to have any communication with his advisers. At intervals during his confinement he was subjected to repeated examinations. The magistrate conducting these interrogatories gave evidence at the trial as to what passed between him and Léotade, and his account is particularly characteristic of French procedure. After detailing the number of interviews he had with Léotade, M. Courbet, the magistrate, stated :—" I told him (Léotade) it was a brutal crime, and could only be accounted for by his being in a state of mind verging on insanity. ' Confess that you yielded to a sudden impulse which took away all your reason, and rendered you no longer master of yourself. If you are really guilty your situation, torn to pieces as you must be by remorse, is deplorable. Confess, and even after such an enormous crime you will find some peace of mind, *and may probably meet with some indulgence from your judges.*' Léotade listened to me with great attention, and replied, ' That may probably excuse the rape ; but the murder ! ' I said, ' Who knows that the author of the crime committed the murder as well ; the deceased may have thrown herself violently against the wall.' *I thought for a moment Léotade was on the point of making a confession.''* How different is all this proceeding to the humane course adopted in England, where a prisoner is fenced round with so many safeguards that it is sometimes by no means easy to get a confession in evidence !

The trial commenced on the 7th February, 1848, before M. de Labaume, President (*a*). The indictment charged Léotade with the murder of Cécile Combettes, and with assault with

---

(*a*) It is necessary here to observe that there were two trials of Léotade, one in February and the other in March in the same year, both lasting about twenty days. The first trial was very nearly completed— the evidence being entirely closed—when the Revolution of February broke out. The court then adjourned for about three weeks, when the evidence was repeated before a second jury, the only difference between the two trials being that in the first trial the jury had a view of the premises, and in the second they had not. The following report is taken from a very voluminous and apparently verbatim report, published at Toulouse by *Jougla*, and collated with that contained in the *Gazette des Tribunaux* for 1848. There is also a very accurate report, of which much use has been made, in the *Journal des Débats* for the same year. Some slight information has been derived from a work entitled *Mémoire Justificatif de l'Innocence du Frère Léotade*, by *Cazeneuve*, published at Toulouse in 1859. The author's aim is, however, entirely directed to making out a case for Léotade, and such portions only of the evidence are given in the work as suit his purpose. But the plans and diagrams are interesting ; and the work contains some documentary evidence not inserted in other reports. Copies of both the *Gazette des Tribunaux* and the *Journal des Débats* for 1848 are in the British Museum [pp. 9466, and pp. 9433 being the press marks for each respectively]. The plan accompanying this work has been taken from the one given in the *Gazette des Tribunaux*, with some slight alterations and additions ; but it is not easy to give a satisfactory description of the premises, owing to its being impracticable to show in a plan the formation of the two walls, one of the main features in the case. Nothing but an actual examination of the Institute garden and walls, and of the vestibule, will enable the very intricate evidence in the case to be thoroughly understood.

intent to commit rape, and with rape, varying the crime very much as in an English indictment. The *acte d'accusation* was then read, detailing at considerable length the facts of the case. In French trials, where no opening speech of counsel is customary, the *acte d'accusation* is generally a most efficient substitute, and frequently is prepared with great literary ability and skill. In the present instance the document had been drawn with more than ordinary minuteness and attention, and the reading of it occupied a considerable time. At the conclusion of the reading of the *acte d'accusation,* and before any witnesses were called, the President commenced a further interrogatory of the prisoner. This interrogatory, previous to any witnesses being called, is another peculiarity of French procedure, and as it stands out in striking contrast to the procedure in the English courts, some of the more important parts of it are given nearly verbatim.

The President.—Before the prosecution proceed to give evidence in detail of the various charges enumerated in the *acte d'accusation,* it is necessary to interrogate you on the various contradictions and tergiversations observable in your previous interrogatories. The court therefore appeals to your sincerity. Reflect before you make any answer, and remember that your replies will have a considerable effect on your ultimate fate. Were you acquainted with the deceased, Cécile Combettes ?

Léotade.—No, I never saw her or knew her.

The President.—Were you not in the habit of going to Conte's house?

Léotade.—Sometimes, on business for the Institute, but I have never seen there any of the apprentices, as far as I can remember.

The President. — You have already introduced that reservation into your preliminary examinations. Let the court have no equivocation. Have you ever seen, or have you not seen, any apprentice at Conte's house, and did you or did you not know the deceased?

Léotade.—No, I was not acquainted with her.

The President.—Is it true that a few days before the crime you were at Conte's house?

Léotade.—I do not remember.

The President.—I must now call to mind the object of your visit, which will refresh your memory. You went to ask Conte for a memorandum book.

Léotade.—I beg your pardon; I remember the circumstance now.

The President.—Did you not say on that occasion to Conte, "Send me the book by Cécile?"

Léotade.—Not having any knowledge of the deceased, I could not say so.

The President.—That remark of yours, if you had made it, would have implied two things; one is, that you were aware that Conte had apprentices, and the other that you were acquainted with one of them, as you mentioned her by name. Do you still mean to say you did not make use of that remark?

Léotade.—I have never seen any apprentice at Conte's house.

The President then passed on to the proceedings of Léotade on the day in question, all of which were enumerated by him in detail. The day commenced with mass, celebrated in memory of a deceased brother at Paris. After mass was breakfast, which finished a little before nine o'clock. At nine he went to the work-room to give out work for the pupils, and afterwards wrote a letter to his superior at Paris, containing his " Compte de conscience." [It is during this time, after nine and before twenty minutes past, that the deceased arrived in the vestibule, where, according to the prosecution, Léotade and Jubrien were present. The writing of this letter between nine and half-past by Léotade, the very time he was said to be in the vestibule of the Noviciat, is therefore a matter of importance, and the prosecution did all they could to disprove it.] At about half-past nine he went to the kitchen, where he remained until ten, and examined the bread. At ten he had seen the director of the Pensionnat, and had given him the letter for the superior. At half-past ten he fed the birds, got up some wood out of the cellar, and at eleven went to chapel. After chapel he had dinner, and after dinner went into the town, and on returning again fed the birds; and the rest of the day he passed in the observance of the usual religious exercises until bed-time. He did not go to bed at the same time as the other *frères*. He went to the cellar to get up two barrels for the purpose of sending for some wine from Saint-Simon the next morning, and did not go to bed until after the rest. He himself wanted the barrels, and they were gauged the next day (Friday) by Jubrien. On that night, therefore, he did not go to bed until after the other *frères*, but stayed up alone. In the course of this interrogatory, which is extremely lengthy, Léotade was examined, or rather cross-examined, on points which seemed at variance with his previous declarations, but none of them are of much moment, and any discrepancy may fairly be accounted for by the pressure that was put upon him during the course of his long solitary confinement. Léotade complained bitterly that he had been treated with much unfairness by the *procureur général* in the first interrogatories, and of the rigour of his solitary confinement, exclaiming, " *On me faisait pleurer au secret.*" The interrogatories then proceeded :—

The President.—On the 3rd of May, in answer to a question put to you, you said you had on at that time of the clothes worn by you on the 15th April only the stockings and *soutane*. Search was made for the drawers you had worn, which you said were in the work-room. They were not found there nor elsewhere, and on that point you have never given any explanation.—I remember now that on the 3rd May I still wore the same clothes I had worn on the 15th, except the shirt.

The President.—This is an entirely new version. Why did you not say so to the *juge d'instruction ?*—I was so much troubled in my mind I could not answer.

The President then proceeded to interrogate Léotade relative to an illness he alleged he was suffering from, which was likely to leave traces of blood on his clothes, which, however, does not appear from the evidence afterwards given to be of much importance. No blood was ever found on the clothes worn by Léotade on that day. The shirt he wore had been changed, and he was pressed closely as to when and where he had changed it, and to whom he had afterwards given it ; all of which questions were answered with clearness and decision.

The shirt to which any suspicion attached was that numbered 562, and found in the *Noviciat;* and there was an entire absence of any proof that Léotade had ever worn that shirt on the day in question. But he admitted that on the Sunday after the murder he did not put on the clean shirt given him because, as he said, it was too small, and irritated a blister he had, but he returned it to the *infirmier.* He was asked if he had any key which would open the lock of the door where the clothes were kept in the *Noviciat,* and replied he did not know. On his own keys being produced one of them was proved to open this particular lock, as to which he offered no explanation.

The President.—Were you in the vestibule of the *Noviciat* at a few minutes after nine on the morning of the day in question in conversation with Frère Jubrien ?—No, I did not leave the *Pensionnat* at all that morning.

The President.—Yet Conte is very positive on that point. He mentions the hour, the place, your position, and your dress. When before the *juge d' instruction* you heard Conte give all these details in evidence, you merely replied, " It is possible; I do not remember." And then you denied it. Jubrien being questioned, his statement confirms yours. Later on you deny having spoken to Jubrien on that morning. It still remains for the prosecution to know whether you were or were not in the *Noviciat* on the morning of the 16th of April ?

Léotade (with firmness).—I solemnly declare, and will declare up to the hour of my death, Conte has stated what is not true. I was not in the *Noviciat* on that day, and did not speak to the Frère Jubrien. I spoke to him on the 16th, but whether in the vestibule or not I do not remember. I had gone to the *Noviciat* to give some money to the shoemaker, but I met Jubrien in the corridor close by the shoemaker's workshop, and gave it to him instead. I do not know whether I had passed by the door of the room where the linen was kept before I met Jubrien. [It was always suggested by the prosecution that it was on this morning, the 16th, on the occasion of Léotade's visit to the *Noviciat,* when he passed close by this linen-room, that he slipped unnoticed into the room (of which he had a key) and got rid of the shirt No. 562, taking another one instead.]

The President.—You ought to be able to remember whether you spoke to him in the vestibule or outside. Consider the position in which you are placed by having such a good memory for certain events and so little for others.

Léotade.—I cannot remember.

The interrogatory then passed on to other points posterior to the day of the murder—Léotade's statements as to the footmarks in the garden, which it was sought to show he had in the first instance admitted to be his, and afterwards retracted : a visit made by him to Conte's wife on the day after the murder, and to a person of the name of Lajus, with whom it was endeavoured to prove he had held a conversation reflecting on Conte's character and antecedents. All these allegations and inferences he denied. On the whole Léotade's answers were given with firmness and precision, and he went through the ordeal without being entrapped into saying anything contradicting his previous statements on any important points, and without hesitation or confusion. It is quite impossible to give these interrogatories and answers in full, nor is it necessary. The only points of any moment affecting Léotade were,—was he in the vestibule of the *Noviciat* on 'the morning of the 15th when the deceased arrived? Was the shirt No. 562 found in the *Noviciat* his own, or could it be traced to his possession? And were the footmarks in the garden made by him? On the more important of these points Léotade's answers have been given nearly verbatim, and the rest may fairly be omitted.

The court then proceeded with the examination of the witnesses. The first witness called was a man of the name of Raspaud, the grave-digger of the cemetery, who deposed that on the morning of the 16th he, in company with Lévêque, the *concièrge*, went into the cemetery. His attention was drawn to a body lying on the ground near the angle formed by the wall of the garden of the Institute and that of the Rue Riquet. He at first thought it was some one praying, as the body was in kneeling posture. On examination it was found to be that of a girl, dead and cold. He touched it without interfering with the position in the least, slightly moving the head without moving the rest of the body. The body was lying on its face and knees, supported by the elbows. The head was towards the Rue Riquet, the feet towards the Institute garden. The body was lying across the angle formed by the two walls. The cemetery door was fastened when he got there; but there was a church in the course of building inside the cemetery, and the workmen were at work when he arrived. Lévêque went for the police, and witness remained near the body. Several persons came and climbed on the wall of the Rue Riquet whilst he was watching the body. The evidence of this witness was corroborated by Lévêque as to the position of the body, and by a *commissaire* of police, M. Lamarle.

M. Estévenet, surgeon, deposed that on the 16th April he arrived at the cemetery at about two o'clock. He examined the body and the surrounding walls and ground. What struck him first were some particles of dust or earth on the head and body of the deceased. He noticed on the wall of the Institute, on the side next the cemetery, below the level of the branches of cypress forming the top of the wall of the Rue Riquet, marks of friction and appearances as of earth having fallen from the wall. The particles of earth on the head and body of the deceased corresponded with the earth rubbed from off the garden wall of the Institute. He then procured a ladder and made an examination of the top of the wall of the Rue Riquet. He found no traces of any body having passed over the top; on the contrary, there were appearances which entirely negatived such a proposition. On the top of the wall, where it formed an angle with the wall of the Institute, there were some tall plants which had not been touched. On the top of the wall of the Institute there were plants of groundsel flattened down, and a plant of geranium. This latter had three flowers, one withered, the second not fully flowered, the third in full flower, but deprived of one of its petals. There was also found a plant nearly entirely rooted up, but hanging by one of its roots, and quite fresh. On the other, the garden side of the wall of the Institute, there was a brick on which plants were growing; these plants were pressed down. The appearance of the plants on the wall of the Institute generally gave the witness the idea that a body had passed over and flattened them. On examining the dress of the deceased he found a fragment of straw, and in the

inside of it, next the skin, some particles of clover. The body
was quite stiff.   He made a *post mortem* examination of the
deceased.   The witness then gave some important evidence
as to the condition of the body :—" The face was swollen, the
nose slightly crushed. Neither the mouth nor throat presented
any appearance of strangulation or suffocation.   There was a
depression about the left eyebrow.   Some dry earth was
incrusted on the surface of the skin, which was broken.
The left cheek was scraped, and earth incrusted on it ; the
lobules of both ears torn.   The wrists were bruised, and
showed traces of great compression; the hands torn and
scratched." The witness then gave some further evidence
to the effect that a felonious assault had been perpetrated on
the deceased.   " The stomach, on being examined, showed
that the follicles were developed as in the first stage of
digestion : the food would probably have been taken two or
three hours before death."   [This would bring the time of
the murder to about ten o'clock.]   " The throat, on being
carefully dissected, showed no signs of compression, and the
deceased had evidently been neither suffocated nor strangled.
There was a large bruise on the left temple, and about ten
others over the surface of the skull; the right parietal bone
and the occipital bone were fractured."   In his opinion the
wounds had been inflicted during life, and would cause almost
instant death.   He thought it possible that the body might
have been thrown from the garden of the Institute without
causing any depression in the soil of the cemetery : the head
might have struck against the inner side of the wall of the Rue
Riquet and so have broken the force of the fall. The weight of
the deceased would be about sixty pounds (French measure).
On being asked by the court the kind of weapon he thought
would inflict the wounds, the witness excluded the fist or
a stick, and thought it more likely to have been a hammer
or violent blow against a wall, or a fall from some height.
Asked as to some conversation with Léotade as to the footmarks in the garden, he said he believed Léotade had said
to him one day, but what particular day he could not remember, " It is probably we who have made the footmarks ?"
[Léotade, being interrogated, denied this, and said on the 16th
of April he was not in the garden with M. Estévenet, but on

another day, the day the ladders were seized, the 17th. The witness was, however, positive that Léotade made use of these words.]

[Evidence was then given as to the construction of the wall of the Rue Riquet and the garden wall, and of the flowers growing on each, and also as to whether there was the appearance of any recent fracture or breach on the top of either. The most important point was that on the top of the garden wall were found growing plants of geranium, one of which, in full bloom, had lost a petal, whilst on the top of the wall of the Rue Riquet there were no geraniums. There was a slight breach also on the top of the wall of the garden, and the appearance as if a hand had been placed there. The finding of the petal of geranium in the hair, and other articles on the dress and person of the deceased, was also proved.]

M. Gaussail, another doctor, corroborated M. Estévenet's evidence as to the examination of the body. He thought the deceased might have been thrown from the Institute into the cemetery without causing any impression in the soil, and without the clothes being disturbed. M. Filhol, chemist, deposed that from the state of the digestive organs he was of opinion that the deceased was killed about three hours after taking food. He had examined the clover found upon her, which was identical with the clover found in the stable of the Institute. The petal of geranium found in the hair was precisely identical with the flowers on the top of the wall of the Institute. He could not, however, state that the shreds of tow or oakum found in the hair were part of the piece of rope found in the garden. He had examined the shirt No. 562. The grains of fig on it were identical with those on the dress of the deceased.

M. Noulet, professor of botany, proved that there was a perfect identity between the particles of clover found on the deceased and the clover in the stable ; also that the grains of fig on the clothes of the deceased and on the shirt No. 562 were of precisely the same character. He stated that in nearly 200 cases in which he had made the experiment with the ordinary figs of commerce he had never found any grains identical with the grains found on the deceased and on the shirt. On being closely pressed as to this and the nature of the experiments he had made, the witness said, with much assurance, "I am positive that the grains on the shirt and the grains on the deceased's clothes proceeded from the same fig."

Ignace Martial Coumès, *brigadier de gendarmerie*, deposed that on the morning of the 16th April he was called to the cemetery, where he saw the body of the deceased. He detailed the position in which it was found. He afterwards went to the Institute and examined the garden. At the foot of the garden wall, near a building called the *Orangerie*, he found traces of "*numerous*" footmarks, and also the marks of a ladder having been placed. Several ladders found in the Institute were successively applied to the marks in the soil, and one of them corresponded with the marks. At the foot of the wall, near the angle formed with the *Orangerie*, was found a piece of cord recently cut. The witness asked some of the *frères*, and amongst others Frère Lorien, the gardener, if they could account for the marks. The gardener did not at that time assert that the footmarks had been made by him, but he did a few days after. The footmarks on the flower-bed were made by some person wearing shoes, and not clogs (*sabots*). On the same line as the footmarks witness also found traces of a ladder; both the footmarks and the impress of the ladder were freshly made. He asked the gardener who had made the marks with the ladder, and he said he did not know. As to the footmarks, a *frère*, whom he believed to be the Frère *Visitor*, said they would be made by *frères* who had been in the garden that morning, and had heard the noise in the Rue Riquet. Witness also examined along the garden wall in the direction of the Oratory, and found footmarks on the beds, and traces as if a person had tried to put his foot on the wall and had slipped. He asked the *frère* who was with him who had made these marks, and he could not tell; and then two *frères* came up and said they had made them that morning; they had heard a noise, and wanted to know what it was. Then the gardener came up, and said the marks on this side (near the Oratory) were made by him as he was trying to catch a mole; "but," said the witness, "when I asked him how he made them he put him-

self into a position which was not at all the position to catch
a mole in." Afterwards, on another occasion, witness was
making a further examination of the premises, and Frère
Lorien, the gardener, came up and said to witness spontaneously, "The day you asked me about the footmarks I said
it was not I who made them. I now, however, remember I
did make them." Witness then pointed out that on the 16th
Lorien was wearing *sabots,* and the footmarks were made
with shoes. The witness's deposition before the *juge
d'instruction* being put in, it was found that on the 16th of
April he had stated that there were only two or three footmarks on the flower-beds, and the traces of them were very
slight. The contradiction between his present statement
that there were "*numerous*" footmarks, and his previous one,
was pointed out to the witness by M. Gasc on behalf of
Léotade, but the witness was unable to give any explanation
of it.

Jacques Dinat deposed that on the morning of the 16th
he examined the top of the wall of the Rue Riquet. He
noticed a stake fixed on the wall, and some blades of
grass growing. From the inspection he made it was impossible in his opinion for the body to have been thrown over
the wall from the Rue Riquet. [The stake fixed on the top of
the wall (*piquet en bois blanc*) was fixed near the angle
formed by the wall of the Rue Riquet with that of the wall
of the Institute garden, and appears to have been placed
there for the purpose of taking measurements or levels, it
being proposed to extend the Rue Riquet. Without this
explanation it is difficult to understand why a stake should
have been planted on the top of the wall : being there,
however, near the angle, it formed an obstacle to a body
being thrown over from the street]. Witness was entrusted
by M. Lamarle with the examination of the cemetery. He
examined the ground along the wall adjoining the Institute
garden throughout its entire length, and at the angle formed
with the Rue Riquet, and .found no footsteps save those of
a dog. (Lévêque being also questioned on this point, said he
had examined the ground in the cemetery and found no
traces of any footsteps, though the grass was tolerably
thick).

Marie Combettes, the mother of the deceased, deposed that her daughter was fourteen years and nine months old. On the 15th, between half-past twelve and one, when witness came home, she learnt that her daughter was missing. Witness sent her mother to Conte's to inquire, and her mother *told* her on her return that Madame Conte had said there was no cause for alarm, as Cécile had often gone to the Institute before. Afterwards she sent her sister to the Institute, who told her on her return that the porter had said he had seen the deceased enter, but had not seen her leave. [It will be noticed that hearsay evidence is admissible in France : in fact a good deal of the evidence given in the course of this trial was hearsay evidence.] Witness deposed that about twenty days after the murder a woman came to her and expressed much sympathy for the loss of her daughter, and offered her money ; the woman said that some one else would give her more. Witness refused the money. She identified the woman who offered the money as a person of the name of Madeline Sabathier. [The prosecution laid much stress upon this offer of money, asserting the woman was an emissary of the *frères*.]

Guillaumette Gestas, a companion of the deceased and fellow apprentice, proved seeing her eating some bread and peas on the 15th, about eight or half-past eight in the morning [this was to fix as far as possible, from the state of the digestive organs, the time of the deceased's death]. She saw her leave the workshop at a quarter past nine. The witness stated she had never seen the deceased the subject of any attention on the part of Conte, nor had the deceased ever complained to her about him. Witness had been to the *Noviciat* two or three times, but had never been allowed to pass beyond the vestibule.

Roche Lafitte, in religion Frère Lorien, the gardener of the Institute, was then called. He was the first witness examined belonging to the community, and at the previous trial, owing to the serious contradictions that were apparent between his evidence and that of Coumès, he had been given into custody, and remained in prison until the close of the proceedings, nearly twenty days. It was expected that the interval between the first and second trial affording ample time for reflection, would have induced him to modify his evidence, and his examination was looked forward to with the greatest interest. The important point was that he claimed to have been the person who made the footmarks on the garden bed near the spot from which it was suggested the body was thrown, and that he stated this to Coumès on the morning of the 16th, whereas Coumès said it was not until some days after that Lorien acknowledged the footmarks. The suggestion of the prosecution was that Léotade having in the first instance admitted that the footmarks were probably made by him, found that it would be fatal to his case to continue to admit them, and sought to thrust the responsibility upon Lorien, who, being an old man and not at all suspected of the murder, might acknowledge them without any danger, and that Lorien was accordingly tutored by his superiors to admit having made the marks.

The witness stated that on the 16th he went to the garden about a quarter to eight. No one was there when he arrived, but the garden door was not locked. Whilst he was in the garden two *frères*, the Frère Sacristan and Frère Isolier, came in before eight o'clock. At that time Coumès had not arrived. The two *frères* went towards the wall of the cemetery, but witness having received an order from the director of the Novices not to allow any one to go near that wall, he would not permit them to approach. Witness, on his entering the garden, had himself gone to the wall, and had trod on the bed and made the footmarks. [Witness here remembered that another *frère*, the director of the *Noviciat*, had by this time also entered the garden.] He could not remember when Coumès arrived, but it would be about eight or a little after. Coumès did not ask witness who made the footmarks, but he (witness) spontaneously told him that it was he who made them. Being asked if he was sure, he said he was, and that there were *five frères* present who heard him. [On being reminded that he had said there were only three *frères* who had entered the garden, he added the porter to the number, and by counting himself as one, made up five. Coumès being here recalled and confronted with the witness, said it was impossible that he (Coumès) did not enter the garden before eight, as by that time all was over, and besides, two *frères* accompanied him into the garden, and when he arrived Lorien was at work. He (Coumès) then asked him who made the footmarks, and it was not until two days after the 16th, when again in the garden moving some boxes in the *Orangerie,* that Lorien came up and said it was he who made the footmarks.] The witness Lorien on being asked if on the 16th he wore shoes or *sabots,* said that he had been that morning to chapel in his shoes, in order to make less noise, but that on his entering the garden he had changed them in the *Orangerie* for *sabots.* The footmarks were, however, made with the shoes before he changed them. Asked why he did not give this explanation when before the *juge d'instruction,* when Coumès observed in his presence that he (Lorien) on that morning wore *sabots,* witness denied that Coumès ever said so. On being further pressed by the President, the witness became confused, and fell into other contradictions with the testimony of Coumès, and on the application of the *procureur général* he was given into custody.

Madeline Sabathier, the next witness called, was one who at the previous trial had also been given into custody for perjury, and had continued in custody until the end of the proceedings, when she recanted what she had said and was discharged. Of the witnesses called in the whole course of the trial, there was probably not one who so fatally damaged the defence as did this witness, apparently actuated by nothing but an excess of religious zeal. Her evidence at the first trial was to the effect that she had seen the deceased *outside* the Institute on the morning of the 15th ; had spoken to her, and had seen a man in a cloak come from the direction of the Institute (assumed to be Conte), with whom Cécile went away. If her evidence had been true, it was a complete exculpation of the Institute, for the crime then must have been committed elsewhere. Unfortunately for the *frères* they believed in the first instance that her testimony was correct, and it was curiously enough corroborated by another witness present in the vestibule at the time, who said quite spontaneously, actuated likewise by the same fatal excess of zeal, that he had seen the deceased go out, " and had stepped on one side to let her pass." Madeline

Sabathier was therefore set up by the Institute, though called by the prosecution, as *the* witness who was able to exculpate the whole body. Now it is obvious that even assuming them to have been entirely innocent of the crime, nothing could have been more fatal than endeavouring to prove a point of this importance which was not true, though they might have been quite innocent of any attempt at fabricating the evidence. In the second trial of Léotade, though the same evidence was not given by the witness, the effect of her previous evidence could not but have weighed on the minds of the jury, as the interval between the two trials was short, and her first evidence was well known, and public feeling had been terribly excited against the Institute in the meanwhile. The witness was besides reminded in court of her previous testimony before giving her evidence at the second trial, and indeed repeated it and retracted it (a).

Madeline Sabathier, after repeating the evidence given by her at the previous trial, which she confessed was not true [the evidence was to the effect that on the 15th she was passing in front of the Institute, about a quarter past ten, when she saw the deceased sitting against a wall, that she spoke to her, and that a man came up from the direction of the Institute, and took Cécile away with him], admitted she had been to the deceased's mother and had offered her money, but asserted it was her own, and she had worked for it. She then formally recanted her previous testimony, but said no one had influenced her to give it or tried to induce her to keep back the truth. That she had only spoken of seeing the man with the cloak because she had heard it talked about outside,

---

(a) It will probably be remembered that in the case of *The Queen* v. *Catherine Wilson* (C. C. C., Sept. 26, 1862), who was tried for murder before Mr. Justice Byles, this point, the fabrication of evidence, was referred to by him in his summing up, and he alluded to a very peculiar case which had come under his own knowledge. A man was put on his trial for the murder of a child against whom he had been heard to utter threats. The child suddenly disappeared, but the body was never found. The prisoner applied for an adjournment from one assizes to another, and was told that if he did not produce the child he would at the next assizes be undoubtedly tried for murder. At the next assizes the prisoner did produce a child, but it turned out not to be the child that was missing. He was therefore convicted, and mainly on the fact of his having fabricated the evidence, though the child in question was afterwards proved to be alive.

and that the money she had offered to the deceased's mother (four francs) was her own, and part of her monthly wages of 25 francs (which the President observed was very unlikely). She had been to the Institute twice, once to tell them what the report was outside, and to inform them of the evidence she could give, and the second time to return a book.

Anglade, in religion Frère Lacténus, deposed that he was porter at the *Noviciat*. On the morning of the 15th the deceased arrived with her master and a workwoman, Marion, with two baskets of books, about nine o'clock. Marion went out after leaving the books, but the deceased remained. He locked the door when Marion left, and helped Conte to carry up the books. He had the key of the door in his hand. When he came down again he did not notice whether the deceased was in the vestibule or not; there was a ring at the door, and he hastened to open it [when in a hurry this witness explained he notices nothing]. The deceased might have been there without his seeing her, as there were several of the *frères* there with their relations. He could not remember who was at the door when he opened it. It was a fair day, and several visitors called. When Conte came down from the library he asked for Cécile, and witness told him she had gone out without his seeing her. Conte said as she was gone he would leave the baskets. Pressed by the President, the witness became confused as to whether he opened the door with the key or without when he came from the library, and inclined to the opinion it was without the key, that is, that when he had gone up with the books, he had closed the door and not locked it, which was in contradiction with the previous portion of his evidence. When the Almoner called he spoke to him at the entrance with the door partly opened, and it was then in his opinion that the deceased passed out behind the Almoner and without witness seeing her. Asked to explain how this could be, when on coming down from the library he did not see the deceased in the vestibule, witness said it was still possible she might have been there without his seeing her. He admitted that when afterwards asked by relations of the deceased what had become of her, he had said that he believed he had seen her sitting in the parlour, but was not sure.

The President.—Explain yourself more clearly: in all probability it is you who know the secret of the whole affair. When you came down from the library, the door of the parlour was obstructed by some of the *frères*; you could not therefore see in. The deceased was not in the vestibule, according to your statement; why then did you say, when inquiries were made about her, that you had seen her sitting in the parlour?

Witness.—I thought I saw her.

The President.—Was it not to put a stop to the inquiries?

Witness.—No; I thought I saw her.

The witness further stated that he heard about the finding of the body the next morning about half-past seven or nearer eight, when the *commissaire* of police came for him to go to the cemetery to see if he recognized the deceased as having been in the *Noviciat*. He said he had, and that she had gone out without his seeing her. [The President contradicted him in this, and said at that time he said he had *not* seen her go out.] On the return of the witness to the Institute with Coumès he went with him into the garden, where Coumès noticed the traces of footmarks near the *Orangerie*, and Frère Lorien said they had been made by him.

The President here commenced another interrogatory of Léotade as to the changing of bedrooms after the murder, one of the most suspicious circumstances alleged against him, from which it appeared that the murder being committed on the 15th, the body discovered on the 16th, on the 17th Léotade was removed from the room he then slept in, from which communication with the garden and the stable where the body was hid was easy, to a room from which the garden was inaccessible.

Marion Rougmanac, the workwoman who accompanied the deceased to the *Noviciat*, stated they arrived there a little after nine. She merely entered, put down the basket she was carrying, took the cloth from the basket Cécile was carrying, and went out, leaving the deceased and Conte inside. Pressed as to whether if two *frères* were talking together in the vestibule she could have seen them from the position in which she was placed, she stated she remained only a short time, and had a large basket on her head, and

Conte was standing before her; she might therefore not have seen them. It appeared from a question put by Léotade at this point, that on the 18th the witness, on being confronted with him, had stated she had not seen any one in the vestibule but the porter, which the prosecution explained away by saying that at that time the prosecution did not attach much importance to the fact of Léotade and Jubrien being in the vestibule. The witness was only asked whether she saw anyone, not whether she *might* have seen anyone.

Bertrand Conte was the next witness called. It was on this man that suspicion in the first instance fell, and it was he who first threw suspicion on Léotade. His evidence was listened to with the utmost attention. After some minor matters had been deposed to, he stated that he arrived with Marion and the deceased at the Institute on the morning of the 15th, a little after nine. He rang at the bell, and all three entered the vestibule. The first persons he saw in the vestibule were Léotade and Jubrien talking together. Léotade had a small black scull-cap on his head (*calotte*). Jubrien had his back towards him, and had his hat on. Witness said to Jubrien "Good day," but was not certain he heard him. Léotade stood facing the entrance door and Jubrien facing the door leading into the court. Witness put down the baskets in the vestibule on the left of the porter's lodge, and told Marion she might go home. He placed his umbrella against the wall and told Cécile to wait until he returned. He then went with the porter (who carried the key of the front door in his hand) to the library. The director came, and witness remained with him half or three quarters of an hour. He had been there about a quarter of an hour when Jubrien entered and whispered a few words to the director, who gave a sign of approbation. When he had finished his business with the director witness said he was going that night to Auch, and if the director had any commissions for him there he would execute them. He then left and came down-stairs, and at the foot of the stairs found Lorien, who was washing his hands. In the vestibule the porter was sweeping. The umbrella he had left with Cécile he found still leaning against the wall. Witness said to the porter, " Where is Cécile?" The porter replied, " I don't know; perhaps she is gone out, or perhaps—pointing to the tunnel—she has gone to the *Pensionnat.*" Witness went into the parlour and looked for her. She was not there. He put down the baskets and went out, saying he would send Cécile to fetch them. [The witness then detailed the employment of his time for the remainder of the day. The defence always threw suspicion on some of Conte's proceedings after the murder, especially on a visit he made to his uncle's immediately after leaving. This uncle lived close by the Institute in a street (the Rue de l'Etoile) of very doubtful reputation, and assuming the deceased to have left the Institute she might have gone to Conte's uncle's house (by Conte's direction) almost without being seen, and that there Conte might have met her and murdered her. All this is, however, mere presumption, and is not supported by a particle of evidence beyond this, that the term of the deceased's apprenticeship was nearly out, and that Conte was alleged to have said he would carry her off before she left him.] The following is Conte's explanation of how he passed the rest of the day.

He first went to his uncle's and then to the *diligence* office to take a place that evening for Auch. He got home about half-past ten. On entering, his wife said, " Where is Cécile? " and witness replied, " She has probably gone to see her mother, who is ill." After breakfast he went to purchase some wheels in company with his uncle. [The defence laid great stress also upon this as unnecessary, the cart for which they were required not being yet made, and alleged that Conte's proceedings in going about contrary to his usual custom, and on matters foreign to his ordinary business were suspicious, and that he was acting with a view to proving an alibi.] He then went and bought a pair of shoes. On his return he saw his wife and the deceased's aunt. The latter said they had been to the Institute, and the porter had said he had seen Cécile sitting on a chair in the parlour, and had not seen her go out. One of the women said she was sure once Cécile entered the Institute, she would never come out. Witness to this replied that she should not speak ill of the *frères*; that the deceased had most likely gone out. The deceased's father then came, and they went together to the police. Witness suggested they should go to the Institute; the inspector said not, as the *frères* had not retained Cécile. Witness sided with the inspector, as he did not wish to throw suspicion on the Institute, and that evening, with the consent of the police and of the deceased's father, he went to Auch on business. On his arrival at Auch his first business was to take a place for his return. He had gone to Auch for the following purpose. Having occasion for money he had drawn two bills on the director of the branch of the Institute at Auch, and he had gone there to raise money to meet one of the bills which fell due on the 20th. He afterwards went to the director there and paid him the amount of one of the bills, 115 francs. [This journey to Auch was always a point regarded with great suspicion by the defence, and they alleged that Conte had no actual business there, and that it was unnecessary.]

On being examined by the President, witness stated he was on very good terms with the Institute. He was a musician. and was useful to them, and they in business matters were useful to him. He alleged as a reason for not saying in his first deposition he had seen Léotade and Jubrien in the vestibule, that he had not been asked. He denied that there was one of the *frères* standing in the doorway of the parlour masking the interior completely [in this being entirely in disaccord with Frères Navarre and Janissien] ; on the contrary, he said he saw in, and that there was a woman sitting there with a handkerchief in her hand. Witness being asked as to his knowledge of the habits and morals of the accused gave some deplorable details [which Léotade, in a speech of some little duration, and delivered with much emphasis and great appearance of truth, most positively denied.] Witness went on to state that he had other relations with the *frères*. He made for them account or memorandum books, for which he never charged. That Léotade, as *pourvoyeur*, had more need of them than the others had. One day witness said Léotade came to his shop and asked for one of these books, and witness showed him one, a very handsome one, which Léotade refused on account of his vow of poverty. Witness therefore showed him another much plainer, for which Léotade was to supply some parchment.

He asked witness what it would cost. He refused payment, but later on he said to Léotade, " You have a fine collection of rabbits ; you may as well give me one." Léotade promised witness one accordingly. Witness delivered the book about twenty days previous to the murder. Léotade never complained of or found fault with it, though witness saw him several times after he delivered the book.

The President.—Yet Léotade in one of his examinations has explained that the reason for calling at your shop on the 16th, the day after the murder, was that the book was imperfect, that there were not sufficient leaves in it.

Witness.—The book was quite complete. I could never understand the reason of Léotade's calling about it.

[In order to understand the exact bearing of this portion of the evidence, it must be remembered that the prosecution maintained that Léotade had promised Conte some rabbits ; that these rabbits were kept in the stable, supposed to be the place of the murder ; that Léotade having met Cécile in the vestibule, had enticed her to the stable on the plea of giving her the rabbits for Conte ; that he there murdered her ; and that his visit to Conte on the 16th was to warn Conte not to say he had seen him (Léotade) in the vestibule on the morning of the 15th. It is rather singular that both Léotade and Jubrien, both of them asserted to have been in the vestibule on the 15th, should both have called at Conte's shop the morning of the 16th within a few minutes of each other, and have asked to see Conte, both alleging reasons for their visit equally unlikely.]

The witness was then examined by the President upon points touching his own morality, and was obliged to admit facts against himself showing great depravity, but he asserted no one could say anything against him since the year 1840.

The President (to Léotade).—You have heard what this witness says. His evidence touches on some very important points, and particularly that you were present in the vestibule on the morning of the 15th, between nine and ten o'clock.

Léotade (with much warmth).—I do not wish to refer to anything the witness has said. All I can say is that he is telling what is not true. I was not in the vestibule on the morning of the 15th. In support of his testimony Conte refers to his antecedents from the year 1840 to the present time. I refer to mine for the whole course of my life. . Ask those who have known me in my own province, from my birth to the time of my first communion, and they will tell you that I was the only one out of sixty who was allowed to take the vows. This I owe, not to my ability or to my birth, but to my good conduct. It afterwards happened that missionaries came to my village. I listened to their exhortations, and as I had always an inclination to enter religion I communicated my wish to the *curé*, who caused me to be admitted as *novice* in the Establishment at Toulouse. There I remained three years, and afterwards I went to Mirepoix, where I remained another three years, from thence back to Toulouse to the *Pensionnat* as *linger ;* then I was appointed *pourvoyeur.* Léotade then continued with considerable animation to give details of his life, speaking with much force, and listened to with the greatest attention. At the conclusion of his speech the court adjourned amidst considerable agitation and excitement.

On the re-opening of the court Conte was again asked whether he was positive that on the morning of the 15th he saw Léotade in the vestibule, and he again stated he was certain of it. Léotade being questioned on the point denied it, whereupon

The President (addressing Léotade) said :—When Conte's statement was first made known to you, you contented yourself with saying that you did not remember. [The interrogatories administered to Léotade on this point were here read.] On the 18th you said, questioned on the same point, you were not in the vestibule nor in the parlour, you were in the *Pensionnat.* Confronted with Conte, who described your costume, you then said you did not remember. On the 23rd of April, asked again if between eight and ten in the morning of the 15th you were in the *Noviciat,* you said you were certain you were not there, and added you had not seen Conte since the Monday previous ; so that first you said " You did not remember," then you said " No," and then again, when Conte had described your dress, " that you did not remember."

Léotade.—It was not difficult to describe my dress.

The President.—But Conte said you wore your *calotte* and Jubrien his hat. Now the *frères* do not wear their hats except when they go into the town. It happens you did not on the 15th of April go into the town, and Jubrien did. [The President was evidently mistaken in this, as Léotade had, in giving an account of his employment on the 15th, distinctly stated he was in the town that day, though not in the morning.] Léotade in reply to this still maintained with much firmness that he was not in the vestibule, and that Conte was lying, to which Conte replied he had often found the *frères* out telling lies. Léotade then turned to the jury and addressed them with much volubility, saying he would rely on their verdict with confidence ; the witnesses would show whether it was he or Conte who was lying. The President remarked upon this that it did not follow because four or five witnesses spoke to a particular point they would necessarily prevail over one ; that the court did not estimate evidence by the number of the witnesses, but by the weight of the testimony. (La justice ne compte pas les témoignages; elle les pèse.) The following portion of a dialogue then took place between the President and Léotade on the relative positions of human and divine justice, disclosing a theory on the part of the President not a little startling. As no translation would do justice to this singular opinion it is given in the original.

Léotade.—Il (Conte) sera jugé plus tard par Celui qui nous juge tous.

The President.—Nous aimons cette confiance dans la justice divine, mais vous aviez jusqu'ici trop de tendance à l'isoler de la nôtre. *La justice divine est l'auxiliaire de la justice humaine, et si vous étiez frappé par les hommes, vous trouveriez dans l'autre monde la sanction de la sentence prononcée.*

Léotade.—J'ai confiance en Dieu; mais Conte a bien menti dans tout.

Léotade then proceeded with much volubility to deny that he had ever promised Conte rabbits. He had sold him them, and he was wanting to get paid for them before he paid for the book Conte furnished him with.

M. GASC.—Conte has stated that he saw a woman sitting in the parlour. How is it that he mentioned that in the first instance, and did not mention that he saw Léotade and Jubrien in the vestibule?

Witness.—I was not asked about it.

M. GASC.—When did the *juge d'instruction* inform Conte of the death of the deceased?

Witness.—On Sunday, the 18th.

M. GASC.—How is it then that on the 17th you began to entertain suspicions as to the cause of Cécile's death.

Witness.—I did not form any suspicions.

M. GASC.—But in your first examination, on the 17th, you said, "She very likely had been enticed into some disreputable place and there murdered."

M. D'OMS, *Procureur Général.*—It is not unlikely that Conte, though arrested on the 16th, may not have been informed of the death before the 18th, and what proves it is that he said, when arrested, "I do not know what the fate of the girl is, but whatever has happened I am innocent."

M. GASC.—But on the 18th, directly he learnt of the death, he exclaimed, "Ah! she has been assaulted and murdered."

M. SAINT-GRESSE.—Conte left on the evening of the 15th for Auch, to take up, according to his own statement, a bill which was not payable until the 20th: in doing this he spent 12 francs, and solely to settle a bill of 115 francs before it was due. [M. Saint-Gresse here read the depositions of Conte on this point, in which the *juge d'instruction* remarked to him how very suspicious this voyage appeared under the circumstances.]

The President.—When the prosecution has kept a person in prison for six months, it is evident that they had at the time strong suspicions against him. All this is, however, matter for your address to the jury.

M. GASC.—Was Léotade acquainted with Cécile?

Witness.—Yes, but whether he had spoken to her or not I cannot say. He knew her as he knew my other apprentices—by seeing her at the *Pensionnat,* and once I remember in the *procure* of Frère Luc, Cécile being present, dropped the cushion she used when carrying on her head the baskets containing books, and Léotade stooped and picked it up, and replaced it.

M. GASC.—In the first instance, on returning home, did Conte inform his wife that he had seen Léotade and Jubrien in the vestibule?"

The President, however, objected to the question being put, on the ground that it was useless, that he would not allow useless questions to be put, and that he was the sole judge whether a question was or was not useless. The question, therefore, though as touching the credibility of Conte on one of the main points of the case of some importance, was withdrawn. With this the examination of Conte concluded. At no other part of the trial was Léotade so much moved as during Conte's examination.

Jean Rudel, one of the five persons present in the parlour when the deceased arrived, deposed that he went to the Institute with a young man named Vidal to see Frères Navarre and Limen, on the morning of the 15th, about nine o'clock. He saw no one enter or leave whilst he was there. He was on the point of leaving, when Vidal remembered he wanted to see Laphien and Janissien, and Navarre went for them. He and Vidal then went again into the parlour, and talked there with the *frères* for some little time. No one stood in the doorway of the parlour during this conversation [contradicting Navarre and Janissien flatly on this point]. No one rang at the front door whilst he was in the parlour. There was no one in the vestibule when he left except Laphien, Janissien, Navarre, the porter Lacténus, and Vidal. The next day Frère Floride sent for him and Vidal to the Institute, where he found a musician named Crouzat. He was asked if he had seen Cécile, whose dress Frère Floride described to him. Both he and Vidal said they had not. When Frère Floride spoke to him about Cécile he said she had a blue neckerchief. He remembered that on going to the cemetery with Vidal, the latter said he wished to see if the body was that of the girl he had seen leave the vestibule, at which he (witness) was much astonished. Later on, the director at Lavaur spoke to him about the matter, and said as Vidal had seen her leave, witness ought to have seen her also. Witness replied, " Vidal may say what he likes ; he (witness) should not say he had seen her leave." The director then said, " Well, don't prevent Vidal from saying it." The director spoke to witness very sharply, and he (witness) ceased to go to the drawing class at the Institute in consequence, and though the *frères* had since sent for him he had not been there again.

The President.—I must here remark to the jury that the evidence of this witness is valuable, from the sincerity he has shown both in the first trial and in this.

Vidal, his companion, was then introduced. Except Madeline Sabathier, there was no witness who so seriously damaged the Institute, and especially some of the directors, as this witness. It was he who, as before stated, in the first instance corroborated Madeline Sabathier as to the deceased having left the *Noviciat.* Before giving his evidence he was warned by the President as follows :—

The President.—Your name has acquired in this affair an unfortunate notoriety : you have withdrawn your previous depositions. Remember that you are now going to be subjected to a further and decisive test. Speak the truth, therefore, calmly and sincerely.

Vidal then related his visit to the Institute on the 15th, at about nine o'clock, in company with Rudel. He had been in the Establishment three times, the 14th, the 15th, and the 17th. He remained in the parlour with Navarre and the *frères* some little time. They all left together and remained only three or four minutes in the vestibule before he and Rudel left. There was no one in the vestibule, and he did not hear the bell ring nor see the door open. No one could ring without his hearing. He saw neither the deceased, nor any girl or woman, nor the Almoner. The next day he heard that the body of a girl had been found in the cemetery, and he went to see it, and again the day following the 17th, but whether he went before or after seeing the *frères* at the Institute he could not remember.

The President.—Had you said to Rudel, " I want to see the body, to see whether I can recognize the girl whom I believe I saw in the vestibule ?"

Witness.—I said this on the Saturday, in the cemetery; it would be after I had left the Institute.

The President.—When you were at the Institute on the 17th, and being interrogated, did you say you had not seen the deceased?

Witness.—I said to Rudel I *believed* I had seen her. It was then that the idea first came into my head.

The President.—But you said to the *frères* at the Institute you had seen no one. Did they describe the deceased's dress to you?

Witness.—They said she wore a blue neckerchief with white spots.

The President.—From thence you went to the office of the *diligence* for Lavaur, where you saw a man named Bonhomme?

Witness.—Yes, and I said to him that I had seen the deceased.

The President.—Did not Rudel express himself much astonished that you should see what he had not seen himself?

Witness.—Yes. But I had got the idea into my head that I had seen the deceased, and I believed it.

The President.—But when a person does not habitually tell falsehoods, he does not believe he sees anything that he does not in fact see. Had any one asked you to say you had seen the deceased?

Witness.—No one.

The President.—Did you really see her or not?

Witness.—I did not.

The President.—Did you see the empty baskets in the vestibule?

Witness.—Yes.

The President.—Did you really see them, or do you merely believe you saw them?

Witness.—I am certain I saw them.

The President.—I very much fear you did not see the baskets either, as you must in that case have seen the deceased also.

Witness.—I am quite positive I saw the baskets.

M. GASC.—His statement is positive on this point.

R

The President.—There is always a danger when a witness has once commenced a system of untruths. He has been living all alóng in a world of illusions, and I am quite justified in asking him whether what he is saying belongs really to the domain of truth or falsehood. (To the witness.)—Vidal, you have deposed before the *juge d'instruction* that it *appeared* to you you had seen the deceased leave the vestibule, and since you have stated that it was a falsehood. Do you now tell the jury that what you said at the first trial was untrue?

Witness.—I did not see any one. What I said then was false.

The President.—And you all five left the parlour together.

Witness.—Yes.

The President.—If therefore you did not see any one, the others could not have seen any body either.

Witness.—No.

M. Gasc.—I wish to observe that Vidal saw the baskets: and I take him, as the prosecution takes him, with all his hallucinations.

M. Saint-Gresse.—The witness also says that on the 16th he told Bonhomme he had seen the deceased leave; that was before the interview with the *frères* on the 17th.

The President (to witness).—How is it that you said that on the 16th?

Witness.—Because then I thought it was true, but now I do not.

The witness then went on to state that the director at Lavaur, the Frère Auricule, after speaking to him on the subject, asked if he had seen the deceased. Witness said he *thought* he had seen her leave; thereupon the director said, "If you think you saw her, it must be because you did see her, and you must say so." The director then paid the fare for witness to Toulouse, and took him to the Institute. On his arrival Laphien, Navarre, and Janissien were sent for, and he was asked what he knew. A representation was made on the spot of how the *frères*, Rudel, and the witness were placed on the 15th of April. Afterwards they all went up into the library, where the Frères Floride, Irlide, Auricule, Laphien, Janissien, and, as witness believed, Liéfroy, also were present [most of them, as the President remarked to the jury at this point, the highest dignitaries in the Institute]. Frère Irlide put questions : the other *frères* said what they knew : that they had seen the Almoner : that he had put his head into the parlour : and one *frère* said he had heard the word *dinner* mentioned. Witness was also questioned. At first he said he had not seen the Almoner. Then he was asked if he had seen the deceased, and witness said he believed he saw her.

The President.—Have you not said you saw the Almoner's *soutane ?*

Witness.—I said so here at the last trial.

The President.—You now acknowledge it was not true?

Witness.—I knew at the time it was false, only as the others said so, I did as they did.

M. Saint-Gresse here read the deposition in which Vidal had stated this fact about seeing the Almoner, and remarked that two *frères* examined previous to Vidal had stated they had not seen the deceased, and that Vidal afterwards said that he (Vidal) did see her. The statement therefore came from the witness first, whilst the prosecution sought to assign to it a different origin.

M. D'Oms. — The witness first said that he saw the Almoner, that he heard the bell ring, and that he *believed* he saw the deceased leave the Institute. He retracts everything now ; the statements therefore take their origin from this pre-arranged meeting in the Institute with the directors.

Navarre Antoine, in religion Frère Marie Liether, deposed that on the 15th he went to the parlour at about half-past eight o'clock, where he saw Vidal and Rudel. He saw Frère Jubrien arrive and speak to two men in the parlour. Jubrien took one of them by the arm, and they all three went away. When Rudel and Vidal were on the point of leaving, one of them asked to see Janissien and Laphien, and witness went to ask Frère Liéfroy's permission. The witness, who gave his evidence with much dramatic action and entirely without being questioned, proceeded as follows :—" I said we would return in five minutes. The director said to me, " My friend, we will see whether you remain five minutes or longer.' I looked at the clock, which wanted five minutes to nine." [It will be seen this is in contradiction with the original statement made by him, and embodied in the *acte d'accusation*, p. 210. He here says the *second* interview commenced at five minutes to nine, whereas it was, according to his previous statement, the first that commenced at that time. As a question of credibility, this discrepancy is not unimportant.] He continued :—" I went down, opened the door of the parlour and saw that Frère Floride and another person were there. After the interview, I got up, opened the door, and stood on the threshold in this manner." [Here witness rose up and showed with several expressive gestures the position in which he stood.] " At this instant I saw M. Conte, who was entering the vestibule. I noticed two females behind him, one of whom was taller than the other. M. Conte removed the cloth from the top of the basket which was over the books. Then I made a turn of the head in this manner [witness again showed with considerable self-possession how he stood] and saw M. Conte on the point of leaving the vestibule for the library. I then returned into the parlour and rejoined Vidal, Rudel, and the other *frères ;* they were looking at the portrait of St. Joseph, and talking about drawing. I rang the bell for the porter to open the door for them, and we all went into the vestibule together. We stood in this manner—M. Vidal was close by me ; Janissien was talking, and so loud it was almost impossible to hear any one else speak ; Laphien was near Janissien. At this moment Vidal changed his position to listen to Janissien, who turned to him and made some inquiries about an old schoolfellow. The porter seeing that Vidal and Rudel did not go out, and tired of waiting, pushed to the door which he had opened, but without closing it entirely, and retired a little way off, and began to tell his beads. Suddenly there was a ring at the bell ; the porter advanced to open the door ; he had the key on his left arm, the palm of his right hand across his breast. It was the Almoner Perlès who had rung, and he stood talking with the porter. At that moment I saw a female behind him, who tried to look in. Rudel and Vidal then left, and I went back in the interior of the Institute. On arriving at the school-room door I found M. Conte. It was then twenty minutes past nine. [Considerable sensation followed the deposition of this witness. After concluding it he sat down, crossed his arms over his chest, and slightly hung down his head, waiting to be questioned].

On being interrogated by the President (who expressed his opinion that there was not a word of truth in his statement) the witness fell into several contradictions, and his memory, on being tested on minor points, was found defective. He could not say how the female behind the Almoner was dressed, but was quite sure he saw the Almoner. [The porter being confronted with the witness, they did not agree as to the time when the door was opened for the Almoner.] Asked if he heard the Almoner speak, he said he did not, but he gathered from the way in which the porter stood, he was listening. Pressed as to the rehearsal scene in the library, he could not say who was present; and asked why he had not mentioned the two men whom Jubrien went to meet in the parlour and took away with him before, he said he had only just thought of it. Being asked if they were in the parlour when he first went to see Rudel and Vidal, he said he thought they were. [These two latter, being confronted with him, said they were not; and being asked whether Navarre at any time stood in the doorway of the parlour and remained there some minutes, they distinctly and emphatically denied that he did, but on the contrary, said that Navarre was sitting down with them the whole time inside. This contradiction is important, because Navarre, from his alleged position, would be enabled to deny, and in fact did deny, the truth of Conte's assertions, that on his (Conte's) arrival with the deceased into the vestibule with the books, Jubrien and Léotade were present. On the witness being further pressed as to the rehearsal scene, he said it was Vidal who put the *frères* in their places, whereas Vidal being confronted with him, said the *frères* placed chairs to represent themselves.]

Clausade, in religion Frère Laphien, proved that he went with Janissien to the parlour to see Vidal and Rudel. No one else was there. He saw Conte enter with some baskets. Afterwards saw the porter open the door (but whether with a key or not he could not say), and the Almoner entered a little distance. He saw something pass behind the Almoner, but could not say what it was. Asked as to who was present at the rehearsal scene, he said he thought Auricule was there, that Irlide was not. Floride he believed was there, but could not say for certain, and Liéfroy he believed was not. [Navarre being recalled, said Irlide and Auricule were there, but he did not see Floride.]

Marcellin Pellié, in religion Frère Janissien, deposed that whilst Rudel, Vidal, Laphien, and himself were in the parlour, Navarre stood at the door. Then there was a ring at the door, which was opened, and he saw the Almoner, who entered and came partly into the parlour.

L'Abbé Perlès, the Almoner, deposed that on the 15th, between nine and half-past, he called at the Institute and spoke for a few minutes to the porter. The door was closed when he arrived. He entered a step or two and remained about five minutes. He believed there were others in the vestibule at the time besides him, but was not certain.

Frère Liéfroy, the director of the schools, gave evidence as to the visit of Conte on the morning of the 15th with the books. He first heard of the body being found at about eight o'clock on the morning of the 16th. He had occasionally seen females inside the *Pensionnat*, but he always directed that they should go out. He denied most positively that any overtures had been made to any persons to procure witnesses to say they had seen Cécile leave the Institute. On being asked whether on the 15th, between the hours of eight and half-past ten, the letters containing the *compte de conscience* were required to be written, he said it was not so in the *Noviciat*, but might be so in the *Pensionnat*. [This writing of the *comptes de conscience*, it will be remembered, was one of the points relied upon for the defence as engaging Léotade in the *Pensionnat* at the time he was alleged to be in the *Noviciat*.]

Pierre Aragon, in religion Frère Jubrien, deposed that on the 15th two persons had come to see him at the Institute. He went to the parlour between eight and nine and saw M. Salinier and a horse-dealer who was with him. They went together to the stable to examine a pony, and remained there three quarters of an hour. He could not remember whether he saw Léotade on that day or not. He admitted that he and Léotade had had an interview together relative to sending for some wine from Saint-Simon, and believed that conversation took place on the Friday, the 16th, between seven and eight in the morning, and in the *Noviciat*, but was not sure. [The prosecution contended that it was on the Thursday, the 15th, and at the very time that Conte arrived with the deceased, and that Léotade had gone to the *Noviciat* for the purpose.] The witness, however, denied most positively seeing Léotade in the vestibule on the morning of the 15th, and he denied seeing Conte. This latter being confronted with him, asserted he had not only seen him but saluted him and said " Good day," and that Jubrien never returned the salute or made any answer. Asked as to the *compte de conscience*, the witness said the *pourvoyeurs* were not exempt by the regulations from having to render it. [Léotade was *pourvoyeur* for the *Pensionnat*, and witness for the *Noviciat*], but they might be exempt personally on account of their duties. He admitted having gone to Conte's house for some pasteboard on the morning of the 16th, and that he asked to see Conte, who was absent.

Madame Conte deposed that Jubrien called at her husband's house at half-past eight on the 16th, and Léotade a few minutes after. Jubrien asked if Conte was in ; witness said no, and he left. Léotade also asked for Conte, and said his memorandum book was not what he wanted. He afterwards said, " The deceased worked with you ;" and witness replied, " You knew her well enough ; she entered your place and never came out again." Léotade turned his back and made some exclamation.

M. Dambarbe Lajus deposed that on the 16th, about ten or half-past, Léotade and another *frère* came to his shop to pay a bill. Witness spoke to Léotade about the body of the deceased having been found in the cemetery, and that he understood she had been to the Institute the day before with a bookbinder. " That person was Conte," said Léotade ; " we have just been to his house ; he has left for Auch, the wretch ! If we had only known his antecedents, he would have had nothing to do with the Institute." He then left, saying, " One cannot positively say it is Conte, *but* ——."

On the 19th, Léotade again came to his shop, and witness questioned him about Conte, who at that time had been arrested. Léotade said, "The police brought Conte to the Institute yesterday. He was very crestfallen; he kept his head down. When a man has nothing to fear he holds his head up." Witness said, "It's all your fault. So long as a man goes to mass, you believe in him." Léotade denied the truth of this conversation, and said the remarks about Conte proceeded in the first instance from the witness, and took place, not on the 16th, but on the 19th. The witness, pressed by the President as to whether he was confounding the two dates, was positive he was not : the conversation took place on the 16th. Asked by the President whether he mentioned the fact of the conversation to his wife, he said he did. [A question similar in character, as to whether Conte had told his wife that he had seen Léotade and Jubrien in the vestibule on the morning of the 15th, it will be remembered, was not allowed, on the ground that it was useless.]

Suzanne Canal, a servant of Lajus, and Madame Lajus, his wife, both confirmed the testimony of the last witness as to the conversation about the antecedents of Conte taking place on the 16th. The latter said her husband told her of it the same day.

Baptiste Lamorelle, a servant in the Institute, deposed that on the 15th he went into the town to get an iron gate which had been ordered, and returned with the workmen about seven o'clock. He then got his breakfast, and afterwards went to work, but where he could not remember. About twelve or before, he went to the stable with a workman called the Parisien. He saw Léotade that morning in the cellar, but could not remember the exact time.

M. GASC.—Were you in the loft on the morning of the 15th?

Witness.—Yes, I went there to give food to the horses about twelve.

M. GASC.—If you had seen a body there you would have said so?

Witness.—Yes : even if it had been my own father who had committed the crime. In reply to the *procureur général,* he said the window of the loft, which looked into the garden, was used to get in the hay by, and that he occasionally left the key of the stable underneath the door instead of carrying it about with him.   M. Gasc here applied that the jury should be allowed to visit the Institute, but the *procureur général* opposed the application, and the President refused it, on the ground that it would be " inconvenient and would prolong the trial." At the previous trial this inspection of the localities had been allowed (*a*).

Frère Ibramion, the *linger* of the *Noviciat,* and Frère Luciolat, the *linger* of the *Pensionnat,* gave evidence to the effect that they could not identify the shirt No. 562 on which the stains were. It was not impossible for shirts belonging to the *Noviciat* to get mixed with those belonging

---

(*a*) The incident of the visit of the court to examine the Institute at the last trial was effected with much solemnity, and it was undoubtedly of great service in enabling the jury to understand the very intricate nature of some portions of the evidence. Both Léotade and Lorien (who was then in custody on a charge of perjury) were present. Léotade was frequently interrogated on the spot by the President on certain points touching his conduct or employment on the day in question. Though the Institute was inhabited by several hundred *frères* and a large number of novices and scholars, together stated to be nearly 500, not the slightest notice was taken by any body of the visit, though conducted with some considerable amount of pomp. The *frères* were found going about their usual duties when the court arrived, and they continued them without the least interruption.   Even the few scholars and novices who were seen at the windows did not evince the slightest surprise at the unusual and unexpected appearance of this large body of visitors, and scarcely looked at them. The few *frères* who came in contact with the court during the course of their visit, in the corridors, dormitories, garden, or elsewhere, saluted calmly and cheerfully both Léotade and Lorien, but as far as the other personages were concerned they might not have been in existence, so utterly was their presence ignored. The calmness and self-command of Léotade whilst visiting the places supposed to be connected with the murder, and which, if a guilty man, must have been a terrible ordeal, are described as being perfectly wonderful. The only person in the least affected during the visit was Lorien at seeing the havoc inflicted by the *gens d'armes* and visitors on his flower beds.   On entering the doors of the Institute the court seemed to come in contact with an atmosphere of resistance and opposition, none the less effectual because it was passive, and which probably tended not a little to prejudice the minds of the public against the *frères*. The visit, however, as an inspection of the localities, was of importance, as it went to show the almost insurmountable difficulties Léotade would have had to contend with if he had committed the murder, and to suggest the impracticability of his being able to perpetrate the crime and conceal it, without an accomplice. For this reason he was probably refused the inspection at the second trial.

to the *Pensiônnat*. All of them were nearly alike. They could not say the number of them in the Institute.

Joseph Bacon, in religion Frère Leri, deposed that the shirts of the *Noviciat* and *Pensionnat* were used in common. He saw Léotade on the 15th in the corridor of the *Pensionnat* between nine and ten. Léotade asked him to get some plaster to cover the holes some workmen had made in fixing a gate.

Marie Melet, the mother of the witness Conte, who described herself as a money changer, and in fact did get her living by changing copper money in the markets, deposed that on the 16th April she met Jubrien, and said to him, " Is it true that a girl has been found in the cemetery who works at my son's." Jubrien said he did not know anything about it. On the same morning Jubrien came to her son's shop, and asked for him. On being told he was at Auch, Jubrien went away without asking for anything.

The President to Jubrien (who was confronted with this witness).—There is something very important in this statement. On the morning of the body being found you go to Conte's house, for what purpose, or what you would have said to him if he had been at home, we do not know, but probably to tell him not to say anything about you and Léotade being in the vestibule when the deceased arrived. Conte not being there, however, you do not know what to say. Your own statement is that you went to ask for some pasteboard, but you come away without asking for any. Of all the questions put to you, the only one which you have answered clearly and positively is, " Were you in the vestibule with Léotade?" At first you said you did not remember, and then when Léotade denied it, you denied it as well. Jubrien, in reply to these remarks, said it was possible he did make the remark to Madame Conte that he knew nothing about the matter, but was not sure. He insisted he had only gone to Conte's shop to get some pasteboard [which, however, as the President remarked, he did not ask for], and admitted on the 15th he was in the vestibule between nine and a quarter past, but denied positively meeting Léotade there. [In his evidence in chief he said he (witness) was there between eight and nine.]

M. Thoulouse deposed that he was employed to make inquiries from a pupil in the Institute named Laporte whether it was true what he had said that he had seen Léotade in the work-room at nine or half past on the morning of the 15th. Laporte on being pressed, said that the *frères* had questioned him three times on the matter, and that they repeated so often that he had seen Léotade in the work-room that he finished by saying it also. Laporte himself being called, corroborated this, and said he told the untruth in the first instance from a fear of being punished. At the first trial he had been summoned by the defence, and had given the same evidence, and on his afterwards going to the Institute Frère Floride treated him very harshly, called him *polisson, drôle,* &c., and said he had brought scandal on the Institute.

Auguste Amilhau, in religion Frère Floride, deposed that on the 16th (the *juge d'instruction* having authorized him to collect information) he sent to Crouzat at Lavaur to send Rudel and Vidal to the Institute. On their arrival witness asked them if they had seen the deceased. They said they had not, and so the interview terminated. He denied having given them any information as to how the deceased was dressed. On the 24th April Vidal was brought again to the Institute by the director of Lavaur, and said he had seen Cécile leave. Witness replied that on the 17th he had said he had not seen her. Vidal answered it was because he had been told to mind his own affairs. Witness urged on him not to say anything but the truth, whereupon Vidal said he was sure he had seen the deceased, and had stepped on one side to let her pass. Witness asked how she was dressed, and Vidal replied he did not pay sufficient attention. Witness did not hear of the handkerchief with the white spots until three months after from M. Plassan, chemist. Witness said all this took place in the parlour and in the vestibule, and that Vidal did not enter into the court. Vidal received two francs from witness to get his dinner with, as he did not think it right he should dine at the Institute. Witness protested against the imputation made by the prosecution that the directors of the Institute were instructing the *frères* in the parts they should play.

Towards the end of July witness said he heard that a shirt had been found which the prosecution looked upon as important, and he went to the *juge d'instruction* to request, as there were upwards of 100 novices who had not been asked anything about the linen, that further inquiries might be made. He denied being present at the scene in the library. [Vidal being confronted with him, said the director of Lavaur, Frère Irlide and the witness were all present]. As to Laporte's evidence he admitted he had impressed upon the witnesses the necessity of putting their depositions into writing, lest they should forget it.

Pradoni, in religion Frère Luce, proved that about eighteen months ago he gave to Léotade a key which opened the door of the room where the clothes were kept.

Jean Cazeneuve, in religion Frère Irlide, deposed that he heard of the finding of the body on the morning of the 16th. He himself suggested that the footmarks should be covered with boards and preserved. Near the *Orangerie* he found a piece of cord, which he picked up and gave to Coumès. He was not present when the footmarks there were first discovered by Coumès. [Lorien had said he was.] Asked as to the changing of rooms by Léotade, he said that the change took place on the night of Saturday, the 17th. Léotade had slept in the dormitory from which he was removed [his bed was next to the witness's] about three weeks. Witness admitted, with some hesitation, that he was present at the rehearsal in the library, and that Floride, Laphien, Janissien, and Liéfroy were there with Vidal. The interview between Rudel, Vidal, and the three *frères* was talked about, and Vidal said he had seen the deceased leave the establishment. Witness said to Vidal that he ought to be quite sure of it before he said so, and Vidal replied he was positive. The advisability of producing Vidal on the part of the defence was talked of. Witness was opposed to it, and Frère Floride also. At this interview each of the *frères* said what he knew. Afterwards they all went down to the vestibule, and each showed the place he occupied at the time. Asked as to the interview with the witness Laporte, witness said he had seen him two or three times to ascertain if he was telling the truth, but denied that he suggested to him anything. Asked as to whether, after the first trial, when Laporte called for his expenses, he had treated him harshly and called him names, witness said, amongst some laughter, that he could not remember the precise terms he used. He admitted having procured from some of the pupils a statement in writing, in order to ascertain those who had come in contact with Léotade on the morning in question, but he alleged, more by way of fixing their memories than for the purpose of instructing them what to say.

With the evidence of Frère Irlide the case for the prosecution may be considered closed. Several of the witnesses called by the prosecution gave evidence in favour of rather than against Léotade; and in order to make the trial as clear as possible they have been inserted, not amongst the witnesses for the prosecution, but amongst those for the defence. The witnesses generally appear to have been examined entirely without reference to what the purport of their evidence might be, and to have been called quite indiscriminately. Some of them who have been retained in the foregoing report as witnesses for the prosecution in reality gave evidence more for Léotade than against him,—such as Navarre, Lacténus, Jubrieu, Marion, and others. On analyzing the evidence obtained the net result seems to be this :—That the deceased was seen to enter the vestibule on the 15th, about a quarter past nine: that there were present there undoubtedly Navarre, Laphien, Janissien, the porter Lacténus, and Rudel and Vidal: that the deceased was found dead next morning in the cemetery, and from the *post mortem* must have met her death about ten o'clock on the morning of the 15th : that there were found upon her, and especially in her hair, particles of clover and some flowers, similar in character to the clover in the hay-loft in the Institute, and to the flowers growing on the top of the wall of the garden, and *dissimilar* to the flowers on the top of the wall of the Rue Riquet : that there were footmarks on the garden bed, and marks of a ladder on the soil of the garden, and, as exclusive of the probability of the deceased having been *carried* and placed where she was found, that there were no footmarks on the grass in the cemetery. These, with the rather doubtful evidence of the experts as to the "perfect identity" of the grains of fig found on the deceased's clothes with those found on the shirt No. 562, and which will be seen was contradicted by two other experts on the part of the defence, form the whole of the evidence, not against Léotade, but against the Institute, as being the locality where the deceased was last seen alive. That the deceased was never seen to leave the Institute seems to be the only fact proved in the whole course of the trial with anything like certainty; and if instead of the Institute being a place inhabited by 500 persons, it had been an ordinary house inhabited by one man, and that man Léotade, this fact alone would probably have been sufficient to bring the crime home to the prisoner. But the only evidence connecting Léotade with the murder was the simple assertion of Conte that he and Jubrien were in the vestibule at the time of the deceased's arrival with the books. This point is spoken to by Conte alone; neither Marion nor Vidal and Rudel, all three unconnected with the Institute, corroborate him, and he is directly contradicted by Navarre, and in the first instance by Marion also. One curious point in the trial is (and of five reports examined all of them are unanimous on this point) that neither Lacténus nor the other *frères* present in the parlour, nor even Rudel and Vidal, were ever *asked* whether they saw Léotade at the time when the deceased arrived at the Institute—an important and unaccountable omission. Such are the facts as drawn from the witnesses for the prosecution alone : when considered in connection with the witnesses for the defence the case set up by the prosecution against Léotade becomes even less tenable.

The first witness called for the defence was

Louis Bonnhour, a horse-dealer, who deposed that on the 15th, a little after eight, he went to the Institute with a man named Salinier. They went into the parlour, and about a quarter of an hour afterwards Vidal and Rudel entered. After them came Jubrien, and the witness and Salinier spoke to Jubrien about a mare that was for sale, and they all three went out to see the mare in the stable, and after that they went and saw the cows. At that time it had struck nine. Witness was positive when he entered the parlour no one was present, but that Vidal and Rudel came in afterwards. These latter being confronted with the witness, they declared they did not see him in the parlour on the 15th on their arrival.

M. Salinier, the companion of the last witness, deposed that Vidal and Rudel *were* in the parlour on the 15th when he and Bonnhour arrived; that there were four persons present, and only one of them a *frère*, and he was not Navarre, being much stouter.

[The President here remarked that it appeared these two witnesses left a little after nine, which would not make it impossible for *Jubrien*, after their departure, to have been in the vestibule at a quarter past nine, when Conte and the deceased arrived ; but Jubrien being there does not of course affect Léotade.]

Frère Adelphe, sub-director of novices, deposed that he was in the garden on the 15th April, and that the traces remarked near the Oratory must have been made by him and another *frère* who accompanied him. The witness further stated that at the time when he was examined by the *juge d'instruction* on the subject of the *comptes de conscience,* he said no one was excused from making them, and that they would be made in the November preceding his examination as well as in April.

The President.—As you draw the attention of the jury to the *compte de conscience* it is right to put the matter before them exactly. Léotade in the account he gave of the employment of his time on the morning of the 15th mentioned the time which he was engaged in writing the *compte de conscience*. It is stated that these *comptes de conscience* are made in the Institute every two months. When inquiries were made on the subject it was the 15th of December ; and after receiving this account given by Léotade the Frères Floride and Jubrien were questioned on the same point, and they replied they knew nothing about it. It was then endeavoured to ascertain when the last *compte de conscience* was made, and Frère Luce said he could give no information on the matter. Frère Adelphe, questioned, said they would be made in November, and that there ought to be a letter from Paris acknowledging their receipt, and showing they were made on the 1st of November.

These contradictory answers being thought very suspicious, interrogatories were issued, directed to the Superior General at Paris, who stated that he received the *compte de conscience* at the time indicated.

Later on he produced a letter from Frère Irlide fixing the date of the *compte de conscience* the 6th October. Three days after that the Superior General voluntarily sought out the *juge d'instruction*, and said he had made a mistakè, it was in the month of November that the *comptes de conscience* had been made. It is, however, important to bear in mind that at the same time that inquiries were being made at Paris on this point, inquiries were also being made at Toulouse, and that sufficient time had elapsed since the inquiries had taken place at Toulouse for the Superior General to be informed of what had taken place.

M. D'OMS.—There were two inquiries, first, to ascertain if the *comptes de conscience* were made on the 15th of April at Toulouse, and secondly, as it was alleged they were made every two months, to ascertain if they were also made on the 15th December, on which day, according to the above calculation, they would be again due. On the 17th December, Jubrien being examined as to his *compte de conscience*, said some of the *frères* were excused from making it, and that he was one of them. Frère Floride, examined on the same point, said he did not know whether the *comptes de conscience* were made on the 15th December or not; and other *frères* stated the same. At the same time, in Paris, Frère Jorson declared he had not received any letter in December or November, and the jury will notice that whilst Frère Adelphe asserts he sent his *compte de conscience* on the 18th November, Jorson at Paris denies that he received any, except in October; but on the 21st December, by which day letters from Toulouse could be received in Paris, Jorson declares that it was by mistake he said he had not received any but in October; the letter accompanying them was dated the 6th October, but it was a mistake, it ought to have been dated on the 6th November. Frère Adelphe here asked for his second deposition to be read, from which it appeared

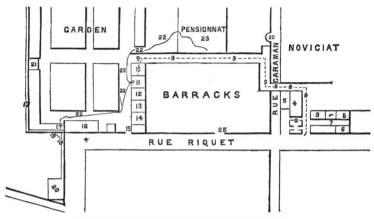

EXPLANATION OF THE ABOVE PLAN.

1. Entrance into the Vestibule of the *Noviciat* in the Rue Riquet. 2. The Porter's Lodge. 3. The Parlour. 4. The Stairs leading to 5, the Library and Rooms above. 6. The Linen Room belonging to the *Noviciat*. 7. The Corridor leading to it, and to (8) the shoemaker's workshop; 9, and the dotted line running from the Vestibule through the Tunnel under the Rue Caraman, represent the supposed route of Cécile from the Vestibule to 10, the Stable, and 11, the Hay-loft above, where the murder was supposed to be committed. 12 and 13. Another Stable. 14. Cart-shed. 15. Entrance into the Garden from the Rue Riquet. 16. *Orangerie*. 17. The wall separating the Institute Garden from the Cemetery, the figures in the angle near the *Orangerie* being where the footmarks were found. 18. The Wall separating the Cemetery from the Rue Riquet. 19. The place where the Body was found. 20. The Oratory belonging to the Cemetery. 21. The Oratory in the Institute Garden. 22. The route supposed to be followed by Léotade from the Dormitory in the *Pensionnat* (23) on the second floor to 11, the Hay-loft, which he would have to enter by the window, and from thence to carry the body to the angle (17) formed by the *Orangerie* with the garden wall where the ladder was placed. 24. Separate Entrance to the *Pensionnat* from the Rue Caraman. (In the plan these figures are erroneously printed "20" instead of "24.") 25. Entrance to the Barracks, where a sentry was on guard the whole night. At the Cross × in the Rue Riquet was a lamp, fixed on the Wall of the *Orangerie*, which rises considerably above the level of the Walls 17 and 18. The lamp would light the corner in the Rue Riquet where a person would have to stand to throw a body into the Cemetery so as to fall in the place where Cécile was found, but would throw the corner *inside* the garden, at the figure 17, where the footsteps were found, and where the ladder was supposed to be placed, into comparative darkness. A person on the ladder, with his back to the wall of the *Orangerie*, would run scarcely any risk of being seen, owing to this shadow. The Stables and Cart-shed, 10, 11, 12, 13, 14 on the Plan, are not quite drawn to scale, owing to the space not being sufficient to show them all clearly : the whole of them do not in reality extend much further down than the end of No. 12.

s

that he fixed the 18th November as the date of sending the *compte de conscience*, and that by means of a letter from Jorson himself.

Briol and Lacour, both tailors in the Institute, deposed to seeing Léotade in the work-room several times during the morning of the 15th, Lacour between nine and eleven, Briol *" à tout moment."*

Julien Bessières, in religion Frère Léopardin, cook at the *Pensionnat*, deposed that he saw Léotade four times on the morning of the 15th, the first time between six and seven, the next between seven and eight at mass. Between nine and a quarter past he saw him in the kitchen, when he asked witness where the gardener was, and again at dinner. He also said he saw him again between ten and eleven. The President having pointed out to him that on the 23rd April he could only remember seeing Léotade once between six and seven in the morning, and though pressed by Léotade then, he could not think of any other time that he saw him, witness said he remembered these interviews afterwards, but did not think it necessary to mention them. [At the first trial this witness only spoke to four interviews ; he now spoke to five, two of them, as to time, very important.]

Antoine Sabathier, the gardener, proved that he was in the garden at nine on the morning of the 15th, and went into the stable between nine and ten to feed the horses and remained there some time on account of the rain. [This was the very time and place the prosecution fixed for the murder.] Being pressed by the President as to how he remembered the hour and the day, the witness said he heard the clock strike.

Jean Marie Cazenave, in religion Frère Illuminat, deposed that he saw Léotade on the morning of the 15th at the Infirmary at half-past four, afterwards at seven, and again at ten feeding the birds. At eleven he came and lighted the fire for the Count de Jarut Salvi, who was ill. Léotade gave him on one occasion a clean shirt, which witness kept for one of his patients. [Léotade, it will be remembered, maintained he had not changed his shirt at the end of the week, alleging the one offered was too small and irritated a blister he had. It was therefore a very important point to account for the clean shirt that was given him in due course the Saturday after the murder.] The witness's original deposition being put in, it appeared that when asked if Léotade had on any occasion returned him a clean shirt, the witness had said he had no recollection of it.

The President.—The jury will appreciate the great importance of this evidence. Léotade pretends he did not change his shirt. On being asked what he did with the clean one delivered on the Saturday, he replied, " I gave it to the *infirmier*." The latter, however, in the first instance denied it, but when he learnt what Léotade had said, he mentioned it for the first time. (To the witness.)—" Is not this the proper explanation of your testimony?"

Witness.—No. Léotade told me at the time the shirt was too small for him.

M. GASC.—The prisoner since his arrest has asked for larger shirts.

The President.—The ones he rejected were measured, and one of them indeed was put on by M. Gaussail, who is much stouter than Léotade, outside his clothes, and it was found to be amply large enough.

Frère Liède deposed that he was ill in the Infirmary at the time of the murder, and had occasion frequently to change his linen in the course of that and the following week. [This was to show that the clean shirt which was given to Léotade on the Saturday, and which he did not use and returned to the *infirmier*, was worn by this witness, and so far to corroborate Léotade's statement.]

Henri Cousent and Félix de Savy, pupils, proved seeing Léotade on the 15th, one from about half-past eight to a quarter past nine, and the other in Léotade's own *procure* about twenty minutes past nine. Another pupil also proved seeing him at ten o'clock in his *procure*. Three other witnesses, Frère Esdras, Frère Julien-Marie, and Frère Yves-Marie, also proved seeing Léotade in the course of the morning of the 15th, but the reports do not state the time when they saw him.

Marie Duprat deposed that she had heard Cécile complain of the overtures made to her by Conte.

Messieurs Dulac and St. Hilaire, professors, of Montpellier, deposed that it was impossible to distinguish the grains of figs of the same quality. M. Noulet, who had stated it was

s 2

possible to do so, being called in, argued at some length, and said that before the Academy of Sciences he would always maintain that the grains on the shirt No. 562, and on the dress of the deceased, came from the same fig, though he added he had found different kinds of grains in one fig.

Several witnesses in succession were then called to prove that the declaration of Vidal that he had seen the deceased leave the vestibule whilst he and Rudel were there, was made by him spontaneously on the 17th before he was confronted with the *frères* at the Institute, and clearly showed that they had taken no part in endeavouring to influence his testimony. Hearing that Vidal had said to several persons that he had himself seen the deceased leave, it was only natural that the *frères* should inquire into the truth of the matter, which was of considerable importance to them.

Etienne Gatimel, in religion Frère Stéphanus, deposed that on the 16th he went into the garden with a *gendarme*, and heard Lorien tell the *gendarme* (Coumès) that he (Lorien) had made the footmarks near the *Orangerie*, on this point entirely contradicting Coumès. Pierre Cahuc, in religion Frère Isoldus, corroborated this witness's testimony.

Crouzat, a musician, gave some evidence to the effect that he had seen Conte act roughly to the deceased, and had heard him speak violently on several occasions against the *frères*. On one occasion, three or four days before the murder, he had seen him come out of the Institute red with passion at something that had taken place. Pressed as to the day when he saw the proceedings between Conte and Cécile, he fixed it for a day when he dined there, when the deceased was present. Conte and his wife thereupon both said that the deceased had never dined there.

Frère Irlide, recalled, proved that on the 15th after breakfast the *compte de conscience* was made in the *Pensionnat*.

Gaja Guillaume, in religion Frère Luc, deposed that on the morning of the 16th he heard of the discovery of the body; he felt afraid to sleep any longer in a room by himself (he was sleeping then in a small closet or work-room called a *procure*), and asked the director for leave to change his room. The director sent him to take the place of Léotade, and this latter was removed to another dormitory in consequence of the application of witness. The director, on the morning of the 15th, ordered witness to collect from the *frères* the letters containing the *comptes de conscience*. He did so, and they were afterwards sent off to the Superior in Paris by *diligence*. M. Gasc here read the deposition of Frère Phillipe, the Superior, on this point, to the effect that a packet containing these *comptes de conscience* did arrive in Paris from Toulouse in April, and that there was one among them from Léotade, but whether it was dated on the 15th of April or not he could not say.

With the evidence of this witness the case for the defence closed, and the court adjourned until the next morning.

On the meeting of the court the next day M. Rumeau commenced his address to the jury on behalf of the plaintiff in the civil action represented by Bernard Combettes, the father of the deceased. The action was brought to recover damages for the murder; and this form of procedure is one of the peculiarities of French criminal law. The defendants were not only Léotade himself, but also Frère Irlide, director of the *Pensionnat*, and Frère Liéfroy, director of the *Noviciat*, as the heads of the community of which Léotade was a member.

M. Rumeau, after alluding to the absence of M. Joly, who in the interval between the two trials had been promoted to high office in the government, proceeded, after the usual tumid flourish which seems a characteristic of French oratory, as follows,—immaterial portions of his speech being omitted : —

" The case set up on the part of the defence rests entirely upon three hypotheses ; the first is that the position of the body and the state of the clothes render it impossible that it could have been *thrown* into the cemetery. None, however, of the experiments that have been made relative to the position of the body negative the possibility of this projection : if the body were *carried* there, as the defence allege, how did it get to the place in which it was found ? Not by the gate of the cemetery, for that was locked by Lévêque, the *concièrge ;* nor from the opposite side of the cemetery near the canal ; nor by the gap in the wall near the *Boulevard St. Aubin.* There is no trace of any ladder having been used, nor of the footsteps of the murderer ; and the grass surrounding the body is not even disturbed. Everything, on the contrary, excludes the possibility of the body reaching the place where it was discovered from any other direction than the garden of the Institute.

" Consider well the proofs demonstrating that the body was thrown over from the garden of the Institute—the state of the wall on the side of the cemetery; the summit; the inside fronting the garden. The experts have described the marks that existed on the portion of the wall facing the body, the plant of groundsel torn up, and hanging only by one of its roots. How have these marks and this appearance been produced? By the pressure made from above on the cypress boughs forming the crown of the wall in the Rue Riquet. On the garden side of the wall of the Institute other plants of groundsel were found disturbed and pressed down, a proof that either a hand or the ladder used by the murderer had been placed there. What deduction, therefore, can be drawn from all these proofs but that some heavy and bulky body has passed over the top of this wall of the garden? What that body was there is no difficulty in proving; for in the hair of the deceased was found a petal of geranium, and a similar flower is only to be found on the top of the wall of the garden of the Institute.

" I pass now to the second hypothesis,—that of the possibility of the projection of the body over the wall of the Rue Riquet. But if the body was thrown from that direction, what becomes of the arguments drawn by the defence from the state of the clothes and position of the body, as negativing the possibility of any projection? Besides, witnesses of intelligence and respectability have been heard, capable of forming an opinion, and they all state that such an hypothesis is untenable, and the projection of the body from the Rue Riquet impossible. Independent, however, of the evidence of these experts there are other facts which tend to the same conclusion. The wall of the Rue Riquet is found to be unmarked; the plants growing on the crown of it intact; the stake placed on the top, near the angle formed by the meeting of the two walls, unmoved. This latter obstacle alone renders the projection from the Rue Riquet impracticable.

" Then again, is it to be supposed that the murderer would

have had the hardihood to throw the body from the Rue Riquet, when at two paces from him there was a lamp burning, and at a short distance a sentry on duty who would inevitably have noticed the assassin?

" The body, therefore, was thrown from the garden of the Institute, and must have been thrown from that direction. Particles of clover were found on the dress of the deceased, and clover of the same description was found in the stables of the Institute, and no clover similar in character has been discovered elsewhere. To persons at all open to reason this conclusion must be sufficient, even if not supported as it is by two facts, which are rendered still more decisive by the falsehoods and subterfuges of which they were the object— the marks of the ladder and the traces of the footsteps in the garden of the Institute.

" The theory of the prosecution on this subject is neither difficult of explanation nor improbable. These marks are the marks made by the murderer when seeking for the spot most suitable for the projection of the body. On consideration he discovered a place more convenient than that which he selected in the first instance ; therefore the marks discovered on the flower beds were feeble, as the murderer did not at that spot mount on the ladder with his victim. It has been sought to dispute the nature of these marks, and to show that they are unimportant, that they were only two or three in number, and were not measured : but what does that matter, when the material point remains that they are in fact the marks made by a *ladder?* Who made them? that is the question. We say the prisoner Léotade made them : the defence says, Frère Irlide says, they were made whilst pruning the trees in the garden ; but it has never been proved that there are any trees in that direction that require or in fact were pruned : besides, on the day after the murder it was set up by the directors of the Institute that the marks of the ladder were upright, and that no one could have mounted on it in that position.

" As to the footmarks, it may probably be objected that they were very indistinct, and that Frère Lorien made them ; but that objection is not difficult to be met. Lorien, who says he made them, has been arrested, and is now in custody for perjury, and the footmarks were indistinct owing to the necessity the murderer was under of effacing them.

"Then again, in the *Pensionnat* six shirts were seized, but on one only, the shirt No. 562, were those terrible and overwhelming proofs—the grains of fig—discovered. You will not seek to draw any argument from the counter-propositions of the witnesses for the defence, which ended in nothing, and in no way upset the evidence of the experts called on behalf of the prosecution. The identity of the grains must strike you at once as convincing, and on no other shirt but the one numbered 562 were there found any grains of fig at all. Neither can you seek to attach any importance to the depositions of the *frères* who have been examined before you : none of them can have any weight. In each the same baleful influences which suggested them, in each the same sentiment, in each the same form of language are to be noted. It is not necessary even to discuss them.

"But in order the better to appreciate the arguments which I have yet to address to you, let me say a few words on the subject of this Institute, on its origin, on its purpose, on its doctrines, and on its management."

M. Rumeau here entered upon a long history of the Institute of the Christian Brethren from its foundation in the year 1651, tracing it through all its vicissitudes down to modern days.—"It was indeed a magnificent idea, that of the Founder of this Establishment, to give to the children of poor persons a gratuitous Christian education, and to call to the work of aiding in the realization of that idea men strong in faith, constant in charity, firm in self-denial and brotherly love. But unfortunately, as with men so with institutions : they have but a short career here upon earth : they become feeble, degenerate, and grow old. What therefore was fitting and useful once, at a time when the Catholic religion was the exclusive or even the dominant religion in France, becomes a mere anachronism under the reign of liberty of conscience, and in the absence of a recognized State religion. What was a benefit at a time when a people possessing nothing but burdens had no rights, becomes a mere usurpation of the duties of the State under a government which ranks amongst its first obligations that of giving to all its children the benefits of gratuitous instruction.

" If you were to ask me what is my opinion of the principle of this Institute of the Christian Brethren, I should tell you that it is an admirable Institution, for it holds everything subservient to the interest of God. Why then has fanaticism so impaired its original purity? Why is it that the successors of the Abbé de Lassalle have placed it under the dominion of retrograde ideas and evil passions!

" The organization and inner discipline of the Institute seem copied from those of that famous Order [the Society of Jesus] whose yoke it has since voluntarily accepted. At the head a perpetual *Superior General,* nominated by a chapter composed of thirty of the oldest members : then follow *directors* for each of the establishments spread over the country and abroad ; then *visitors* charged with the inspection of those establishments, each, like the *directors,* elected for three years ; then the *professed brethren* who form, properly speaking, the body of the Institute, and then *novices* only admitted after certain proofs and for a certain fixed definite period.

" Amongst the most important of the vows taken by the members of the Institute are the vows of poverty, chastity, and obedience. These vows, it is true, are taken only for three years, but they are renewed at the end of each period of three years : during that time the member who has pronounced them cannot by the terms of their statutes be relieved except only by the authority and on the interference of the Pope.

" I own I must admit that for Congregations in general, and particularly for Congregations exacting such vows as these, I have but a very moderate sympathy. The vow of poverty is easily forgotten : of the two other vows, chastity and obedience, one is surrounded by such dangers, the other has facilities for abuses so grave, that we are often inclined to ask—and in the present day more than ever to ask—if the existence of these vows is compatible with a morally organized and properly regulated social existence."

M. Rumeau then proceeded to descant with much force on the vow of obedience exacted of the members of the Establishment, quoting largely from the writings of several of the most distinguished members of the Society of Jesus, whose rules were binding on the Institute. It must be borne in mind that M. Rumeau was pleading for the plaintiff in the civil action, who sought to recover damages from the heads of the Establishment of which Léotade was a member, and that the question of passive obedience to their Superiors, which all the *frères* were bound to recognize, had an important bearing on the credibility of the witnesses called on behalf of the Institute. He sought therefore to show that this vow of obedience was with them far different from what it is with us in the ordinary affairs of life: in civil life obedience does not prevent the exercise of either reflection or reason, but in religious life, he argued, the vow of obedience, fully and faithfully observed, excludes morality, religion, truth, duty, everything except the one point of passive obedience to the wishes and orders of a Superior. As such it becomes a fearful and powerful weapon in the hands of a stern, unflinching, and uncompromising man. The member of a Congregation who has taken this vow remains, M. Rumeau submitted, no longer a man : he becomes a dead body. It was this moral deadness to everything except the orders of a Superior, this loss of life as a separate and independent being (*perinde ac cadaver*), that M. Rumeau sought to demonstrate from the authors whose writings he then proceeded to quote :—

" I know," he said, " no Jesuit who, after Escobar, has so clearly expressed his views on this question as Eudæmon Joannes. In his *Apology for Henry Garnet* he says:—' I cannot understand all these outcries against equivocation; it must be because it is regarded either as a lie, or if not a lie, as none the less deceiving him against or towards whom it is used : or because in the daily commerce of men and in the ordinary affairs of life it banishes all good faith. But none of these reasons have any weight. Equivocation is not a lie, because to lie is to speak contrary to one's thought, and he who uses equivocation gives to the words which he uses the meanings of the words that are present to his mind. As to the point that it deceives him towards or against whom it is used, I cannot perceive what advantage my adversaries can draw from it, because the use of it is not permitted on all occasions without choice. If the interest of Society require the observance of good faith in all conversations, if it be true that the destruction of good faith would necessarily destroy or put an end to Society also, Society would be equally destroyed if the right every one now possesses over his own thoughts—to conceal or disclose them to others as he thinks fit—were taken away' (a).

" Suarez does not explain himself less clearly:—' Equivocation in conversation is not always a lie, and the reason is that a lie is a thing said contrary to the thought of him who says it, because it is the duty of the person who speaks to make his words conform to his own thoughts, and not to the thoughts or understanding of the person addressed; from which I conclude it is not perjury to state upon oath what is said in this manner, for by the oath God is not called upon to witness a lie, since there is no lie.'

" Such is the doctrine published and taught in Lyons in 1714 by the Jesuits of that town, with the permission of the Provincial and the approbation of the General Aquaviva and of a great number of the doctors of the Society. Let us see now what application is made of these principles, drawn from the most celebrated and learned casuists :—

" A man plunges his dagger into the breast of another named Lecoq : you are called as a witness : you have some motives for not giving evidence in the matter : how reconcile the obligation you have to speak the truth with the reasons and motives you possess ? A Jesuit Father teaches you at once what to do : You may swear in safety and in good conscience that you did not see the prisoner stab Lecoq, but by reservation you say to yourself ' le coq de la basse cour,' for it is certain that that cock at least has not yet been put to death.

"Another case. You are in Hungary, where Latin is spoken. You are asked to give evidence respecting a murder. It is well known that gallus signifies equally a Frenchman and a cock. You have, as in the previous case, reasons for not giving

---

(a) The adversaries alluded to above were the adversaries with whom Eudæmon Joannes was arguing on the disputed point whether Garnet was or was not implicated in the Gunpowder Plot.

evidence; you therefore say you know nothing of the affair, meaning, by reservation, "the affair of the cock."

"Again. You arrive in a country governed by an atheistic prince. You are required to take the oath of allegiance. You, who are an excellent Catholic, are not willing to swear fealty to a person excommunicated. How do you propose to get over the difficulty. A Jesuit Father will again show you: You say aloud, 'I swear' and to yourself quite low, 'that I will be faithful to my own king.'"

M. Rumeau then proceeded to give further examples of the danger arising from the vow of passive obedience and the doctrines of the Jesuit Fathers on the subject of equivocation. Amongst others he mentioned the proposition made by Stroz, a German Jesuit, in a book published with the authority of the Superior General, to make a dictionary for one's self to call a "man" a "horse," a "horse," a "man," to understand by the word "pound" a "shilling," and by the word "cow" a "cat," and *vice versâ;* and then to quote an extract from a work by *Barnard,* the *History of the Progress of the Society of Jesus,* on the subject of passive obedience:—"Let every one understand that those who live in obedience ought to allow themselves to be led by the orders of their Superiors as if they were a dead body, which lets itself be carried in all directions, and in such manner as may be required, or like the walking-stick of an old man (*sicut baculus senis*), which is in the hand of him who holds it to be used in all places and for every occasion as he may desire."

"Again, in a catechism for the use of schools, *Noviciats,* and Congregations, written by one of their own body, is this doctrine, in which, in answer to a question as to the duties imposed by the Second Commandment, and whether the rigorous observance of those duties could not be evaded, the reply of the pupil is, 'Yes, they can be evaded by the judicious employment of mental reservations, such as to swear aloud that you will keep the conditions of such and such a treaty, and to say to yourself at the same time by mental reservation, *that is, if I do not change my intention.*' And in answer to a further question whether this doctrine is approved of by other learned men, the pupil is taught to say, 'It is approved by all the theologians of the Society of Jesus, who unanimously teach that on all occasions where there is any necessity to conceal the truth an oath may always be taken with a double meaning' " (a).

M. Rumeau then, after citing other works and documents more or less bearing on the same question of passive obedience, proceeded:—

"You" (the Institute) "may say you are not *entirely* Jesuits. That may be : but you have with them many things in common; and what is worse you have accepted their dominion. Your tendencies in temporal matters are the same; your principles on the subject of obedience identical. If the tricolour floats proudly on the roof of your buildings, the oriflamme of the Congregation of the Society of Jesus glitters on your altars within. And can there be any more striking proof of the influence of that Society than the very fact of this trial, and the opposition of which it has been the object?

" Nevertheless, my reproaches do not attach to the virtuous Founder of the Society, nor to his immediate successors. His idea, as I have already stated, has been corrupted and mis-

---

(a) Thoroughly to appreciate the bearing of these extracts and quotations on the question at issue, it is necessary to bear in mind the circumstances under which the trial took place. It originally commenced on the eve of the outbreak of the Revolution of 1848, and was adjourned in consequence of that event for a period of about three weeks. In the interval between the first and second trial a fierce and excited crowd, such as can be met with only in France in times of great political disturbance, besieged and eventually broke into the Institute, devastated the gardens, plundered the buildings, desecrated the chapels, and pulled down the crucifixes from the altar. The director was afterwards ordered by the authorities to send all the pupils back to their own homes, and a body of seventy-eight soldiers was quartered in the Establishment, and occupied the buildings at the time of the second trial.

In the Revolution of '89 religious institutions of this, and indeed of every description, had all been swept away, and at the Revolution of '48 there was a strong hope in the minds of the great bulk of the populace, that they would be swept away again. The observations and address of M. Rumeau were therefore directed, not only to show that *Léotade* must be guilty of the crime, but that the Institute also were guilty, and that their tenets and rules were incompatible with an advanced state of enlightenment and civilization. Hence these quotations on the subject of passive obedience, which though in undoubted bad taste, yet would have a considerable effect upon the minds of a jury drawn from amongst that excitable class of politicians and free-thinkers which forms so large an element in revolutions in France. That in the midst of such religious and political excitement Leotade could have a fair trial is of course out of the question.

understood. But the germ of that corruption is to be found in the rules themselves, and also in those solemn words which the Founder pronounced on two memorable occasions during his long life, ' I exhort you to observe a perfect union and a perfect obedience ;' and again, on his death-bed, ' I exhort you to be submissive to the Church, to exercise a particular devotion to the Virgin Mary, and to St. Joseph, the Patron of the Society, to have an intimate union and fellowship one with another, *and a blind obedience to your Superiors.'* This principle of blind obedience, fertilized by Jesuitical influence and contact, has become what you have now seen it to be in this present trial.

" Suppose a religious corporation with these principles and these alliances in the presence of or arraigned by the civil authority ; suppose a social interest, the repression or punishment of crime for example, at war with the private interest, or what is supposed to be the private interest, of this Society ; is it necessary for me to state that the one will stifle the other, and that if the Society persist and resist, the truth can only by the most gigantic efforts be discovered ?

" That which I am now putting as a hypothesis merely is a deplorable reality in this trial. It is not the first time that Justice has required an account from an Institute of *frères* of crimes committed within the bosom of the Institute. The case of the *frère* of the Institute at Metz, guilty of a crime similar to this, and never discovered, is one example. Another less known but not less authentic case took place lately in Paris. An assault was made by a *frère* on a child, who was afterwards murdered, as in this instance. The parents denounced the crime to the Minister : the Minister demanded inquiries should be made by the Superior General. Do you know what was the reply made to the Minister ?—that the accusation was true ; that the *frère* had been punished in the interior of the Institute, and sent into the Sardinian States !

" It would perhaps have been dangerous to have acted in this manner with respect to the crime of the 15th April : Justice indeed did not allow sufficient time. But if the Institute could not dispose of, they at least could endeavour to conceal the culprit. It is then that was organized that system of opposition which we have seen, and which, commencing at the rehearsal, developed itself by calumny, subornation, and falsehoods, and culminated in perjury!

" Now let us examine the question of the culpability of the accused; and it is under the influence of the ideas which I have just been uttering that this question ought to be examined. In the first place it is necessary to put on one side the suspicions and accusations which have been thrown upon Conte. Not that I purpose to constitute myself the champion of that witness, but I wish to expose and destroy that system whose aim is only to silence the voice of Truth.

" The accusation against Conte can be made in a double form. He can be accused as the accomplice of the authors of the crime, or as having sold Cécile. To say he is the actual murderer is to assert what is simply absurd. My argument will not be long, but it will be conclusive. Conte accounts for the whole of his time from the moment when Cécile entered the vestibule to his departure for Auch, and was not at Toulouse when the body was thrown into the cemetery.

" Was Conte simply an accomplice of the crime? I admit that for some time I shared in an error pretty generally accepted by the public; but the more I have studied the case the more convinced I am that that accusation is inadmissible.

" So, therefore, there is nothing possible, nothing reasonable in these accusations. The defence then seek to throw suspicion on the evidence of Conte, and to rake up his antecedents. Conte has to reproach himself undoubtedly with a grave crime perpetrated more than seven years ago, a crime since expiated by conduct free from all reproach. Conte even received forgiveness for the crime within the walls of the Institute itself. As to the witnesses Marie Duprat and Crouzat, who seek to make you believe that Conte has been guilty of certain proposals towards Cécile—proposals which, if true, she must have tolerated, as she made no complaint of them—these witnesses are simply a libel on the character of a young girl whose virtue, contested by no one, is spoken to by the whole town.

"There are, besides, reasons, and decisive reasons, for believing Conte's testimony. He had no interest in saying what he does. On the contrary, he had every reason to shield the *frères*. Remember, too, what he said to Madame Baylac, that she should not throw suspicion on the Institute.

"Let us now examine the question of the culpability of Léotade. Who is it that must necessarily be suspected? Naturally those who were present in the vestibule when all trace of Cécile was lost. Now who was there in the vestibule at the time? On this point we must avail ourselves of the evidence of Conte.

"Conte states that he saw in the vestibule Léotade and Jubrien. He has described to you their position and their dress. If he is speaking the truth, then those *frères* are either guilty or know the secret of the crime. On all points the assertions of Conte are positive; his statements the statements of a man uncontaminated by the stain of Jesuitism.

"Is this evidence of Conte unsupported—isolated? No. It is supported indirectly by the evidence of Marion. A deposition thus supported is true, and cannot be disproved but by other evidence, and I find no other evidence. Could Conte prepare his plan, could he foresee the questions that would be addressed to him? No. He is arrested on descending from the *diligence* from Auch, and he declares he saw Jubrien and Léotade in the vestibule, and he never varies. No tergiversation is to be noticed in his deposition. His evidence continues always the same. Marion is on the whole affirmative. Lacténus denies nothing; he has no memory, he says, and the most simple facts escape his notice. The evidence of Conte therefore remains intact.

"Then as to the denial of Léotade that he was present in the vestibule on the morning of the 15th, I will not trouble you much about that: it is the province of the prisoner always to have to deny that which is brought against him. As to the denial of Jubrien, that is different. That denial, if true, would naturally have on your minds a certain influence, but it is suspicious for several reasons. If Jubrien is not under suspicion to-day, he has been under suspicion; his denial and the denial of Léotade are therefore the result of an understanding.

"The agreement between Jubrien and Léotade to deny their presence in the vestibule is the more possible, because arrested only on the 26th of April, the proceedings on the part of the prosecution were not in the first instance absolutely secret to them. They have been enabled therefore to agree upon what they should each say. They had each the same interest to defend. Take their depositions from the time of the second interrogatory until now, and you will find them of one accord on all points. You will find in them both the same energetic denial; but the pure simple real truth you will not find at all. If they are thus tenacious and persistent in their denials, it is because they have the same interest at heart, not the interest merely that an accused person naturally has, but the interest of the Institute, the *esprit de corps*.

"As to the alibi, if it is true, its effect is immense; but is it true?

"It is necessary to notice relative to this alibi that there are two distinct periods in which it originates, and each period has a different version; the first, prior to Jubrien's discharge from custody, the second afterwards. The first version was this: Jubrien did not fix the exact time; he was uncertain: some time between eight o'clock and ten o'clock, or half-past ten, he could not say positively. But during that period of time he pretended that he went to the bakehouse at a quarter past eight; that he remained there with Iboncien half an hour, that he then went to his *procure* (a), where he remained about as long, and then he went out into the town. Such was Jubrien's version when in custody, and if I had no other version to contend with than this, it would not be difficult to refute it.

(a) The word *procure* means a sort of study or office, a small room set apart in Institutes of this description for the use of the director, *pourvoyeurs*, and one or two of the other chief officials, each of whom generally has one to himself. The *Procure des Livres* has in all cases been translated *library*, the nearest English word attainable to distinguish it from the other *procures* alluded to in the course of the trial.

" But Jubrien, released from prison, gives an entirely different version: he was with Bounhour and Salinier in the stable,
and in their company from ten minutes past eight to a
quarter past nine. Compare the two statements. You find
Jubrien in two places, the stable and the bakehouse, at the
same time! You cannot say this time at least [turning to
some of the directors who were present] that no falsehoods
have been uttered. This is Jubrien's statement : one of the
members of your body: the *Frère Procureur* : one of the
heads of the Institute !

" Of the two versions Jubrien naturally will sacrifice the
one in which Iboncien appears, and will excuse it on the
ground of the error into which Iboncien has fallen. But
how is it that the fact so useful to the defence was not discovered until four months after. Is not the discovery of
this important fact so late in itself suspicious?

" But Salinier and Bounhour are not themselves agreed.
One of them saw two *frères*, the other only one. Neither of
them agree as to time, nor the duration of the interview, nor
the length of time they remained in the Institute. Vidal
and Rudel completely contradict them. Abandon Vidal if
you like. As the learned President has observed, he may still
be living in the dominion of illusions, but Rudel has never
said anything that was false, and Rudel states that he never
saw either Salinier or Bounhour.

" I do not believe that Jubrien is guilty, and I gather the
proof of his innocence from the proceedings themselves.
Jubrien, at a few minutes past nine, was in the *procure*
with Frère Liéfroy—conclusive evidence that he could not
have committed the murder.

" Is it necessary for me to state the hour of the deceased's
death, the place? The hour is ten o'clock, the place the
stable. Is it to be said that it is impossible for the crime to
have been committed without the person committing it being
seen? I answer, No. At that time the ordinary occupations
of the *frères*, of the servants, would leave Léotade free, and
because it is said no one saw the crime committed, is that a
reason it was not committed? It is said the crime could
not be committed without the cries of the deceased being

heard, but Cécile was not able to cry, terror had paralyzed her senses, and besides if she had cried, was there any one there to hear?

"Then as to the alibis. Léotade was in the kitchen, in the work-room, in the cellar, fetching wood, in the Infirmary amusing one of the invalid pupils with a *serinette.* How is it, however, that in the Institute this alibi was not mentioned in the first instance, whilst Léotade was *au secret,* when with one word they could have saved, not only Léotade, but the Institute as well? Why are they silent for ten months, and then, after the lapse of that long interval, bring forward the evidence of *frères,* of servants, of children, and of scholars?

"Examine well the alibi which Léotade sets up. After the crime, at the time when everything was fresh in the memories of the witnesses, no one came forward to speak to or to confirm this alibi. But to-day the witnesses to it are *legion;* they are brought forward in profusion : the Institute seems to have a whole army in reserve, and if any doubt should fall on the matter, to be able to produce others as well! Léotade states that on the 15th he wrote the letter containing the *compte de conscience,* but that assertion comes forward very late, and yet it was much more important than that which he gave in the first instance, that he fed the birds.

" Gentlemen, do not let it for a moment be said that the commission of the crime was unknown in the Institute! It could not be unknown! If it were unknown by the *frères* generally, *Frère Irlide knew it!* (Great sensation.) The director is necessarily the confidant of everything which takes place in the Institute. Did not the director receive all the *comptes de conscience?* Did not the director have his doubts aroused by the extraordinary event which had taken place? A crime had been committed. There was necessarily a criminal : that criminal was not far off : the director knew everything!

" And then consider the subject of the shirt discovered in the *Noviciat,* which every one disowns, because, like the tunic of Deianira, it consumes the person who wore it. Is not that shirt the shirt of Léotade? Again, do not all the visits made by Léotade in the town to the tradesmen of the

Institute, his idle and imprudent remarks, do not they all come forward in support of the prosecution now?

"You denied (turning to Léotade), you denied the conversation held with Lajus—those words which in the day of your trouble you so unwittingly let escape you, and which to-day doubtless you so bitterly repent having used. Compelled to admit a certain portion of that conversation, you try to fix it as taking place on the 19th instead of the 16th. Before the *juge d'instruction*, overwhelmed with remorse, you were on the very point of making a confession of your guilt. Well! that confession I demand of you to-day! In the name of everything which you hold sacred : in the name of that unhappy family plunged in grief for whom I am to-day lifting up my voice : in the name of that unfortunate child over whose body the grave has so recently closed : in the name of that religion of which you yourself are one of the representatives, I demand of you—speak! confess! (After some moments of intense silence, during which the eyes of the whole of the audience were directed towards Léotade, who bore the ordeal with considerable firmness and self-possession :) Ah! (turning from Léotade to the jury) he is silent! He is the guilty man! Human justice will now pronounce his doom, waiting for the judgment of God!"

On the conclusion of M. Rumeau's speech, the *procureur général*, M. D'Oms, commenced his address to the jury on the part of the prosecution. His speech, which is very long, may be divided into two portions, one in which he endeavoured to localize the crime within the walls of the Institute; the other, in which he analyzed and discussed in a very able manner the evidence as it affected Léotade. In the following summary everything that is immaterial to the real point at issue has been omitted, as also those points which have been already dilated upon by M. Rumeau.

After alluding to some of the evidence given at the trial by the witnesses put forward on behalf of the *frères*, to the marks of the ladder, and the traces of footmarks in the garden, and after describing and pointing out to the jury, on the model of the two walls, the position of the flowers which had been rooted up, M. D'Oms proceeded :—

"You have already considered, from the arguments that have been adduced, the difficulties that present themselves to the body being carried from any place exterior to the Institute and placed in the position in which it was found. But if in imagination you put yourselves in the garden of the Institute, you will be struck with the facilities which that position affords for the disposal of it. No indiscreet, obtrusive, curious eye can overlook the premises. On the right is the desolate Cemetery St. Aubin ; behind, the vast deserted garden of the Institute ; on the left the high wall of the *Orangerie*. The *juge d'instruction* caused experiments to be made in order to ascertain if from any of the houses adjoining the cemetery it were possible to see the assassin when in the act of disposing of the body. The result was entirely negative. Even if the night of the 15th April had been a beautiful clear moonlight night (which it was not), and if all the neighbours had been looking from their windows, no one could have seen the murderer."

After referring to, and discussing at some length, the state in which the dress of the deceased was found, the particles of clover discovered adhering to the body, and the evidence of the experts, MM. Filhol and Noulet, as to the identity of those particles with the clover found in the stable in the Institute, and the " perfect identity " proved to exist between the grains of fig on the shirt No. 562 and the grains found on the clothes of the deceased, the *procureur général* next proceeded to lay before the jury the arguments from which he sought to fix the hour of the deceased's death :—

"The grandmother of the deceased saw her eating some bread at seven o'clock in the morning, and her young companion (Gestas) some bread and peas at eight. The experts prove that the bread eaten at those two meals, though taken at two different times, was found assimilated together in the *duodenum*, whilst the peas eaten at eight were in the stomach. The digestive tables compiled by *Beaumont* prove that bread never remains in the stomach more than three hours. As, therefore, some portion of the bread was taken at seven, the death of the deceased must have

occurred at or a little after ten. Where then can
you fix elsewhere than in the Institute the place of the
murder? What time would Cécile have had to leave the
Institute if you endeavour to show that the murder was
committed outside? At a quarter past nine Cécile was
alive and well in the vestibule of the *Noviciat*. She must
therefore have met with her death at an hour not far distant
from the time when she entered the Institute. There is
also another remarkable fact : in the deceased's shoes was
discovered, adhering to the mud, a particle of hay. Now
that implies that when Cécile entered the hay-loft (for it is
there that the crime must have been committed) the mud on
her shoes was still wet, consequently that she had only
recently left the soil from which that mud had been produced.

" You will gather from the evidence that has been given
in the course of the trial that on Thursday, the 15th, from
eight to eleven, the *frères* would, in the ordinary course of their
duties, be assembled together in the *salle des exercises;* that
the approaches leading from the vestibule to the garden and
stable, as well as those places themselves, would necessarily
be deserted. Even if Cécile had been *seen*, the prosecution
are quite justified in asserting that no one would have given
evidence of the fact. It would have been still easier for the
defence to have obtained the silence of any of the *frères*
who might have seen Cécile than it was for them to procure
the perjured testimony of Frère Lorien. Cécile, who outside the Institute would have hesitated in accompanying a
stranger on any pretext, would have had no suspicion or
hesitation with reference to the *frères*. Remember the evidence that has been given as to the terms of familiarity and
daily intercourse that existed between the *frères* of the
Institute and Conte's house. Nearly every day apprentices
of Conte were in the habit of going either to the *Noviciat*
or to the *Pensionnat*. Cécile herself had been there in the
very week in which the murder was committed. Any one of
the brethren, therefore, meeting Cécile in the Institute would
have had no difficulty in inducing her to follow him. Once
at the door of the stable, the mention only of rabbits, of
pigeons, which the murderer would promise to show her,

would have induced her to enter. From the loft where the pigeons are kept to the loft where the hay is stored, and which the prosecution assert is the place of the murder, is but one step.

"How, it will be said, is it possible to suppose the assassin capable of such audacity? All along the route indicated he must have encountered the gaze of several curious scrutinizing eyes, and in the garden, labourers; Frere Lorien, the gardener, too, amongst others, must have been at work. None of these objections raise in my mind the least hesitation or difficulty: none of them, plausible as they may be, can get rid of this fact, *that Cécile was seen to enter the vestibule alive, and was never afterwards seen to leave.*

"It will be said that in order to pass from the *Noviciat* to the *Pensionnat* it is necessary to traverse a court commanded by several windows. But nothing proves that there were any *frères* stationed at the windows at the time when the deceased must have passed; besides, if they were, every one would have denied having seen her. The prohibition against females passing from the *Noviciat* to the *Pensionnat,* attempted to be set up, is not proved. The porter himself said to Conte that it was possible the deceased had gone to the *Pensionnat,* though he afterwards modified it by saying that he thought Conte might have taken her. Two points therefore are proved from these facts, one is that Cécile if accosted by a *frère* would have had no hesitation in accompanying him, the other, that means of communication between the two establishments were accessible and easy. By them, we bring her to the door of the stable, the key of which is often in the lock, and when not in the lock, underneath the door. Remember that in this stable the rabbits were kept. Cécile would have learnt at Conte's that Conte had been promised a rabbit by Léotade. She would have followed him therefore without suspicion. The possibility of her arrival at the stable is thus indisputably shown.

"It will be said that Cécile must have cried out, and that no one has heard any cries, and this argument is put forward as an important, indisputable fact! Nothing is easier than to refute it. If Cecile did in fact cry out, she must have been heard by some one. But that some one would be the *Frère*

Superior. Frère Irlide does not come forward to state he heard these cries. Therefore she did not cry out, or if she did no one has heard her, in which case the objection falls to the ground. If the crime had been committed elsewhere would she not also have cried out? There would have been a score of witnesses to prove these cries. The houses adjoining the Institute are much frequented, and it would have been impossible for the deceased to have cried out without being heard! It is therefore within the walls of the Institute, in the midst of the body of *frères* who inhabit it, that we have to seek for and seize the murderer. The crime being thus localized, the prosecution demands, why therefore these struggles against evidence? why this endeavour to show, in the interests of the Society, that it is *not* within these walls that the murderer is to be discovered? Is it because if the murderer be discovered amongst the *frères,* the respect for the Body will be lessened? Far from it! The respect for the Institute would increase by reason of the efforts made to discover the criminal! The disgrace of one member does not re-act on the whole Body, except in so far as the whole Body may cover with their protection the member who has dishonoured them.

" What then has been the attitude adopted by the Institute as a Body with reference to this inquiry? The consideration of this point is indispensable in order to arrive at a satisfactory estimate of the value of the evidence adduced by the prosecution against Léotade; for according as you may feel convinced in your own minds either that the Superiors have given their assistance to justice, or have by underhand means caused any proofs to disappear, so will you appreciate differently the evidence that has been laid before you and the evidence that may be wanting. If you are convinced that the Superiors have always been actuated by a desire of delivering a criminal to justice, you will be surprised that there cannot be found in the whole Institute a single witness who can come forward and give evidence of a crime committed in open day. But if, on the other hand, you think the apparent support and assistance offered by the Institute were merely a stratagem to enable them the better to undermine the prosecution, then you will not be surprised if the proofs are found in some particulars to be defective!

" I do not assume to assert for a moment that members of a religious community could accept gladly a partnership with crime in endeavouring to conceal a criminal, or that the crime of murder committed by one of their own members could so influence the Body generally as to induce them to conspire together to obtain immunity for the guilty. But I maintain that the Institute, carried away by prejudices which two revolutions have not been able entirely to uproot, have been desirous of disputing with the secular power the right to the possession of a criminal because that criminal is invested with the habit of a religious order.

" No one will deny that the society in which we live does not exercise an important influence on our feelings, and does not modify our judgments, or that a religious community does not form in the midst of our great social body a separate society of its own, with its own laws and its own discipline, its own customs, its own jurisdiction. Doubtless the civil body exercises control to some extent over a religious body, but that control is without influence on the most powerful element of its constitution—on its habits, its customs, and its morals. In societies so organized men often learn obligations different from those which influence ordinary society. I therefore feel that it is necessary for you, in investigating this case, to study the organization of this Community of Christian Brethren, and I think you will learn by this study that the errors, the reticences, the dissimulations, of several of the *frères* will be found on investigation to be the errors, reticences, and dissimulations of one ; and that you will understand the agreement of several witnesses on a particular point is worth no more than the evidence of a single witness.

" From the moment a member of this Institute clothes himself with the dress of the Order he no longer belongs to Society. The link connecting him with his own family is not more thoroughly broken than is the link connecting him with society at large. All that which in ordinary civil life or in his own family denotes or distinguishes a man disappears in the new life and the new family which he enters. First, he is stripped of his name; and you will have formed an opinion from those names which have come under your notice in the course of this trial how it appears almost a matter of importance and obligation for the members to take and impose names which by their very strangeness testify how fully the metamorphosis is complete.

" Then the uniformity of dress, the clothing held and used in common, further show how all individuality disappears in the Body which absorbs them. Add to these a complete resignation of self, a perfect submission to the orders and wishes of the Superior, and you have constituted a Society representing in the highest degree the reality of absolute power. The Superior of a Society thus composed does not command the *actions* only of its members, he commands their *wills,* and to a certain extent is master of their opinions and convictions also. To form an opinion in a religious society—a belief in any particular event—does not require the effort that is necessary in civil life for the acceptance even of the most self-evident truism : all that is required is a single word.

" The day on which the Superior declared in the midst of the Institute that Cécile had been seen to leave the vestibule : that she had met with her death outside the Establishment : that her body had been carried to the foot of the wall of the garden in order to throw suspicion on the Institute—on that day the opinion of the whole of the *frères* was formed; and there was not one single member of the whole Body who, though without having seen or examined anything for himself, did not come to the firm conviction that conspiracy alone had accumulated together those proofs which now press so heavily against the Institute.

" Would you therefore feel surprised if in a Society so organized there were found a member who on seeing the body hidden in the *Pensionnat,* and knowing of the crime, should say to himself, ' To cause the traces of the crime to disappear to save a criminal is not actually forbidden by the law. If a brother were to discover in a house traces of a crime committed by his own brother, would he denounce the crime or efface the traces of it ? Are we not all brothers, all members of the same family ? Are the bonds of a religious brotherhood less strong, less sacred, than those of natural brotherhood ? The murderer is no doubt a great criminal, but he must be kept for those punishments which Religion reserves for such criminals: he is a member of our family, and we must save him, and in saving him save also ourselves.' These words and reasons are no longer the words and reasons of *our* time, but they explain, without justifying, this struggle of the Institute against Justice.

"Is it possible that there can be any doubt that some directing mind, working within the Community, has not organized a plan of resistance against Justice? Scarcely is any suspicious fact revealed before it is made to disappear. Footmarks are noticed at the base of the wall: Léotade, who believes that to admit in advance any damnatory fact is to weaken it, says *he* made them when going to the garden that morning out of curiosity. Lorien, asked about them at the same time, is silent. But three days afterwards the plan of resistance is agreed upon: Léotade, against whom suspicions are beginning to be aroused, must no longer assume the responsibility of these footmarks; but Lorien, whose age excludes him from all imputation, is put forward to admit them!

"Does not the appearance of a plot still more reveal itself when the director, Frère Irlide, under the most idle of pretexts, two days only after the crime, removes Léotade from the chamber where he was then sleeping, in order to send him to some distant garret, the very isolation showing the horror which his presence created? This fact, which touching the guilt or innocence of Léotade is of the gravest importance, is also of importance as showing the actual part taken by Frère Irlide in the schemes devised against Justice. To remove Léotade from the bedroom which he occupied on the 15th, from which he could descend into the garden, only to take him to a dormitory which he could not leave without being seen, reveals not only that he who caused the removal knew the culprit, but also that he was acquainted with the means employed to dispose of the body."

The *procureur général* having thus disposed in a manner, and with arguments which certainly are entitled to consideration, of two of the main points in the case, one, that the crime had been committed in the Institute, the other, that there was a conspiracy formed in the interior of the Community of which

Frère Irlide was the head, for the purpose of concealing the criminal from justice, proceeded next to discuss the evidence as affecting Léotade himself.

Respecting the presence of Léotade and Jubrien in the vestibule at the time of the arrival of the deceased, M. D'Oms remarked :—

"It was on the 18th that this question was put for the first time to Conte, who stated that on the 15th he saw Jubrien speaking to Léotade near the door. The two *frères* being themselves questioned on this point—and I beg you to consider well their replies—Léotade said, ' I was not in the vestibule on the 15th. I was in the *Pensionnat.*' This was his first reply. Confronted with Conte, he says ' he does not remember,' an important modification of the first answer, and to which I draw the particular attention of the jury.

" Jubrien, in his turn, when questioned, said, ' I did not see Conte in the vestibule, but I did afterwards when in the director's *procure.*'

" But on being also confronted with Conte, he says, ' he does not remember.' There would have been nothing remarkable if in the first instance Jubrien had said he did not remember. He is of the *Noviciat,* and his duties as *pourvoyeur* take him to the vestibule several times a day. Léotade, on the contrary, belongs to the *Pensionnat.* He could not therefore be in the vestibule of the *Noviciat* except on some special occasion. He ought therefore to have remembered, if on the 15th he had been in either the vestibule or the parlour.

" But interrogated again on the 20th they are no longer uncertain. They declare both of them that they were *not* there ! As for Conte, pressed repeatedly by the *juge d'instruction,* in upwards of thirty different interviews, told that his assertion bore most heavily against Léotade and Jubrien, he never hesitates: during the whole term of his long detention, nearly six months, he never varies. Conte had no interest in accusing the *frères :* he gained three or four thousand francs a year from the Institute, and his father also worked for them : their business was the existence of the whole family. Since this event he has lost the business, which has been followed as far as Conte is concerned by total ruin, by bankruptcy, and by arrest !

"Take the hypothesis that Conte wished to throw suspicion on the *frères*, would he have fixed as being in the vestibule both Léotade and Jubrien? It would have been quite sufficient to have mentioned only one. He could then have said, 'Between one who denies and one who asserts, my word will not be suspected.' But when he declares he saw Jubrien as well, he insures contradiction by another person also. Jubrien at first stated he had not been to the vestibule that morning, but later on he was compelled to admit he had been there twice. One fact is fully admitted by all parties, that Jubrien and Léotade had to arrange together for sending for some wine from Saint-Simon ; Léotade could not send there by himself. Interrogated separately on this point, they both of them fix on a time, place, and day, different from the time, place, and day on which the affair was agreed upon. On the 2nd of June, Jubrien stated that on the Friday, about half-past six in the morning, he went to the *Pensionnat* to seek Léotade. He found him in the court, and asked if he would send for his wine, as he (Jubrien) was going to send for his. Léotade agreed to do this, and Jubrien thereupon stated he went to obtain a *permit* for him. Asked if he had endeavoured to find Léotade before this interview, he stated he had sought for him either on the Wednesday or Thursday, but could not meet with him. Pressed by the *juge d'instruction* on this point he said, 'I saw Léotade on the Friday at half-past six in the morning.' Jubrien, therefore, interrogated twice as to this meeting, twice fixes the same day, the same hour, the same place. Let us see now what Léotade says about this !

"The day Léotade in the first instance fixes upon is the day *before* the Friday, and before the barrels were got up. Now the barrels were got up on the Thursday evening. He then asked for time to reflect, and the next day he said it was the Friday at *eight o'clock*. So he does not agree with Jubrien as to the time ; and then at this present trial he again says it was on the Thursday night.

"Then as regards the alibi.

"The alibi of Léotade presents a whole mass of contradictions, and the alibi of Jubrien rests solely on the interview with Salinier, which has risen up in a wonderful manner in the very midst of the trial. On that point alone is Jubrien found to speak positively—he who is never positive, and remembers nothing about other matters! Now let us examine this interview with Salinier. Jubrien affirms that Salinier and Bounhour saw Rudel and Vidal in the parlour, but these latter did not see them. Rudel, who was not, like Salinier, interrogated on this point six months after the event, but was asked about it on the 25th April, replied that on the 15th he saw no one in the parlour. Vidal said the same. Navarre, who had not then received his instructions, said on the 18th no one came into the parlour during the time Vidal and Rudel were there with him: no one could have come in. So there are several persons who, at the time the inquiries are first instituted, say they did not see in the parlour either Salinier or Bounhour. These latter, however, remember it after a lapse of six months.

"Bounhour and Salinier, interrogated separately on the point, contradict one another. Bounhour says when he entered the parlour with Salinier there was no one there : Salinier, that Vidal and Rudel were there. Bounhour says he saw a group composed of two *frères* and two laymen. Salinier saw three laymen, and one more *frère* than Bounhour did. Even this is not all. Bounhour says, ' We arrived in the parlour at ten minutes past eight. We waited for Jubrien ten minutes (which would bring it to twenty minutes past eight). We then went to the stable, and left a few minutes after nine.' Bounhour thus fixes about one hour as the duration of the interview ; Salinier half an hour. Take the mean between the two statements and say three quarters of an hour, and that you will find will not preclude the possibility of Jubrien being in the vestibule at a quarter past nine, when the deceased arrived with the books !

"Léotade, after the discovery of the crime, is interrogated on the employment of his time on the morning of the 15th. He then indicated four persons who could corroborate his statements. The first, Léopardin, does not, in spite of Léotade's efforts, when confronted with him, remember anything. The servants Baptiste and Bonnet contradict him, as does also the porter. On the 23rd, interrogated afresh, he stated he had been to the Infirmary, and had lighted a fire there for the young St. Salvy. On the 5th of November, however, he appears before the President of the Assize Court, and then his memory has all the elasticity that can be desired, and he establishes a whole series of alibis. A perfect crowd of witnesses seem to have met Léotade on the morning of the 15th, and passed him from hand to hand. But then Léotade was in communication with the Institute, and their system of defence was already organized !

"Then as to the *comptes de conscience*. That Frère Luc collected these *comptes de conscience*, made a parcel of them, and sent the parcel to the *diligence* office I do not deny. But Léotade said nothing about them in the first instance, nor did anyone else in the whole Institute. None of the directors even ever thought of saying, ' Ask Léotade if he did not write his *compte de conscience* on that day.' And yet the performance of this duty is a solemn thing in a religious society like the Institute. When, however, this fact *is* produced in the urgent necessity of the defence, it is surrounded by several contradictions. We therefore maintain that these *comptes de conscience* have been invented on purpose for the defence.

"Now let us pass on to consider the fact of the changing of bedrooms by Léotade. From the 15th to the 16th Léotade slept in a room having two beds placed close to a door of which Léotade had the key. According to Frère Irlide the change took place in order to give Léotade's place to Frère Luc, because the latter had felt a vague, undefined terror after the discovery of the crime. Why should the murder terrify a *frère* belonging to this Institute of Christian Brethren ? Léotade could from that chamber during the night of the 15th have descended to the garden, and have then taken all the precautions necessary for the concealment of the crime !

"Then as regards the shirt No. 562. The shirt was found in the *Noviciat*. Léotade belongs to the *Pensionnat*. No one, however, has recognized or admitted that shirt as his own—proof, therefore, that it is suspected. Moreover, it often happens that *novices* wear clothes belonging to the *Pensionnat*. Léotade might therefore wear a shirt belonging to the *Noviciat*. Remember, too, that on the morning of the 16th, Léotade was in the *Noviciat*, not far from the room where the linen is kept. His statement is that he went to give some money to the shoemaker, but that meeting Jubrien in the corridor, he gave it to him instead. The shoemaker says he did not see him : Jubrien says he did not see him. Léotade, therefore, was in the *Noviciat* on the morning of the 16th for some reason that is suspicious ; and if he says he saw the shoemaker and saw Jubrien (whom he did not see) it is to account for a fact which he finds it impossible to deny.

" Then as to Léotade's wanderings in the town on the morning of the 16th. His proceedings on that day are of the highest importance. On leaving the Institute he goes to Conte's wife, and he gives as a reason for his visit the memorandum book which Conte had made for him some weeks back, and in which he stated Conte had neglected to insert some leaves of parchment. He asks for Conte, whose services would be very unnecessary for the trumpery alteration, and without leaving the book with any of the workwomen, he carries it away with him. After him comes Jubrien also to Conte's house, to get, as he says, some pasteboard, and he goes away without asking for it. He, like Léotade, also inquires for Conte, and, like Leotade, departs without executing the mission he had in hand. The same day Léotade goes to Lajus. M. Lajus had heard of the discovery of the body : he sees Léotade enter, and he says to him, ' Tell me *cher frère,* what is this that has occurred in the cemetery ; they have found the body of a girl who works at some bookbinder's.' ' I have just come from the bookbinder in question,' says Léotade, ' and if we had known his antecedents we would never have employed him.'

" Now at this time, ten o'clock in the morning of the 16th, the cause of death was completely unknown, the body not having been examined or removed. How is it then that Léotade attaches the murder to Conte on account of his antecedents ? How did Léotade learn anything about Conte's antecedents at all ? Were they made known to him privately by any person ? No : he cannot mention anyone as his informant. Was it public report which within an hour after the discovery of the crime proclaimed aloud these doubtful antecedents of Conte ? Still less is this the fact : for Justice

herself, anxious to inquire into Conte's character, could not
for some days after learn anything about these antecedents
which Léotade knew so thoroughly on the 16th. Therefore,
outside of the Institute we can find no one who could communicate to Léotade anything on this head.

" But *inside* the Institute there is a member acquainted for
many years with these scandalous passages in Conte's life.
Would it not be wanting in the most ordinary logical deductions not to infer from this fact that it was from the mouth
of one of the directors of the Institute that the information
obtained by Léotade had been procured? But you will say
that this supposition assumes that the crime was known in
the Institute from the very moment it was committed, or at
the very latest, on the night of the 15th or the morning of
the 16th April. There is nothing impossible in such a
hypothesis!

" From the very time the crime was discovered we meet
with nothing but facts which testify to the earnest desire of
the Institute to mislead. From this you can draw two
inferences : the first, that the murder had been committed
in the Institute; the second, that their knowledge had been
obtained from the confession of the criminal himself. It is
the great glory of religion to possess consolations for every
sorrow, and alleviations for every grief. The atrocity of
some fearful crime may terrify human, but can never terrify
divine justice. There is no crime so enormous which religion
cannot pardon and absolve. Léotade flies from the scene of
the murder, covered with shame, agitated with remorse!
It is no exaggeration to suppose that the directors, with
that thorough knowledge they possess of each individual placed
under their control, did not notice the trouble that weighed
upon Léotade. Do you think it would be difficult to obtain
a confession on a promise that the crime should not be
denounced? Do you think this confession would not be
easily obtained on its being represented to Léotade that it
was the only way to save him from justice?

" The position of Léotade assumes then quite a different
aspect. He is no longer an ordinary culprit, but a culprit
put forward to do battle with the secular power. On his
head rests the honour of the whole Community. Let him

U

stand unshaken in the combat! Behind, supporting him, are his brothers; and perhaps his very judges will be deceived, and will confound the calm which a sense of security will give him with the serenity of an innocent man!

" If the directors of the Establishment had loyally aided in the discovery of the crime, if it were true that, without subterfuge, they lent to the researches of justice a thoroughly earnest active co-operation, the guilt of Léotade would be inexplicable. One cannot imagine that anyone stained with such a fearful double crime could the very next day pursue his ordinary occupations without his countenance betraying some signs of inward agitation and alarm. But it is quite capable of explanation when an active directing mind is felt from the commencement interposing itself between the criminal and justice. If Léotade had neglected his customary duties, if he had buried himself in solitude, he would have made the whole Institute confidants of his guilt.

" The guilt of Léotade is therefore proved by his own acts and by those plots concocted in the interior of the Institute. Léotade *was* in the vestibule of the *Noviciat* when Cécile arrived with the books! He was there with her for a moment alone; by a look, a gesture, a friendly word, he enticed her in the direction of the *Pensionnat*; then changing his plans, and taking advantage of the perfect solitude in which he found himself, he directed his steps towards the garden: the door of the stable, perhaps half open, gave him the idea of drawing her on to the spot where the pigeons were kept, and there, in the solitude and isolation of the place, the crime was committed! The body would be easily hidden during the rest of the day; and in the night Léotade would descend from his dormitory and throw it over the wall of the garden into the cemetery. Such is, in substance, the explanation of the drama which has so long and so painfully agitated the whole of France!"

The speech of M. D'Oms was listened to throughout with the greatest attention, and the excitement evinced at some portions of it was intense. The above summary can necessarily only give, in a very condensed form, an outline of the contents. It was undoubtedly the best speech that was delivered in the course of the trial; and the effect of it on the minds of the public and of the jury was very great. On its conclusion M. Gasc rose to commence what was indeed, in the face of the prejudices and excitement of the audience, a very unequal struggle on behalf of Léotade.

After some remarks on the atrocity of the crime, and the character of the deceased, made with the object of counteracting the effect of M. D'Oms' speech on the minds of the jury, M. Gasc proceeded to refer to the remarkable case of *Calas*, one of the most singular instances of judicial error that have taken place in France, and which, as it occurred in Toulouse, was urged by him with much force on the jury as a warning against committing another error as fearful in its results. He then went on to contest the position taken up by the prosecution, that there was any similarity between the doctrines and rules of the Institute and those of the Society of Jesus. There was nothing, he said, in common between them; the vows of poverty and obedience were taken, it was true, but they were simply taken relative to the duties each member had to fulfil in the Community. The assertion, therefore, made by them, not only against Léotade, but also against the Institute, was entirely destitute of foundation.

That the prosecution had failed in their endeavours to trace the crime and to discover the criminal, he submitted was simply owing to their having insisted in looking for him within the walls of the Institute; they had committed an error, and had persevered in it, which naturally resulted in the loss of all traces of the criminal.

With reference to the evidence of Madeline Sabathier, M. Gasc remarked that the defence had never relied upon or occupied itself with her at all; she had never been anything of importance to them. He admitted the prosecution had obtained from her a retraction of her original evidence, but denied they had ever obtained from her an avowal that the Institute had influenced her in making it. Even as it was, her original deposition had not been entirely retracted or destroyed; there was one portion which ought, he said, to weigh on the most prejudiced minds. Madeline had offered the mother of the deceased four francs. If the defence had wished to buy over the family of the deceased, surely they would have offered something more than that sum.

Then as regarded Vidal; the prosecution set up the defence had corrupted him; but the jury, who knew the history of that evidence, would say whether the accusation of corruption made against them could be maintained. It was known he had asserted he had seen Cécile leave; he had spoken of it to Rudel and others, and it was a matter of public notoriety. The director at Lavaur, therefore, on hearing of it, sent off Vidal to Toulouse, and up to that time neither Frère Floride nor Frère Irlide had appeared in the matter at all. He ridiculed the idea that because Vidal, who was poor, had his fare paid and two francs given to him to get his dinner with, the Institute therefore suborned and corrupted him.

After reminding the jury that the members of the Institute were of the people, and sprung from the people, and had their interests and welfare at heart, M. Gasc proceeded to enlarge on the improbability of the case set up by the prosecution, that the body had been thrown over the wall of the garden and not over the wall of the Rue Riquet. He denied, however, the fact of *any* projection, and asserted that the body had been carried in and placed where it was found. As proof of this, he argued that the position of the body was exclusive of the possibility of its having been thrown, as it was found resting on the tips of the toes, the knees, the elbows, and the face, and the clothes were not displaced, though the height of the wall was about nine feet. He submitted that the body, if really thrown, ought to have had the clothes completely disarranged, and the body itself at least partly uncovered; and he pressed also on the jury the fact that it had made no mark whatever on the soil of the cemetery, though on the night and morning in question it rained until one o'clock, and had rained heavily for some days previously, and the soil was soft. The jury had not examined the spot, and could not therefore understand how easy it was for the body to have been carried. He denied that the gate of the cemetery was locked on the night in question, and though the *concièrge* said it was, he did not believe it, as the *concièrge* could not possibly admit otherwise. There was still, besides, the possibility of approach by the side of the canal and by the other gardens adjoining.

The prosecution affirmed that Cécile was seen to enter the Institute on the morning of the 15th, and was never afterwards seen to leave. He denied that she was seen by any person in the populous neighbourhood through which she passed; therefore, was it impossible for her to leave without being seen ? On the 16th of April upwards of thirty-eight persons examined on this point, all living in the adjoining streets through which the deceased had passed with the books, stated that they did not see her go by.

As to the petal of geranium being found in the deceased's hair, and similar geraniums found on the wall of the Institute, he argued they were wild geraniums growing anywhere where flowers would thrive ; they were to be found in the cemetery itself. The hair of the deceased was loose, it was a boisterous and windy day, and he submitted the wind could easily have carried a petal of a flower, which might have caught in her hair. It was not likely if the body had been thrown over the wall of the Institute, that the hair would have carried away only one petal ; it would have rooted up the whole flower. As to the tow or oakum found in the hair, M. Filhol himself said he could not identify it with the rope found in the garden.

The distance of the body [the nearest part of it] from the base of the wall of the Institute garden was four inches ; the summit of the wall overhung nine inches ; so that the deceased if thrown over from the garden did not describe the parabolic curve usually followed by projectiles, but fell *inside* the overhanging summit of the wall, which M. Gasc urged was a clear impossibility (*a*).

(*a*) The defence laid great stress upon this point, which certainly tends, at first sight, to show that the body could not have been *thrown over* into the cemetery. If the person throwing the body stood on the ground on the garden side of the wall, it would have been practically impossible for him, to have thrown the body over a wall whose summit overhung the base nine inches, so as to cause it to fall at a distance from the base of only

Passing on to the entry of the deceased into the vestibule at a quarter past nine on the morning of the 15th, M. Gasc proceeded to discuss the difficulties in the way of her being enticed from thence to the stable without being seen :—" Necessarily she must pass along the court-yard of the *Noviciat,* before the kitchen and refectory, along an open passage, well lighted, forty yards in length, in which members of the Establishment are constantly to be found. She would then have to pass into the tunnel, which has nothing dark or mysterious about it, but is lighted by large openings; then along another passage, commanded by several windows, to the stable. * * * * The chamber above is used by the servants, one or all of whom might have entered at any moment; on leaving this chamber she would enter the hay-loft, filled with hay, but having a good number of openings; one window towards the garden ; two doors and another opening looking into the court-yard of the barracks adjoining, so placed that the bayonet of the sentry on duty there is always at the level of the opening. Could *this* be the place of the murder?—the garden close by ; Lorien there at work; *frères* in the Oratory at prayer, and the murder committed without a groan or cry of the victim ! [It will be remembered the medical evidence negatives entirely strangulation or suffocation, so there was no mechanical reason for the deceased not

---

four inches. But assuming a ladder to have been used, the difficulty vanishes, for the body then, instead of being *thrown*, might have been *dropped* over. In that case, however, a further difficulty arises. For a man to have mounted, with the deceased in his arms, on a ladder resting on the wet soil of a flower bed, must have caused a considerable impression on the soil, whereas the impression was admitted to be slight, and also that the murderer did *not* mount on the ladder for the purpose of throwing the body over, but only to reconnoitre (*vide* p. 263).

The position too of the geranium plant on the top of the wall, a petal of which was alleged to have been found in the hair of the deceased, was out of the line of projection, if made from the spot where this impression was found, and so far negatives the probability of the body being thrown from the top of a ladder. The probability is that, if thrown at all, the body was thrown by a person standing in the garden, probably from the walk near the base of the wall (*vide* plan) in order to avoid observation. In that case, however, could the parabolic curve be prevented, and could one person, however strong he might be, throw a body (sixty pounds in weight, French measure, or about five stone) over a wall nine feet high ? Neither hypothesis is free from difficulty.

having cried out.] No trace of the crime to be found in the hay-loft on the 16th, though everything was moved and examined, and no trace of blood. The body left hidden amongst the hay and clover all the day, buried in fact under the hay, and yet only two little filaments, almost defying analysis, found upon her clothes the next morning; and the clover too of the commonest kind, cultivated by everybody!

"Then as to the disposal of the body. It rained all the evening and night, up to one o'clock in the morning, yet the clothes were found to be dry. Allowing every possible care and precaution taken in the removal of the body from the stable, the clothes must have got wet. But if the body had been carried in a bag or box it could have been placed in the cemetery conveniently, and the clothes then would naturally have been found dry. If the crime were committed in the Institute, the murderer must have removed the body at an early hour, probably midnight or one o'clock; he must have got up and left his room, which he could not do without awaking the porter and the Frère *Director*, both sleeping close by, and then have removed the body when it was raining; yet the clothes were found dry!"

M. Gasc then proceeded to discuss the main point of the case, that Léotade and Jubrien were present in the vestibule when the deceased arrived with the books. It is impossible to give more than a summary of his arguments on this point, which were involved and tedious in the highest degree, rendering it very difficult to follow or understand the deductions he sought to draw from them. In substance they were shortly as follow:—Conte *alone* spoke to the presence of the two *frères*. Marion did not see them, though she entered and put down the basket within four feet of where they were said to be standing. The assertion that the basket she was carrying on her head prevented her seeing them was absurd, because it is particularly essential that persons carrying anything on their heads should look straight in front of them. Therefore Marion not seeing the *frères* proved they were not there. Rudel and Vidal also did not see them. He laid much stress on the fact that Conte on his first interrogatory said nothing about the presence of the two *frères* in the vestibule, and also that he said he saw in the parlour a woman sitting down whom no one else ever saw, and who, in fact, was not there at all. He excused the contradictions noticeable in the answers made by Léotade to his various interrogatories, on the ground that he was in the most rigorous solitary confinement from the 26th of April to the middle of August, part of the time being the height of summer, the heat of which in Toulouse is particularly oppressive ; deprived of air ; cut off from all communication with the other prisoners and the outside world, and debarred of the consolations of religion—" no wonder," M. Gasc said, " his mind and memory should suffer from treatment which would have driven other persons out of their senses. In all his experience he had never met with or heard of such cruel treatment" [an observation which drew from the *procureur général* the remark, " *Il n'y a pas de bonne foi chez vous, M. Gasc,*" but which met with many signs of approbation from the public present in court]. He relied on what was known as the " *incident Salinier,*" as a proof of Conte's falsehood, and complained of the way the witness for the defence, speaking on this essential point, had been treated. For merely speaking to it at the first trial Bounhour had been imprisoned four days. He accounted for Jubrien not remembering the interview with Salinier in the first instance by the fact that it was not until his discharge from prison that he met Bounhour, who recalled to his mind the visit to the stable. Salinier, being asked on the point, said he remembered seeing Vidal quite well, who was the son of one of his oldest friends.

Respecting the alleged motive for the meeting between Jubrien and Léotade in the vestibule—the sending for wine to Saint-Simon—M. Gasc observed that it was improbable in the highest degree that two men, each being *pourvoyeur,* and each having a *procure* of his own, should meet for this purpose in the vestibule of the *Noviciat;* and as to the alibi, he dwelt with much force on the conduct and demeanour of Léotade in the course of the morning, arguing from his occupations and proceedings that day, the improbability of his being able to go through with them so shortly after committing such an atrocious crime. He did not, however, examine in detail the exact times spoken to by the witnesses, alleging his unwillingness to make up what he called a mere "*faisceau de dates.*" His arguments and deductions on this point were not at all clear, and it is difficult to discern what he sought to prove from them beyond the fact (which was not denied) that Léotade's self-command during the day of the murder, when at any moment the body might have been discovered in the stable, was marvellous.

On the subject of the shirt No. 562, he urged on the jury that it had never been brought home in the slightest degree to Léotade, and ridiculed the idea propounded by M. D'Oms, that the director had "banished" Léotade from his usual room as soon as he knew of the murder, because he believed Léotade to be the criminal, and wished to isolate him. Nothing could be more absurd. Léotade was sent to a dormitory in which there were sixty beds, and placed amongst the scholars who boarded and slept in the Institute, an arrangement which Frère Irlide could never have been a party to if he had suspected Léotade.

On the conclusion of M. Gasc's speech, M. Saint-Gresse was by right entitled to address the jury and the *procureur général* to reply, but owing to the great length of the trial, it was arranged that both this speech and the reply should be waived. The President thereupon asked Léotade if he had anything to add to what his counsel had said?

Léotade.—I do not wish to prolong the trial, but I wish to say that I have never stated to the court anything that is false. If there have been contradictions in my numerous depositions, it is owing to the solitary confinement I have undergone.

The President then declared the evidence on both sides to be closed, and proceeded with his summing up to the jury.

The summing up of the President was divided by him into two parts, the first relating to the localization of the crime in the Institute. On this point it is not necessary to follow him closely, because it may fairly be admitted without at all prejudicing the case set up on behalf of Léotade, that the fact which can be relied upon with any amount of certainty as proved in the whole course of the trial is that the deceased entered the vestibule of the *Noviciat* on the morning of the 15th of April at about a quarter past nine, and was never afterwards seen to leave; the second part was how the crime was sought to be brought home to Léotade. It is on this head only that the remarks of the President need be given. His summing up as a whole was able and effective. Its great fault is the bias evinced against Léotade. Putting entirely on one side the remarks made on the first head of the summing up, the following is an outline of the observations addressed to the jury on the main point—how out of an Establishment of several hundred *frères*, Léotade alone could be singled out as the guilty party.

"Of the many persons residing in the *Noviciat* and the *Pensionnat*," the President remarked, "there were but few who from their duties on the morning of the 15th could be concerned in the crime. The day was a Thursday, and at the time of the murder nearly all the *frères* were in the *salle des exercises* under mutual *surveillance;* therefore suspicion could not attach to any of *them*. The number of those whose duties would occupy them elsewhere would be about twelve. First, there was the director, Frère Liéfroy. He could, however, not possibly be guilty, because Conte had remained with him in the library upwards of an hour, and when he left Cécile had disappeared. Then there was Jubrien, but he also could not be guilty, nor the porter Lacténus, for the latter went up with Conte to the library with the books, and when he came down the deceased had disappeared. Frère Irlide and the porter of the *Pensionnat* must also be exempt from suspicion. The names of the others he did not know, but amongst the whole twelve there was not one who from his duties had so many facilities for the murder as Léotade. He was *pourvoyeur* for the *Pensionnat*, possessed complete liberty of action, and had no duties in common with the other *frères*. Assuming the stable to be the place of the murder, he of all others was the most likely to be able to entice Cécile there; there he kept his rabbits and pigeons, and the place was to some extent under his dominion.

"It being thus shown that Léotade was amongst the number of those who had facilities for committing the crime, the next question had to be considered—was he in the vestibule on the 15th when the deceased arrived? On this point Conte's evidence was of importance. Now Conte, when he went to Auch, did not know what had become of Cécile, and he did not know when arrested on the 17th. When interrogated the second time as to who was present in the vestibule, he replied, 'Léotade and Jubrien.' In Conte's mind the fact was not at the time of the slightest moment, for he knew nothing of the deceased's end. Léotade and Jubrien, both examined at this time, deny having been in the vestibule. Confronted with Conte, who could not understand a denial of what he considered *then* a fact of no moment, Conte re-asserted his former statement, and remarked to Jubrien, 'I saw you so well that when I had taken down the basket of books from off Marion's head, I said to you, Good day.' Both Léotade and Jubrien then said they did not remember.

"It must not be forgotten that at this time the two *frères* were still at liberty; they could therefore arrange together what to say, and that they did arrange what to say was the more probable from the answers they afterwards gave on the day they were arrested. They then said, 'We are quite sure we were neither of us in the vestibule on the 15th.' The prosecution very naturally wanted to ascertain on which side was the truth. It was known that there was a reason for an interview between Léotade and Jubrien on the day in question, as they both had to send to Saint-Simon for wine. They were therefore separately asked, being then in custody and not able to communicate with each other, *when* this interview took place. Léotade said he saw Jubrien in the *evening* at the *Pensionnat;* Jubrien that he saw Léotade in the *morning* at the *Noviciat*.

"Now how could Conte be deceived as to their presence in the vestibule, and why should he say what was not true? The fact was of no importance at all to him; he had no occasion to wish to throw suspicion on the Institute; he did not even then know the deceased was murdered; he was under considerable obligations to the *frères*, working for them to the amount of 4000 fr. a year. His good faith too was further shown by his answer to the woman Baylac, who wished to throw suspicion on the Institute.

"Compare with Conte's testimony on this point the evidence of Salinier and Bounhour. You will remember the presence of these two witnesses in the vestibule at a time when they saw everybody and no one saw them, unless it were Jubrien, who, however, did not remember the fact until ten months after. Salinier at first did not remember the day he called at the Institute; but ten months after, he remembered having seen Vidal there, whom he knew. Salinier saw *three* laymen and *one frère* in the parlour; Bounhour *two* laymen and *two frères.* Navarre, who had always an invention at the service of the Community, said, ten months after the event, he saw Jubrien take a person by the arm and lead him away from the parlour, and then Bounhour, by a most happy coincidence, said he remembered Jubrien taking him by the arm as described, and that the arm was the left arm !

" Vidal fixed the time of his entry at nine o'clock. He was expressly told not to call before. He asked outside in the street, before he rang, what o'clock it was, and was told it had just struck nine. Bounhour fixed the time of his visit *a little after eight.* Yet he said he saw Vidal ! At half-past eight he went to the stables with Salinier and Jubrien, but they left at a little after nine, which would not make it impossible for Jubrien to be again in the vestibule at a quarter past.

" Léotade, when in prison, gave an account of the employment of his time on the morning of the 15th. He first stated that between nine and eleven he saw Baptiste in the cellar, Léopardin in the kitchen, and another *frère.* Baptiste being asked what *he* was doing between nine and eleven, said he never went to the cellar until the evening; there could not therefore be any meeting between the two. Léopardin at first also denied meeting Léotade in the kitchen. This account remained in force until Léotade was transferred to another prison. Then he underwent another interrogatory, and his answers were in contradiction with his previous statements. He then said for the first time he wrote his *compte de conscience* between nine and ten o'clock in the morning. At that time, however, it was proved he was in direct communication with the Institute (a).

" Then as regards the changing of beds. There was proof that on the night of the 17th, Léotade was sent to sleep in another dormitory from which it was not easy to get out at night without passing through a dormitory containing three rows of beds. The accusation saw in that a species of punishment, and also suspected other reasons. The defence explained the measure by the terror evinced by Frère Luc the night after the discovery of the murder. But it would have been equally easy to have sent Frère Luc where Léotade was sent to. If it were really a proceeding of moment, it was unfortunate it occurred at a time which was strangely coincident with the circumstances arising after the murder.

" With reference to the shirt No. 562. Léotade being asked what he had done with the shirt given to him on the 17th, and which he alleged he did not use because it was too small for him, asserted he returned it to the *infirmier*. The latter being questioned, at first denied it, and also that any one had returned him a clean shirt within the space of six months, but at the trial he corroborated Léotade as to the return of the shirt. Now if Léotade did not use this shirt, it was because it was too small ; but the jury had heard M. Gaussail, and his evidence on that point would show them the reliance they were to place on that statement.

" In order to attribute the shirt which was found in the *Noviciat* to Léotade, it must be shown that he had facilities for placing it there. Now on his arrest there was found in his possession a bunch of keys, one of which would open the door of the linen room of the *Noviciat*. He had admitted he was in the neighbourhood of that room on the morning of the 16th, and gave as a reason that he wanted to pay some money to the shoemaker. But the shoemaker being examined denied having met him, and then Léotade said he met Jubrien outside in the corridor and gave the money *to*

(a) It was not thought necessary to insert the evidence touching on this and one or two other collateral points of no great moment. There is no doubt but that Léotade at that time was in communication with the other *frères*.

him. But Jubrien, examined separately, said he did not remember seeing Léotade at all."

The President then concluded his summing up by a *resumé* of Léotade's proceedings in the town on the morning of the 16th, remarking more especially on the visits to Conte's house by Léotade and Jubrien on the morning of the 16th, and on the conversation held by the former with Lajus. There is no doubt but that the proceedings of both Léotade and Jubrien on the morning after the murder were suspicious, and it is a remarkable fact that they alone, out of the whole number of *frères* in the Institute, should call at Conte's house after the discovery of the body, both alleging as the object of their visit reasons that were equally frivolous. Bearing in mind also that these two *frères* were the two spoken of by Conte as present in the vestibule at the time of the arrival of the deceased with the books, these visits, and the conversation held by Léotade with Lajus, are of undoubted importance in weighing the evidence adduced by the prosecution against Léotade.

Referring to the visit to Lajus, the President remarked :— " Now there was indisputably a reason alleged for this visit. Léotade had to pay Lajus a sum of money ; the only point is that the Institute, contrary to their ordinary custom, should send to pay him such a trifling sum before it was due. The conversation then turns upon the subject of the bookbinder who had taken the girl to the *Noviciat.* Léotade observes, ' That bookbinder is Conte. I have just come from his house. If we had known his antecedents before, we would not have employed him at all ; one cannot say positively he is the culprit, *but '*——. Now Leotade, when in the first instance questioned as to this conversation, says, ' It is not true ; I did not speak about Conte's character first to Lajus ; it was he who said to me that Conte's antecedents were very questionable.' Lajus, confronted with Léotade, says, ' It is impossible ; I was not acquainted with Conte, and I knew nothing of his antecedents.' Léotade then changes his ground, and says, ' I could not have had this conversation with you on the 16th, but perhaps it might have been on the 19th.' Lajus inquires, ' Had you on the 19th just come from Conte's house ?' ' No,' replies Léotade. ' Then,' returned Lajus, ' that fixes it, for you said first of all you had just come from Conte's house, so this conversation could only have taken place on the 16th.' You will also bear in mind that Lajus mentioned the conversation both to his wife and his servant on the same day.

" What has been the conduct of the accused since the time of these denials? He has constantly affirmed he could not have had this conversation with Lajus on the 16th, for then he did not know anything about Conte's antecedents, but on the 19th he believes it possible for him to have done so. The variance between the two on this point still exists, and it is for you to determine whether to give the preference to the statements of Lajus or the statements of Léotade. Lajus does not stand alone ; Léotade does."

On the subject of Léotade's demeanour after the murder, the President observed :—

" It is urged by the defence that the calmness of manner shown by Léotade during the course of the afternoon of the 15th, when the fear of the discovery of the hidden body must have been weighing on his mind, is a proof of his innocence. Undoubtedly this objection would be of weight in an ordinary case, for generally crime *does* leave behind it traces of fear, and of the agitation caused by remorse. But you must remember you have in Léotade to study a character quite exceptional in its nature ;· a character crushed and remoulded (*broyée et repétrie*) by the discipline of that *Noviciat* which works such wonderful transformations. Which of us possesses the secret of those penances and mortifications by the aid of which peace can be restored even to a mind racked by remorse? It is the power of religious habits and influences, —this inner life of the cloister,—that is the problem now submitted to your judgment and experience for solution, in considering the facts and proofs brought to light by the present trial."

The President then proceeded to put the following question to the jury :—

" Was Louis Bonafous, in religion Frère Léotade, guilty or not guilty of the murder of Cécile Combettes on the morning of the 15th April, the said Cécile Combettes being then under the age of fifteen years?"

The President after putting this question pointed out to the jury that by the decree of the 8th of March, a majority of nine out of the twelve members of the jury would be necessary for a verdict, but that the question of " extenuating circumstances " was still left as it originally stood at common law (*le droit commun*), and a majority of only seven to five would be required.

The jury, after an absence of an hour and a half, returned into court with a verdict of *Guilty* by a majority of more than nine voices, but with " extenuating circumstances."

Sentence was then passed on Léotade of penal servitude for life.

The court further condemned him to the payment of costs, but nonsuited the plaintiff in the civil action, on the ground that the proceedings for damages ought to have been taken against the Superior General in Paris.

On the 26th of January, 1850, Léotade died at the *bagne* at Toulon. His conduct from the time of his conviction up to the time of his death was essentially that of an innocent man. His end is described as being calm and peaceful.

When the evidence is doubtful the demeanour of a prisoner after conviction, and especially his conduct and language in his last moments, are often found to have an important bearing on the question of his guilt. Though it does not necessarily follow that the approach of death *always* impels a prisoner to speak the truth, yet at least the motives for falsehood are taken away. On the morning of his death Léotade sent for the chaplain and one of the head officers of the *bagne,* and for the last time solemnly declared his innocence, avowing also his entire ignorance of how or by whom the crime had been committed. Since his death a vigorous effort has been made in France by his brother Francois Bonafous to rehabilitate the memory of Léotade, but up to present time without effect. The late Emperor (Napoleon III.) is reported to have taken a great interest in the case. It is not, however, now likely that anything further will be done in the matter, and the question of the guilt or innocence of Léotade must be left, like a great many similar cases, to the judgment of posterity.

London : Printed by Shaw & Sons, Fetter Lane.

For EU product safety concerns, contact us at Calle de José Abascal, 56–1°,
28003 Madrid, Spain or eugpsr@cambridge.org.

www.ingramcontent.com/pod-product-compliance
Ingram Content Group UK Ltd.
Pitfield, Milton Keynes, MK11 3LW, UK
UKHW010349140625
459647UK00010B/945